The Timucua

The Peoples of America

General editors
Alan Kolata and Dean R. Snow

This series is about the native peoples and civilizations of the Americas, from their origins in ancient times to the present day. Drawing on archaeological, historical, and anthropological evidence, each volume presents a fresh and absorbing account of a group's culture, society, and history.

Accessible and scholarly, and well illustrated with maps and photographs, the volumes of *The Peoples of America* will together provide a comprehensive and vivid picture of the character and variety of the societies of the American past.

Published

The Tiwanaku: Portrait of an Andean Civilization
Alan Kolata

The Iroquois
Dean R. Snow

The Timucua
Jerald T. Milanich

In preparation

The Aztecs
Michael E. Smith

The Cherokee
Gerald Schroedl

The Cheyenne
John Moore

The Incas
Terence N. D'Altroy

The Moche
Garth Bawden

The Nascas
D. M. Brown and Helaine Silverman

The Navajo
Alan Downer

The Sioux
Guy Gibbon

The Timucua

Jerald T. Milanich

Copyright © Jerald T. Milanich 1996

The right of Jerald T. Milanich to be identified as author of this work has been asserted in
accordance with the Copyright, Designs and Patents Act 1988.

First published 1996
Blackwell Publishers Ltd
108 Cowley Road
Oxford OX4 1JF
UK

Blackwell Publishers Inc.
238 Main Street
Cambridge, Massachusetts 02142, USA

Library of Congress Cataloging-in-Publication Data
Milanich. Jerald T.
    The Timucua/Jerald T. Milanich.
      p. cm.–(The peoples of America)
    Includes bibliographical references and index.
    ISBN 1–55786–488–8
    1. Timucua Indians. I. Title. II. Series.
E99.T55M57 1996
975.9'01–dc20   95–40289
                                                                                      CIP

British Library Cataloguing in Publication Data
A CIP catalogue record for this book is available from the
British Library.

Typeset in 11 on 12.5pt Sabon
by Pure Tech India Ltd Pondicherry
Printed and bound in Great Britain by Hartnolls Limited, Bodmin, Cornwall

This book is printed on acid-free paper

For G and G

Contents

List of Figures

List of Tables

Preface

Name, nationality, and ethnic affiliation: Juan Alonso Cabale,
Spanish, Timucua Indian.
Religious preference: Roman Catholic.
Date and place of birth: 1709, mission Nuestra Señora de la
Leche, Florida.
Date and place of death: November 14, 1767, Guanabacoa,
Cuba.
Wife's name, nationality, and ethnic affiliation: María Rosa
Tuslipalea, Spanish, Yamasee Indian.
Children: Juan and Francisco, born about 1741 and 1742 in
Florida.

Taken at face value, these biographical facts provide only a
thumbnail sketch about a native American Indian who lived in
Spanish Florida and died in Cuba more than two and a half
centuries ago. But if we look behind these few particulars from
one person's life, we will find an incredible story. Juan Alonzo
Cabale, who died in a land far from his birthplace and the home
of his ancestors, was the last of his people, the last survivor
of perhaps as many as 200,000 Timucua-speaking Indians
who once had lived in northern peninsula Florida and southern
Georgia.

Almost nothing is known about the life of Juan Alonso Cabale
beyond these facts derived from three historical documents: a
census list in a Spanish archive; a parish registry from the church
of Nuestra Señora Ascuncíon in Cuba; and the minutes of the
cabildo, the town council, of Guanabacoa, Cuba. Even so, these

scanty details reflect the colonial period history of the Timucua Indians and the cultural changes which occurred after the conquest of Florida and Georgia by people from Europe.

For instance, Juan Alonso Cabale was born in a Spanish mission, not a native village, and he had a Spanish name, not a Timucuan one. He was married to a Yamasee Indian woman whose ancestry was from Georgia or South Carolina and whose native language was a Muskhogean dialect very different from the Timucua language; he did not marry a Timucuan woman. When he died, Juan Alonso Cabale was living in Cuba, not in Florida.

The reasons for these facts are found in the chapters that follow. We will learn that the ancestors of the Timucua had made their home in what is now northern Florida and southern Georgia for many generations. For thirteen millennia native American Indians had lived in what would become Timucuan territory, living off the land. The people fished, hunted, gathered wild plants, and cultivated crops.

Literally thousands of archaeological sites – village middens and sand mounds – still dot the landscape, offering mute testimony to the presence of these precolumbian people. Today names like Alachua, Arapaha, Aucilla, and Etoniah dot the landscape of Florida and southern Georgia, remnants of the world of the Timucua.

The Timucua were likely the first native American Indians living in what is now the southeastern United States to come in contact with people from the western hemisphere following Columbus's 1492 voyage. The first documented instance of such contact was with the expedition of the Spaniard Juan Ponce de Leon who landed on the Atlantic coast of northern Florida in 1513.

First Spain, then France, then Spain again sought to place the Timucua within their respective colonial empires. The history of the Timucua and the French and Spaniards in *La Florida*, as the southeastern United States was known, is so entwined that the story of the Timucuan people after 1513 cannot be told without also telling the story of the European explorers and colonists who invaded their land, bringing great changes to the Timucua's indigenous lifeways. Throughout the colonial period the Timucua sought to adjust to these changes and deal with the problems and challenges forced on them by the European presence. To understand the Timucua is to understand the nature of European colonization and its impact. The very nature of Timucuan lifeways was in large part shaped by events of the colonial period.

Using the results of archaeological investigations at precolumbian villages and mounds we can reconstruct the culture of the ancestors of the Timucua prior to 1492, focusing on how they made a living, their material culture – tools and the like – and even aspects of social and political organization and their beliefs. And with both archaeological data and information gleaned from hundreds of Spanish and French documents and, to a lesser extent, English documents from the Carolinas, we can trace the history of the Timucua into the seventeenth and eighteenth centuries, providing insights into the impact of the European presence on native lifestyles.

In the early sixteenth century at the time of first contact with people from Europe native American Indians who spoke dialects of the Timucua language occupied most of the northern third of peninsular Florida, from the Aucilla River east to the Atlantic Ocean and south into the Lake District in Lake County west of Orlando. This large region includes the St Johns River north of Lake George and its tributary, the Ocklawaha. Timucua-speakers also lived in a significant portion of south-central and southeastern Georgia.

The exact region in Georgia inhabited by Timucua-speakers is undergoing revision as more documents from the mission period are interpreted. The best evidence now at hand suggests the extent of the Timucua in Georgia is much greater than previously supposed. Timucua-speakers were living as far north as the forks of the Oconee and Ocmulgee River, which join to form the Altamaha River. The Altamaha River apparently forms the northern boundary of the Timucua.

This is a huge region which encompasses Suwannoochee Creek, the Satilla River, and the wetlands of the Okefenokee Swamp. Along the coast Timucua-speakers lived on Cumberland, Jekyll, and St Simons islands. This large tract of modern-day Georgian Timucuan territory was nearly as extensive as the lands of the Timucua in northern Florida.

The many Timucua-speaking groups, or tribes, in northern Florida and southern Georgia were never united politically or ethnically. Indeed, some were at war with one another. It is their

shared language that allows us to refer to these groups as Timucua Indians.

As we shall see in chapters 1 and 2, specific Timucuan groups
can be correlated with several different archaeological assemblages. This is the result of their living in different environmental
zones and having different histories, some of which can be traced
back in time hundreds of years into the precolumbian period.
Chapter 2 further describes who the Timucuan groups were and
where they lived when they were first encountered by people
from Europe.

In chapters 3 and 4 we will recount the colonial period history
of the various Timucuan groups: the first invasions and attempts
at settlement by Spaniards and Frenchmen, the subsequent successful colonization by the Spaniards, and the establishment of
Franciscan missions among the Timucua.

Chapters 5 to 7 describe aspects of Timucuan culture, such
things as settlements, subsistence systems, social and political
organization, and religion. Both information from archival sources and evidence from archaeology are used to show how these
aspects of Timucuan societies changed as a result of Spanish
conquest and colonization.

In the end the European conquest of La Florida proved cata-
strophic for the Timucua. Although they successfully adjusted to
many aspects of the changes brought by the Spanish, the Timucua could not maintain their numbers in the face of diseases
brought to North America from Europe and, perhaps, Africa.
Epidemics and ill-health resulting from the stresses of colonization and the servitude it brought eventually overcame them. The
final chapter traces the demise of the Timucua. Two hundred
and fifty years after the landing of Juan Ponce de Leon, only one
Timucua remained, Juan Alonso Cabale.

The Timucua were among the many American Indian groups
who did not survive the European conquest of North and South
America. The ancestors of Juan Alonso Cabale and the other
Timucua Indians bore the brunt of colonial expansion, ultimately succumbing to it. Other groups in the eastern United States did
survive the colonial era and their descendants today continue to
live in that region and in Oklahoma.

It is my hope that learning about the Timucua will help all of
us to better appreciate the histories of present-day native American Indian societies and the contributions those groups have

made to our modern world. All our histories have been shaped by the incredible events set in motion five centuries ago when Juan Ponce de Leon first sailed to La Florida.

In writing this book I have relied heavily on the work of my colleagues, both archaeologists and historians. Many of their contributions to our present knowledge of the Timucua are alluded to in the text and referenced in the bibliography. I thank them all, especially John Hann and John Worth, whose respective archival research has provided quantities of new information on the Timucuan missions of seventeenth-century Spanish Florida. John Worth and Dean Snow both read this manuscript and made many comments which improved it immensely. They both have my thanks. I also owe a heavy debt of gratitude to Kathleen Deagan, whose own research on the Timucua was largely responsible for my undertaking this book.

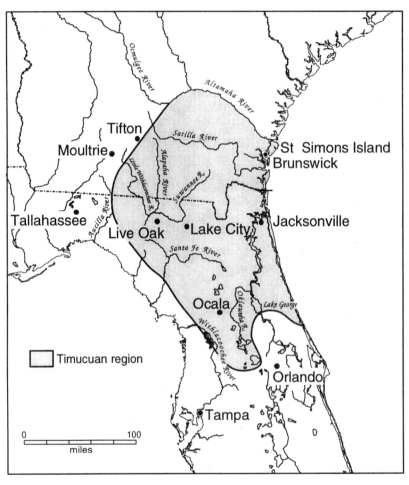

Modern Florida and Georgia with the Timucuan region shaded

1

The Beginning

American Indians lived in the region occupied by the Timucua Indians for at least 13,000 years prior to the sixteenth century and the appearance of soldiers, friars, and colonists from Europe. Throughout those thirteen millennia changes in the native cultures occurred as people adjusted to alterations in climate, increasing populations, new ideas and innovations, and, perhaps, the immigration of new groups.

Numerous archaeological sites, remnants of places where precolumbian people once lived or carried out other activities, have been excavated. Artifacts and other evidence left by early native people at those sites have been used by archaeologists to chart the nature and development of native American cultures through time.

Because there is no written record for these earliest people, names taken from modern geographical landmarks or from other sources have been assigned to the various precolumbian cultures. We do not know what names the people used to refer to themselves. It is only in the colonial period when the Spaniards, French, and other Europeans, as well as some native individuals themselves, provided written accounts containing references to the indigenous societies that the names of native groups were recorded.

Even though we may not know what names the precolumbian groups used to refer to themselves or to one another, we can use archaeological evidence to trace colonial period native groups back into the precolumbian period. In some portions of the large region once inhabited by Timucua Indians we can confidently correlate specific groups with archaeological traditions that extend back in time hundreds of years or even longer. As we shall see, we can show that Timucuan groups and their immediate ancestors occupied a very large portion of northern Florida and southern Georgia for hundreds of years prior to the time when people from Europe first came to what is now the southeast United States, a land those Europeans called La Florida.

In this chapter I will describe the precolumbian cultures, both those ancestral to the colonial period Timucua and those which were present even earlier. This will set the stage for subsequent chapters, which describe the Timucua Indians and the impact of European colonization on them. Our first step into the past, a step of thirteen millennia, is a giant one.

Paleoindians

At about 11,000 BC parts of the region that today is northern Florida and southern Georgia were first colonized by Paleoindians whose ancestors had entered North America from eastern Asia during the Pleistocene era. Sea levels as much as 350 feet lower than present, the result of so much water being tied up in Ice Age glaciers, exposed a huge land bridge connecting Asia and northwestern North America. Hunter–gatherers in search of game and other foods easily traveled across this land bridge, which was as wide as the distance from Orlando to New York City.

At the time of the Paleoindians those same lowered seas gave Florida a total land mass about twice what it is today (Figure 1.1). The Atlantic and Gulf of Mexico coasts were much farther seaward than they are at present. This was especially true for the Gulf coast of Florida which was more than 100 miles west of its present location. The Atlantic coast of southern Georgia and northeast Florida was closer to its present location, but still east of the chain of barrier island marking that littoral today.

With so much water frozen in glaciers during the cold Pleistocene era the climate of Florida and southern Georgia was much drier than today. Many of the present rivers, springs, and lakes were not here, and ground water levels were significantly lower. Plants were those that could grow in the dry, cool conditions. Scrub vegetation, open grassy prairies, and savannahs were common.

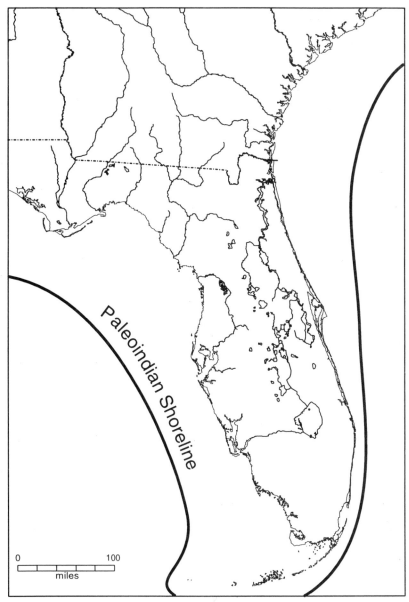

Figure 1.1 The shoreline at the time of the Paleoindians

The relatively few sources of surface water that were available were sought by the Paleoindians and by the animals they hunted for food. Paleoindians found water in deep springs, like Warm Mineral Spring in Sarasota County, Florida near the central Gulf

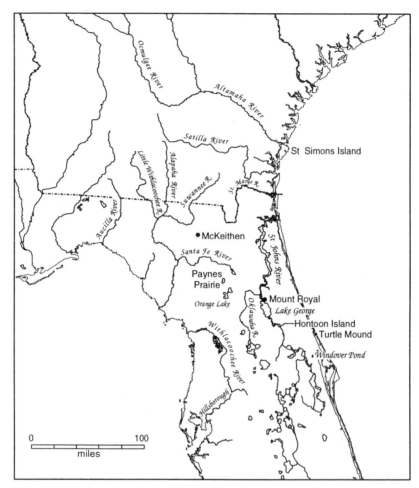

Figure 1.2 Archaeological sites and site locations mentioned in the text

coast or at watering holes or shallow lakes or prairies where limestone strata near the ground surface provided catchment basins (Figure 1.2). Such limestone deposits are found from the Hillsborough River drainage north through peninsular Florida into the Florida panhandle and southern Georgia.

Surface water sources were prime hunting and camping locales for the Paleoindians. Today, with higher water levels, many of these catchment basins are flowing rivers, like the Santa Fe, Withlacoochee, and Aucilla. Some of the hunting sites and camps which were in these basins in the past lie below the present waters of the rivers. Archaeologists, diving in the rivers or excavating the rivers' bottoms, have found bone, ivory, and stone weapons and tools left by the Paleoindians. Also found are bones of animals the Paleoindians hunted and butchered for food.

Some of the animal species hunted by the Paleoindians became extinct shortly after the end of the Pleistocene era. They include mastodon, mammoth, horse, camel, bison, and giant land tortoise. Some scientists argue that overhunting by Paleoindians accounts for the demise of these species. Others claim their extinction was due to climatic changes, while still others suggest a combination of hunting and the onset of a wetter climate in late Paleoindian times caused the animals' disappearance.

After about 9000 bc, as glaciers melted and sea levels rose, the climate in the southeastern United States became wetter than it had been, providing more water sources around which the Paleoindians could camp. But as the sea rose, coastal areas were gradually inundated and the Florida peninsular landmass was reduced. Less land, more water sources, and larger human populations may have influenced the later Paleoindians to practice a less nomadic lifestyle, one which required fewer moves between water sources. Individual bands of Paleoindians could live for longer periods of time at each of their campsites.

Camps inhabited by more people and for longer periods of time resulted in Paleoindian sites much larger than the small sites common earlier. These larger late Paleoindian sites have been found near locales where the more extensive surface water sources were located, such as in the Hillsborough River drainage near Tampa and around Paynes Prairie south of Gainesville, Florida.

As archaeologists continue to assess the nature of the Paleoindian occupation of southern Georgia and northern Florida they are discovering more and more sites. And it seems certain that just as many sites are now inundated under the Gulf of Mexico, land that at the end of the Pleistocene era also was home to Paleoindians.

Archaic Period Cultures

Over time the toolkit of the Paleoindians was altered as people adjusted to the changing environmental and social conditions.

They began to use a wider variety of stone tools, and many of the lanceolate stone points originally used to hunt large animals were no longer made. These changes were sufficient by 7500 BC for archaeologists to delineate a new culture, the Early Archaic. Early Archaic populations were the descendants of the Paleoindians.

The climate of the Early Archaic period was still drier than it is at present, but it was wetter than it had been during Paleoindian times. Early Archaic people continued to live next to water sources and to hunt and gather wild foods.

Excavations at the Windover Pond site in Brevard County, Florida by Glen Doran and David Dickel of Florida State University indicate that at least some of the Early Archaic groups buried their dead in the peat at the bottom of water-filled ponds. At Windover the nature of the peat preserved wooden and fiber artifacts, items not generally found in archaeological sites, providing unique information on the Early Archaic culture.

Sharks teeth and dog or wolf teeth were found attached with pitch to wooden hafts. Other tools made from stone, deer bone and antler, manatee bone, panther or bobcat bone, and bird bone were shaped into pins, barbed points, awls, and throwing-stick weights. The latter, made from deer antler, were used with a hand-held shaft to help launch spears. Paleoindians also used throwing sticks.

Bones of animals eaten by the Early Archaic who used Windover Pond were from otters, rats, squirrels, rabbits, opossums, ducks, and wading birds, alligators, turtles, snakes, frogs, and fishes. The large mammals once hunted by Paleoindians had become extinct. Doran and Dickel also recovered an edible prickly pear pad and a gourd fashioned into a dipper. Weedy, hard gourds grew wild and could be used as containers, net floats, and dippers. These gourds were indigenous to Florida and were growing there even before the Paleoindians lived there.

A sophisticated array of cordage and fiber fabrics were preserved in the Windover peat. Fibers taken from Sabal palms and saw palmettos and other plants were used in twining and weaving. The Early Archaic people, like the people who preceded them and those who would follow, utilized items from their environment that were well suited to their livelihood.

After 5000 BC the climate in the lower Southeast began to ameliorate, becoming more like that of the modern period, the climatic onset of which was reached about 3000 BC. The two millennia between 5000 and 3000 BC are known as the Middle Archaic period.

Middle Archaic sites are found in a variety of settings, some very different from those associated with Paleoindians and Early Archaic people, including, for the first time, along the St Johns River and in the Atlantic coastal strand of Florida. Middle Archaic sites are found in the Hillsborough River drainage northeast of Tampa Bay; along the southwest Florida coast; and in a few south Florida locales. They also are found in large numbers in interior northern Florida and, presumably, southern Georgia. As yet, however, Middle Archaic sites have not been found on the coast of southeastern Georgia where the earliest sites found thus far date after about 2000 BC.

During the Middle Archaic period populations were significantly larger than in earlier times and a more settled lifestyle was present. Some sites are several acres in extent and have yielded thousands of stone artifacts. The Middle Archaic people used a larger variety of specialized tools than their ancestors, perhaps a result of increased sedentism.

Essentially modern environmental conditions were reached by about 3000 BC, the beginning of the Late Archaic period. Expanding populations would soon occupy almost every part of Florida and Georgia. Wetland locales especially were heavily settled. Numerous Late Archaic sites are in southwest and northeast Florida and in the St Johns River drainage, as well as along the Georgia sea islands and the nearby mainland. All of these village sites are typified by extensive deposits of mollusk shells, the remains of thousands of precolumbian meals. Shellfish and fish, in both marine and freshwater locales, were staples for later native groups as well, including most of the Timucua-speaking people. Many of the subsistence strategies formulated by the Late Archaic period continued to be used into the colonial period.

Today Late Archaic sites are found in the coastal salt marshes of northeast Florida and southeast Georgia. When occupied, these sites were on dry land, but rising sea levels and the subsequent encroachment of the marshes have altered the land forms around the sites. Even more Late Archaic sites, as is true of earlier Archaic and Paleoindian sites, probably have been inundated by the rising waters of the Atlantic Ocean and the Gulf of Mexico.

Table 1.1 Post-500 BC regional cultures in the Timucuan region

Colonial period	East Florida	Southeast Georgia/northeast Florida	North peninsular Florida
	Eastern Timucua	Mocama and eastern Timucua	Western Timucua
AD 1565			
AD 1500			
AD 1400			
AD 1300			
AD 1200	St Johns II	Savannah/St Johns II	Suwannee Valley
AD 1100			
AD 1000			
AD 900			Alachua
AD 800		Wilmington/St Johns II — Swift Creek	
AD 700			
AD 600			
AD 500			McKeithen Weeden Island
AD 400			
AD 300			Cades Pond
AD 200			
AD 100	St Johns I	Deptford/St Johns I	
AD 1			
100 BC			Deptford
200 BC			
300 BC			
400 BC			
500 BC			

It is during the Late Archaic period, the time from 3000 BC to about 500 BC, that archaeologists can begin to trace regional cultural developments. One valuable tool in defining individual precolumbian cultures is the presence of ceramics made from fired clay. The first ceramics in the Timucuan region appear between 2500 and 1800 BC in the sites along the lower Georgia and northeast Florida coasts and those in the lower (northern) St Johns River. Early pottery is found elsewhere in Florida and Georgia during the same period as well.

On the Georgia coast the earliest sites are those of the St Simons culture. That culture was contemporary with the Orange culture of north and eastern Florida described below. The ceramics associated with the St Simons and Orange cultures contain vegetable fibers, either palmetto or Spanish moss, which were added to the clay as temper. Some of this fiber-tempered pottery was decorated with incised and punctated designs impressed into the walls of bowls before they were dried and fired.

After about 500 BC fiber-tempered pottery was no longer made and several different pottery traditions, each associated with one or more regional cultures, dominated the region that was to be the homeland of the various Timucuan groups. It is some of these Late Archaic cultures and post-500 BC regional cultures which can be traced through time to colonial period Timucuan groups. Elsewhere in what would become the Timucuan region, however, the succession of regional cultures is not a smooth continuum or it is poorly known. In such areas we cannot correlate the earliest regional cultures with later Timucua Indian groups. Table 1.1 shows the various regional cultures.

East Florida

One region within Timucuan territory where there appears to be great continuity from the Late Archaic period – and perhaps earlier – to Timucuan groups is east Florida. That large region includes the St Johns River drainage from the river's mouth south to Lake George and the area immediately to the east extending to the Atlantic coast. It also includes the Oklawaha River drainage that runs southward from the St Johns River into an area of numerous large and small lakes just south of the headwaters of the Oklawaha in what is today modern Lake County and northwestern Orange County.

The St Johns River, the small rivers and creeks that are its tributaries, and the lakes in this region provided native peoples with the fish and shellfish which were mainstays of their diets. Likewise, along the Atlantic coast the lagoons, estuaries, and salt marshes – and in a few places freshwater wetlands as well – provided quantities of fish and shellfish. In coastal areas where larger barrier islands are present, such as near Cape Canaveral, there are extensive coastal salt marsh and tidal stream systems which rival those of the Georgia coast in extent.

A person in an airplane flying over the relatively flat region which we today call east Florida could not help but notice its most prominent feature: the wetlands. East Florida is dominated by rivers and their tributary streams, freshwater marshes and swamps, lakes, and saltwater marshes, lagoons, and coastal streams.

These wetlands and the adjacent forests provided the animals and plants eaten by the native peoples, as well as other raw resources used for tools, weapons, clothing, and all the other rudiments needed to maintain their way of life. In the later precolumbian period the cultivation of plants, including Indian corn, squashes, and beans, supplemented the native diet. However, farming was never as important in east Florida as it was to the southeastern native peoples who lived farther north in the river valleys of Arkansas, Mississippi, Tennessee, Alabama, inland south Carolina, western North Carolina, and central and northern Georgia.

Following the Orange period, which lasted until 500 bc, there were sufficient changes in pottery technology in east Florida for archaeologists to recognize the St Johns culture, one of the several regional cultures which appeared in the Timucuan region at that time (Figure 1.3). The precolumbian temporal portion of that culture has been divided into two main periods, based on changes in artifact types and other aspects of culture that occurred over time and are observable in archaeological sites. The two periods are St Johns I (500 bc–ad 750) and St Johns II (ad 750–1565).

We can trace the St Johns culture from the Late Archaic Orange culture to the Timucuan groups living in east Florida at the dawn of the invasion of people from Europe. But not all of

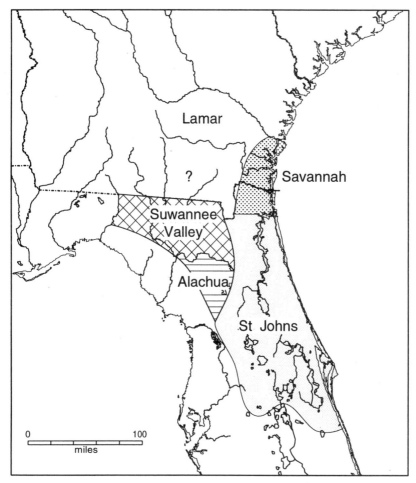

Figure 1.3 Late precolumbian archaeological cultures ancestral to the Timucua

the precolumbian groups associated with the St Johns culture were Timucua-speakers. In the colonial period the St Johns River drainage south of Lake George was the home of the Mayaca Indians, who spoke a language different from Timucua. And St Johns culture sites also are found in central Florida where other non-Timucuan groups probably lived.

The basic life of the St Johns people – hunting, fishing, collecting wild resources, and occupation of villages and camps adjacent to the numerous wetlands in east Florida – was changed little if at all from that of their Orange period predecessors. Indeed, St Johns I sites usually are found on top of Orange period sites. In a region where wetlands were so important the reoccupation of the same sites over many generations would be expected.

Although old locations continued to be occupied, new wetland villages were established throughout the period of the St Johns culture, a reflection of an ever increasing population. Archaeologist James Miller has charted numbers of sites per century for the Orange, St Johns I, and St Johns II periods. He found indices of 4.5, 9.3, and 21.1 sites/century, respectively, for the three periods, statistics which offer strong support to the picture of a growing St Johns culture population. The increase was largest in the later St Johns II period when agriculture is thought to have been most important in local economies.

Even though the basic lifeway of the St Johns culture was established by the end of the Late Archaic period, the culture was not unchanging. After 500 BC inventions and new ideas, the latter reflected in the appearance of new and non-local ceramic styles, along with larger populations and increased use of domesticated plants, led to changes. After about AD 1050, although that date has not been verified with radiocarbon dates, at least some of the St Johns groups along the lower (northern) portions of the St Johns River developed complex social and political structures characterized by large mound centers and, apparently, by a chiefly level of social organization. These societies must have had a great influence on other St Johns groups, including Timucuan groups of the sixteenth century.

St Johns I Culture, 500 BC to AD 750

St Johns I villages were established in both freshwater and coastal zones. Villagers occasionally moved to smaller camps to perform specific activities, such as fishing and gathering shellfish. This pattern is probably the same as that practiced in east Florida in the Orange period. Tools and other St Johns I period artifacts, other than types of ceramics, also were the same as those used in the Orange period. In fact, from the Orange period on, the same shell tools, bone pins, bone awls, and bone points appear to have been used. Other artifacts include stone points, hollow bone sockets, and plummets or net weights.

St Johns pottery, with its distinctive chalky appearance and feel, is ubiquitous at sites. The most common type is undecorated. Some pottery is decorated with incised designs like those found on the earlier fiber-tempered pottery. Pinching, another decorative motif, appears on some early St Johns I vessels (Figure 1.4). The chalky feel of St Johns ceramics comes from freshwater sponge spicules which occur naturally in the clays mined for pottery-making.

St Johns coastal shell middens, composed mainly of oysters, are among the largest shell mounds in the United States. One of the most extensive is Turtle Mound near New Smyrna on the central Florida Atlantic coast. Before its partial destruction, various observers estimated its height at as much as 75 feet.

Figure 1.4 St Johns pottery; the top four St Johns I potsherds are pinched or incised; the bottom three St Johns II potsherds are check stamped

Excavations at coastal sites have uncovered hundreds of bones of the animals the St Johns villagers consumed. They include deer, turkeys, raccoons, opossums, rabbits, panther, and a variety of fishes, especially snook, mullet, shark, and redfish. As elsewhere, fish and shellfish were the most important meat sources. On occasion a porpoise might have been caught and eaten as were a variety of water birds. The wide array of animals represented at the large coastal villages contrasts with the many fewer species found at special-use fishing camps.

Each St Johns village had a leader who helped coordinate activities such as communal ceremonies. Villagers most likely were organized into a number of lineages or other kin groups, each of which probably had a name and distinctive paraphernalia or other symbols of membership.

When a village grew too large for its residents to be supported easily by local resources, one or more of the kin groups broke away, establishing a new village nearby. Traditions and shared lineage membership served to tie old and new villages together. Such a social system was probably present in nearly all of Florida at this same time.

St Johns I ceremonial life appears to have combined indigenous elements with motifs and practices found elsewhere in northern Florida. Many aspects of beliefs must have been shared all across northern Florida. Low sand mounds generally less than four feet high were built, although a few are as high as ten feet. At times red ochre or a similar mineral was mixed with the soil used to build mounds.

Mounds for interment of the dead were used in conjunction with charnel houses where bodies were stored and perhaps macerated before the skulls and long bones were deposited in the mounds. The same mound might have been used more than once for burials, resulting in several mound strata and multiple layers of human burials. Primary burials – either in flexed or extended position – were placed in mounds less frequently. The number of people interred in any one mound ranges from two to one hundred, although most mounds contain less than 25 individuals. Each mound may have been for the members of the same lineage or kin group.

After AD 100 new ideas must have entered east and central Florida along with items exotic to the region. Trade routes brought mica and galena, copper-covered animal jaws and wooden effigies, greenstone celts, quartz plummets, copper discs, copper cymbal-shaped ear spools, and bird-effigy elbow pipes. These items were used and then placed in mounds, sometimes with individual burials. Ceramic vessels, some made in regions far from east Florida, also were placed in the mounds, along with shell objects, including columella beads, drinking cups, tools, and pendants. Mounds of this time were larger than those present earlier and all are constructed in the shape of truncated cones. Two excavated mounds dating from about AD 100 each contained a small log tomb. Log tombs are known from Hopewellian mounds elsewhere in the southeast and midwest United States at the same time.

By the end of the St Johns I period at AD 750, native groups were living in villages throughout east Florida. As was true of other contemporary native societies in Florida, they lived in close proximity to wetlands and made their living by hunting, fishing, gathering, and collecting wild resources. Some gardening may have taken place, or, at the least, the St Johns I people encouraged the growth of wild plants that they used for food, containers, and other purposes.

St Johns II Culture, AD 750–1565

The appearance of check-stamped pottery in the St Johns region at about AD 750 provides archaeologists with a convenient marker that allows St Johns II archaeological deposits to be distinguished from those of the St Johns I period. Although changes in ceramic decoration took place, other artifacts used by villagers remained much the same.

The St Johns II people, like those of the earlier period, used a wide variety of plants and animals. One glimpse into that precolumbian world is provided by Barbara Purdy's archaeological investigations at Hontoon Island, a site just south of Lake George. Although Hontoon is just beyond the southern extent of colonial period Timucua-speakers, it is a St Johns culture site like those found just to the north.

Purdy's excavations, some of which were made in waterlogged shell midden, uncovered a remarkable assortment of St Johns II period artifacts and plant and animal remains, including thousands of woodchips and other debris from wood-working and dugout canoe-making. The water helped to preserve these normally perishable materials.

Small stone arrow points were common as were sandstone abraders used to work wood. The array of bone and shell artifacts is very similar to that found at other St Johns sites: deer ulna awls; bone pins, pendants, beads, a dagger, and fishhook; shark teeth; *Busycon* shell hammers and cups; and a fishhook made from mussel shell.

Animals remains were dominated by freshwater species such as catfish, gar, bass, mullet, aquatic turtles, and alligator. A variety of other fish and reptiles were eaten, along with ducks (some of which are migratory species), Canadian geese, and terrestrial species, including gopher tortoise, rabbit, deer, and turkey. Most popular in the meat diet were snails, catfish, pond turtles, and gopher tortoises.

Analysis of the plant remains by archaeobotanist Lee Newsom identified the species used for artifacts and food. The variety was immense. Thirty wood species were identified along with 82 species of seeds or other plant parts. Several tropical woods not native to Florida were found.

Cypress chips were very common, most likely debris produced in shaping dugout canoes out of logs. One broken canoe paddle was recovered, along with a red cedar bird-effigy ornament, perhaps a hairpin. Posts, fire-starters (parts of bow drills), shafts, plugs, a wedge, tool handles, small points, and a bowl were identified. Also found were numerous notched sticks, some of which could be throwing-stick shafts, while others resemble the pegs used today to anchor tent supports.

Just as the native peoples used a wide range of animals, so did they make use of many of the plants that grew around them. Hickory nuts, acorns, and cabbage palm remains were especially numerous as were may pop, grape, and saw palmetto. At least 17 other plants produced fruit, berries, or seeds that were eaten.

Both a variety of a gourd-like squash (*Cucurbita pepo*) and bottle gourds (*Legenaria siceria*) were identified from the wet deposits. Both plants probably were used as containers rather than as food and neither appears to have been cultivated. As in the St Johns I period, they apparently grew in and around human settlements, encouraged as botanical camp followers.

Near Hontoon Island toy-like ceramic effigies representing a variety of plants and animals were excavated from the Thursby Mound, a St Johns II mound, in the late nineteenth century. Squashes, gourds, acorns, fishes, turtles, panthers, bears, squirrels, turkeys, dogs(?), and beavers(?) all are depicted in clay. Pottery displaying corncob impressions has been found at other St Johns sites. However, the exact importance of maize within the late St Johns culture diet remains uncertain.

Although many aspects of life remained the same during the St Johns II period, larger populations and other conditions did lead to cultural changes that can be seen in the archaeological record. One such new trait is the appearance of large mounds – probably bases for temples and other special buildings – constructed at villages serving as centers of ceremonial and, perhaps political life. Another is the use of special paraphernalia by elite, probably chiefly officials. Together these traits suggest the development of a more complex level of political organization, one characterized by hereditary chiefs who, with their families, ruled over their own towns and the populations of outlying villages.

Because the St Johns II economy was based largely on food collection – hunting, gathering, and fishing – rather than agricultural production, the population of late precolumbian east Florida never reached the density of the farming populations in the interior of the Southeast. Consequently, the large, politically unified societies with paramount chiefs ruling literally hundreds of towns that were present in those regions never were present in the St Johns region. Instead, as we shall see in later chapters focusing on the Timucua, in east Florida it was more common for the chiefs of villages or groups of small villages to form alliances for mutual defense and for other benefits. Large, central towns with multiple buildings and temples erected on mounds from which a paramount chief, a hierarchy of chiefly officials, and other elites ruled vast territories never occurred in the region of the Timucua. Only a few towns are found that had even a single mound used as the base for a building (Figure 1.5).

One such precolumbian St Johns II town may have been the site called Mount Royal just north of Lake George. The site was visited by the naturalist William Bartram in 1765 and 1774, who described the site and its linear earthwork or causeway (1928: 101–2):

At about fifty yards distance . . . stands a magnificent Indian mount. About fifteen years ago I visited this place, at which time there were no settlements of white people, but all appeared wild and savage; yet in that uncultivated state it possessed an almost inexpressible air of grandeur . . . But what greatly contributed towards completing the

Figure 1.5 Drawing of the Grant Mound, a large St Johns II mound
Source: Allen (1896: 366).

magnificence of the scene, was a noble Indian highway, which led from the great mount, on a straight line, three quarters of a mile, first through a point or wing of the orange grove, and continuing thence through an awful forest of live oaks, it was terminated by palms and laurel magnolias, on the verge of an oblong lake, which was on the edge of an extensive green level savanna. This grand highway was about fifty yards wide, sunk a little below the common level, and the earth thrown up on each side, making a bank of about two feet high.

Decorative motifs and artifacts excavated from the mound at Mount Royal by Clarence B. Moore in the late nineteenth century are like those found elsewhere in the southeast United States dating to AD 1050–1150 and associated with early Mississippian centers. These artifacts and symbols are a part of the Southeastern Ceremonial Complex, an assemblage of artifacts and art styles widespread in time and space and associated with various beliefs and practices that transcended the Southeast.

Figure 1.6 Copper plate with forked eye motifs from Mount Royal
Source: Moore (1894a: 3).

Southeastern Ceremonial Complex items from Mount Royal included a copper plate embossed with forked eye motifs like those found at other Mississippian sites (Figure 1.6). Copper beads and copper ornaments also were found, evidence of contact between the St Johns region and societies to the north and northwest.

When excavated by Moore, the "great mount" was 15 feet high and 160 feet in diameter. As with other St Johns II mounds, the mound appears to have been capped with an red ochre-impregnated layer of sand. The mound probably served as a base for one or more buildings associated with the village's religious life and its leaders. At least some of those individuals were interred in the mound. At other times, other people were buried in the mound as well.

Artifacts from the mound included *Busycon* shells, greenstone celts, spatulate greenstone celts, ceramic biconical tubes, and numerous fired-clay vessels. The latter were constructed into a variety of unique shapes and must have had special ceremonial use, such as for brewing and drinking ceremonial teas. Pieces of copper and copper artifacts, such as ear spools, were found throughout the mound.

One of the most intriguing features of the site is the linear causeway described by Bartram. It leads 820 yards from the mound to a small lake. The causeway, which varies from 12 to 25 feet across, was built by scraping up soil from the ground surface and piling it on both sides of the causeway. These parallel piles or, more correctly, ridges, were nearly 3 feet high and as much as 12 feet wide.

In the sixteenth century French colonists visited a Timucuan town called Edelano, located on an island in the St Johns River. They described a walkway 300 paces long and 50 paces wide at the town. Huge trees with their branches intertwined overhead were said to grow on both sides of the walkway. Recent research by Virgil Beasley, a student at the University of Central Florida, suggests Edelano was on Drayton Island on the north end of Lake George where the St Johns River flows from the lake. The site also was visited by Bartram, who described it (1928: 104) as "a very pompous Indian mount, or conical pyramid of earth, from which runs in a straight line a grand avenue or Indian highway."

A similar causeway also was described by the French as having been present at the main town of a Timucuan chief living just west of the St Johns River.

If the evidence from the Mount Royal site is being correctly interpreted, it indicates that at least some of the late St Johns II period societies on the St Johns River must have shared aspects of ceremonial and political lives with other southeast societies, even while retaining their own specific economic adaptations. But although these precolumbian ancestors of the Timucua practiced maize agriculture, their cultivation of crops was not as intensive or extensive as in many other parts of the interior Southeast.

Even though the presence of gardening was less important in east Florida, the practice of cultivating crops went hand in hand with new cultural practices. A desire to understand and try to control such things as agricultural fertility and rainfall, the need for more social cooperation in order to maintain fields and protect territory, and larger populations together led to the development of more complex forms of political organization and new beliefs and ceremonial practices. Village leaders, perhaps like those at Mount Royal, sought to bridge the gap between ordinary people and the supernatural. Often these chiefly individuals were associated with special objects and symbols, such as those found in the Mount Royal site. Those objects and symbols were visible reminders of the power of the chiefs.

Some of the St Johns II sites continued to be occupied into the sixteenth century when they were visited by French and Spanish colonists and soldiers. Most likely, the ancestors of the Timucua had first occupied those same sites many generations earlier, in the precolumbian period.

Southeast Georgia and Northeast Florida

The coastal region between the mouth of the St Johns River and the Altamaha River was home to Timucua-speaking native groups in the sixteenth century. But the succession of precolumbian cultures which inhabited the region during the Late Archaic and post-500 BC periods differs from that found to the south in east Florida. At times archaeological assemblages resembled those found in the St Johns region, while at other times they were similar to the cultures found on the Georgia coast north of the Altamaha River. At still other times the archaeological assemblages found on the lower Georgia coast resembled neither east Florida nor central and northern coastal Georgia, or they were a combination of both.

This ambiguity is due in part to the geographical placement of northeastern Florida and the lower Georgia coast between two regions that have well-defined and distinctive precolumbian cultures. Because our present recognition of the presence or absence of those cultures is based largely on types of pottery, changes in the popularity of ceramic styles give an illusion of much less population continuity in the St Johns-to-Altamaha region than probably actually occurred. It is more likely the precolumbian people in the St Johns River-to-Altamaha region maintained the same lifeways over hundreds of years, as did the coastal populations to the north and south. Only the styles of pottery they made changes as first one type of pottery and then another rose and fell in popularity.

The St Johns River-to-Altamaha River coastal zone is typified by large, linear barrier islands which front the Atlantic Ocean. The islands, some more than fifteen miles long and three miles wide, were characterized by live oak and magnolia forests which provided home for numerous plants and a host of terrestrial animals. Freshwater ponds provided water for the pre-columbian inhabitants and served as sources of freshwater turtles and fish.

But the most important larder was the marsh/tidal stream/estuary system which is extensive on the mainland side of the barrier islands, especially at the mouths of rivers like the Nassau, St Marys, Satilla, and Altamaha. Fish and shellfish, mainly oysters, could literally be harvested from the tidal streams draining the marshes and from the mouths of streams and rivers flowing to the Atlantic. These waters and marshes also provided raccoons, diamond-back terrapins, water and wading birds, and even sea mammals. All of these resources were used by the coastal dwellers from the Late Archaic period into colonial times.

As noted above, the earliest sites on the lower Georgia coast are associated with the St Simons culture, 2000 to 500 BC, which is contemporary with the Orange culture found to the south in Florida. St Simons sites, usually shell middens, some deposited in donut-shaped rings, contain fiber-tempered pottery similar to Orange pottery, but at times with different designs. Orange culture sites also are found in the southern portion of this coastal region.

Following the St Simons and Orange cultures, the succession of archaeological assemblages in the St Johns-to-Altamaha region include artifacts from both Georgia and Florida cultures. Great variation exists and site assemblages through time differ almost by estuarine-river drainage. There is considerable overlapping of assemblages. In general the sequence for southeast Georgia is: Deptford culture, 500 BC to AD 750; Wilmington culture, AD 750 to 1000; and Savannah culture, AD 1000 to c.1565. The contemporary northeast Florida sequence is the same as that for east Florida: St Johns I, 500 BC to AD 750, and St Johns II, AD 750 to 1565. But again, a single site might, for instance, contain both

Deptford and St Johns I artifacts, while another might contain only Savannah materials.

Other archaeological assemblages than those listed in the preceding paragraph also were present in portions of the region for short periods of time. For instance Swift Creek sites have been found in the northern portion of the St Johns-to-Altamaha region. Swift Creek sites, including some with sand mounds, have been found both on St Simons Island and, in small numbers, down the coast and the adjacent mainland into northeast Florida. They are thought to date sometime within the period AD 500–1000. One large coastal Swift Creek site is on the Georgia mainland in the vicinity of Darien just north of the Altamaha River and numerous sites exist in central Georgia, including in the Ocmulgee River drainage. Those coastal Swift Creek sites may represent a movement of people from the interior of Georgia to that zone.

During the late precolumbian period, after AD 1200, the Savannah cultural assemblage, characterized by cord-marked, check-stamped, and complicated stamped pottery, was present at a number of sites on St Simons Island. At about the same time or soon after the Savannah archaeological assemblage was found all along the southeast Georgia–northeast Florida coast from the mouth of the St Johns River northward. Along that section of the coast Savannah sites are later than St Johns II sites. The best evidence we have from Amelia Island in Florida and St Simons Island in Georgia is that the early colonial period Timucua-speakers in the St Johns-to-Altamaha region were associated with the Savannah culture or variants of it.

Excavations on northern St Simons Island provide a glimpse of one late precolumbian/early sixteenth-century Savannah village probably occupied by the ancestors of Timucuan people. The village was on a wide point of land surrounded by tidal streams and salt marsh. Measuring 225 yards across, the area of the village contained a number of small shell middens which probably surrounded houses. Other larger shell heaps accumulated on the north and east sides of the village close to the marsh.

Two buildings were excavated. The first was a large, oval dwelling, 40 feet by 52 feet. Large posts were spaced around the perimeter. The walls may have been thatched, although no evidence of this was found. Interior partitions and the structure's size suggest it was the home of several families. Cooking pits were in evidence as well as debris from everyday activities. The house probably resembled the one described in 1595 by a Franciscan friar for the Georgia coast (Swanton, 1946: 405):

a big cabin, circular in shape, made of entire pines from which the limbs and bark had been removed, set up with their lower ends in the earth and tops all brought together above like a pavilion or like the ribs of a parasol.

Inside near the eastern end of the house a large shallow grave had been dug and the partial skeletal remains of at least 12 adults and a newly born child or fetus were interred in it. Some of the bones showed marks from having been cleaned of flesh. The dead apparently had first been buried or stored elsewhere in the village, then cleaned and interred in the house floor. They may have been relatives of the families who lived there. Other secondary burials, some containing the bones of several people and some individual interments, were also discovered in the house.

Toward the northern end of the village excavations located a squarish building 36 feet on a side. Tightly flexed human burials were placed in individual, shallow, oval graves dug against the inside walls. The location of each grave was marked with a layer of shells 4 to 6 inches thick. Some graves were found which were empty except for a few small pieces of bone, suggesting the individuals buried in those graves had been removed. In those instances the shells marking the grave's location were not present.

Most likely when a person died he or she was buried in this mortuary structure. Later, probably after decomposition, the body was exhumed and the bones cleaned. The cleaned bones, mainly the long bones from the arms and legs and the skulls, were taken elsewhere. At least some of the cleaned bundles of bones may have been reburied in the house described above.

Other burials and empty graves were found just north and east of the mortuary structure. Some of these individuals were buried with stone spatulate celts and other paraphernalia. Two dogs also were buried there. One had a musket ball in its leg, graphic evidence that the village was occupied at the time people from Europe came to the island.

Apparently not all of the villagers' dead relatives were afforded similar treatment. Some may have been interred in a sand and shell mound located 2.4 miles south of the village. The people buried in the mound may have been from one family or kin group.

The mound was constructed by first laying down a square core of shell midden brought to the location from elsewhere. This core was 3 feet high and 23 feet on a side. Six people were buried in flexed positions in shallow graves on the east side of the shell core. Sand was dug up from around three sides of the core and used to cover the shell as well as the location of the graves. This resulted in a horseshoe-shaped borrow pit encircling most of the mound.

On the south side of the mound alternate layers of sand and shell were deposited to form "steps" up the side of the low mound. A human fetus or newly born child dressed in clothing decorated with a shell bead "apron" was placed in a grave dug into the steps.

Later, additional burials were interred in graves dug into the top of the mound and its east side. Before use of the mound was discontinued, a cache of ceramic vessels was deposited in a shallow depression dug on its eastern side. Several large pieces of wrought iron, perhaps ship's hardware, were put with the ceramic vessels before the cache was covered. European coins and glass beads also were found in the mound, offering evidence that it was used in the early sixteenth century.

The Savannah ancestors of the Timucua Indians lived off the wild foods gathered from salt marshes, tidal streams, and the lagoon which separates the barrier islands from the mainland. They also utilized the resources of the estuaries and rivers in the St Johns-to-Altamaha region as well as the oak and magnolia forests. In the sixteenth century the people along that coast grew corn and other plants. Charred corn has been found in a Savannah site near the mouth of the St Johns River. But although these ancestors of Timucua Indians were agriculturists, the importance of cultivated foods within their diets was probably no more than it was for the St Johns people to the south.

North Peninsular Florida and Southern Georgia

A third area of colonial period Timucua-speaking groups was in northern peninsular Florida west of the St Johns River drainage and in southern Georgia. This area extended well into present-day south-central Georgia as far as the Altamaha River and the intersection of the Oconee and Ocmulgee rivers. The archaeology of the post-500 BC region cultures in a portion of south-central Georgia, such as those occupying the valleys of the upper Withlacoochee and Alapaha river drainages and Suwannoochee Creek, is not well understood.

Archaeological surveys undertaken by archaeologist Frankie Snow in the upper Satilla River drainage have indicated the presence of ceramic assemblages that contain Lamar pottery associated with the Lamar culture assemblage found in the late prehistoric period in piedmont Georgia. Several sites have been found which contain Spanish artifacts, suggesting those river valleys were occupied in the colonial period.

The archaeology of north peninsular Florida is better understood. In that area there are a number of Paleoindian and Early and Middle Archaic period sites. Fewer Late Archaic sites have been documented and those sites with Orange fiber-tempered pottery which have been found are small, perhaps representing camps. Likewise early Deptford sites, 500 BC to AD 100, are also few in number and small in size. Perhaps between about 2000 BC and AD 100 the region was not as important to pre-columbian cultures as it had been in earlier times and as it would be later.

After AD 100 late Deptford people began to utilize the region year-round and to establish villages, some with sand mounds and other earthworks. Sedentism quickly brought more cultural changes and by about AD 200 to 300 two distinct cultures had developed. In north-central Florida south of the Santa Fe River was the Cades Pond culture, while north of that river was the McKeithen Weeden Island culture. The latter is related to the other Weeden Island cultures found in northwest and west Florida and southern Georgia.

The economies of both the Cades Pond and McKeithen Weeden Island cultures were based on collecting wild foods rather than farming. If gardening was present, archaeologists have not yet found evidence of it.

Cades Pond sites are found adjacent to lakes and extensive freshwater wetlands, reflecting that culture's dietary reliance on fish, water birds, turtles, and a host of other animals that live in and near wetland habitats. Sand mounds, some with earthen berms and ditch enclosures, served as repositories for the bones of the dead and as platforms on which to erect special buildings, such as charnel houses in which bodies were cleaned and the bones stored before interment.

McKeithen Weeden Island sites, both villages and camps, tend to be located in the Hammock Belt oak and hickory forest of north Florida near small streams, especially in the region between the present-day towns of Live Oak and Lake City north of the Santa Fe River. Smaller sites also are found in the lowland, mixed pine and oak forests of north Florida. Many of the village sites are associated with sand burial mounds which were repositories for bundled, secondary burials. Most likely each mound did serve a specific lineage or other kin group.

Excavations at one village, the McKeithen site, provided evidence that Weeden Island village leaders came from the kin group which had achieved the highest social importance, perhaps because of that group's ability to gain stature through hosting community feasts, ceremonies, and the like. Such leaders, like those of the St Johns culture, most likely were both religious and civic figures.

The McKeithen site itself probably was held in high esteem for several generations or longer, a period during which its leaders assumed greater importance and power than was often the case. That importance may in part have come from the village's central geographical setting and its ready access to a host of food and other resources. But the economic base of the Weeden Island people was not sufficient to sustain continued political elaboration for more than a few generations. The importance of villages, and their leaders, rose and fell.

It was sometime during the period AD 350–475 that the village at the McKeithen site served as an important center. During that period the village covered approximately 120 acres. Three sand mounds were arranged nearly 300 yards apart in a large triangle. A horseshoe-shaped village midden, marking the locations of houses, extended around the three mounds. A central plaza was enclosed by the mounds and midden.

Comparisons of pottery from contexts in the village dating before and after that period showed that high status ceramics were most evenly distributed in the village during that time, reflecting the higher status of the village relative to other periods. The village's importance, and that of its leader, also are reflected in the construction and functioning of the three mounds.

Excavations revealed that all three mounds were built about AD 350 and that their use ended by AD 475; the actual period of construction and use could well have been a much shorter time within that century and a quarter. Mound B was located at the apex of the triangularly positioned mounds. It originally was constructed as a small, rectangular platform with a height of less than 2 feet. A rectangular building with pine wall posts was erected on the platform. Small posts along the interior walls may have supported sleeping and sitting benches positioned around a hearth. Ceramics recovered from in and around the house, many with a raptoral bird motif on them, suggest the house was home to the village leader, a person of great importance.

That person, a woman or very gracile male mid- to late thirties in age, died and was buried in a very shallow grave dug into the floor of the house. He or she was interred on the back with arms bent at the elbows and palms up. Red ochre colored the hair which was decorated with the lower leg bone of an anhinga, a bird also called the water turkey. Cause of death could have been an infection caused by an arrow wound to the left hip; a stone arrow point was found embedded in the bone. Evidence of a severe infection which had lasted at least several months was in evidence around the point.

Once placed in the grave the body lay exposed for an unspecified length of time, allowing rodents and possibly even a dog the opportunity to chew on the body, leaving characteristic toothmarks on some of the bones. Then a small wooden-post tomb was erected over the shallow grave and body within it. Next sand was used to cover the tomb and the building was burned to the ground and the charred remnants scattered. A mantle of earth more than 3 feet thick was used to cover the platform mound, burying the mound and its tomb.

Mound A, the largest mound at the village, also began with the construction of a low, rectangular platform mound. Its purpose was for performing activities associated with cleaning the bones of the dead. Those bones were later interred in Mound C, the third mound.

The cleaning process involved interring bodies in graves dug into the mound, allowing them to decompose, and then exhuming them and cleaning the bones. That portion of the mound where this took place was hidden behind a substantial wooden-post screen. Small fire pits, deposits of red ochre, and evidence of feasts in which deer were eaten were found on the mound.

When the charnel activities ceased and the bones had been removed, the posts from the screen were used for a huge fire atop the mound. Some of the burned debris was cleared to the edges of the platform mound before the platform was buried under a 6-foot thick layer of sand. The resultant oval to rectangular mound measured 145 by 260 feet.

Cleaned bones from the Mound A charnel activities probably were stored in a charnel house erected on Mound C, which was first constructed as a circular platform 3 feet high. At some point in time the stored bundles of bones were removed and the charnel house was burned to the ground. Clean soil was used to cover the burned debris before the bundled burials were placed around the edges of the platform. As a part of this ceremony a small fire was lit on the eastern part of the platform mound atop the clean sand. The participants ate and perhaps drank one or more sacred teas from special ceramic vessels. A number of other ceramic vessels, some portraying animal symbols, were placed on the eastern edge of the mound and, as with Mounds A and B, the entire deposit, bones and ceramic vessels included, was buried under 6 feet of earth. Apparently the importance of the McKeithen village was at an end.

Alachua Culture, AD 600–1539

In north-central Florida the Cades Pond culture was supplanted in about AD 600 by a precolumbian culture associated with a very different archaeological assemblage. All the evidence on hand indicates that the Alachua culture represents a migration of people from south-central Georgia who displaced the Cades Pond population. Investigations in Georgia have shown strong similarities between Alachua pottery and some stone tools and the pottery associated with the Ocmulgee culture of the Ocmulgee River valley of Georgia, especially the physiographic region known as the Dougherty Uplift. The uplift is a highland zone that cuts diagonally across Georgia from Augusta down to northwest Florida.

The people of the Ocmulgee culture may have been the ancestors of the Timucuan groups in at least a portion of south-central
Georgia, but that remains very uncertain. It appears that in
around AD 600 Ocmulgee populations expanded beyond the
boundaries of their Georgia region, moving south around the
McKeithen Weeden Island region in north Florida into north-
central Florida. There, especially in the western part of that
region away from the Cades Pond sites which are located among
the more easterly wetlands, the population derived from the
Ocmulgee culture found a suitable area to settle.

Alachua site locations and the archeological assemblage found
at those sites contrast sharply with those of the Cades Pond.
Most Alachua sites are large middens with little or no freshwater
shell; pottery, bone tools, and lithic artifacts occur in relatively
large amounts. The chert used for the stone tools was easily
mined from local limestone outcroppings.

While Cades Pond sites were situated to maximize access to
extensive wetlands, Alachua villages were in locales where good
agricultural soils are found, mainly in the Middle Florida Hammock Belt which extends from north Florida down into the
north-central part of the state. Differences in the two cultures'
site selections can be seen when individual sites are mapped and
it is evident their locations are mutually exclusive. Alachua sites
are not on top of or contiguous with Cades Pond sites. They are
located on higher elevations where drainage is better and where
deciduous hammocks and loamy soils are found. These locations
reflect economic patterns: the Cades Pond people relied heavily
on wetlands to provide a significant portion of their diet; the
Alachua people grew crops. Less of their diet came from hunting,
fishing, or collecting wild resources. The number of animal
species used for food by the Alachua villagers was fewer than the
number Cades Pond culture used.

Within north Florida Alachua culture sites most often occur in
clusters. New villages budded off from older villages as populations increased and villages were shifted as nearby soils lost
fertility. Site clusters are found at west Orange Lake, north Levy
Lake, the north-central side of Paynes Prairie, the northwest
side of Paynes Prairie, near the town of Rochelle, the Moon
Lake locality, the Devil's Millhopper locality, near the town of
Alachua, and in the Robinson Sinks locality in northwest Alachua County. Except for the first two, all of these sites are south

of the Santa Fe River and north of Paynes Prairie. Villages were placed along trails, some of which were still being used by American settlers when they were first mapped in the nineteenth century.

All of these clusters, except north Levy Lake, contain at least one site where sixteenth- and/or seventeenth-century Spanish artifacts have been found. That the Alachua culture was the precolumbian manifestation of the Timucua-speaking Potano Indians who lived in that area in the early colonial period is certain. It may have been the ancestors of the Potano who entered Florida from Georgia in the seventh century.

Alachua villages were close to lakes, ponds, or other freshwater sources which provided drinking water and access to fish, turtles, and wading birds. Evidence of the use of nets to catch fish and for filleting and, perhaps, drying them has come from excavated sites. Using snares, traps, and bows and arrows, the latter tipped with small triangular projectile points made of local chert, the Alachua people caught and hunted forest animals, of which the white-tailed deer was the most important to their diet. Deer were butchered at the kill site and the haunches, hide, lower jaw with the tongue, and antlers were taken to the village.

Evidence for Alachua plant use is still scarce. Palm berries, acorns, and hickory nuts have been found and corn kernels have come from one late precolumbian/early colonial period site. That corn was grown is certain. The surfaces of many ceramic vessels were roughened with corn cobs, some of which still had kernels, a practice that left impressions of the corn. In 1539 members of the Hernando de Soto expedition saw cornfields at Potano villages when they marched through the region.

Excavations at the Richardson site, an Alachua village on the west shore of Orange Lake, provide some of our best evidence of what a village was like. The village covered an area 200 yards on a side. Houses were circular, about 25 feet in diameter, and placed about 70 feet apart. They were built with wall poles placed 2 to 3 feet apart. Tops of the poles were probably bent over and tied together to form a dome-like structure which could have been thatched with palmetto or palm fronds. Drying racks and storage cribs were situated around the houses. The size of the village suggests it contained 15 to 20 households.

Within the houses cooking fires were lit in shallow hearths. Much deeper sub-floor pits were probably lined with hides or

grass and used for storage. Along the inside walls were low
sleeping and sitting platforms. To ward off mosquitoes at night,
the villagers lit small smudge fires under their beds.

A variety of stone and bone tools were in use. Triangular
Pinellas arrow points are very common. Other stone tools include drills, gravers, spokeshaves, bifacial-ovate knives, and
hones. Flakes and blades of various sizes were used as knives and
scrapers. Grinding implements, both mortars and manos, were
used to process maize, nuts, and seeds. Hand-axe-shaped implements were used as choppers, perhaps for working or cutting
wood; some were used as hoes. Bone pins and awls which were
sharpened on stone or ceramic hones are the most common bone
tools.

Shell was also used as a raw material. Shell earpins made from
the columella of *Busycon* shells and *Busycon* drinking cups were
used. A shell gorget with a spider motif came from an Alachua
site in eastern Levy County.

Pottery of the Alachua culture is distinctive from that of the
earlier Cades Pond culture. Alachua vessels were cylindrical
pots, smaller than those of the Cades Pond people, and simple,
small, bowls 10 inches or less in diameter at the mouth. Prior to
firing nearly all of the clay vessels had their surfaces malleated
and roughened. Perhaps this helped to compact the clay coils,
adding strength to the vessels. The roughening was done with
fabric- or cord-wrapped wooden paddles or with dried corn cobs
(Figure 1.7). About half of the vessels were then smoothed over;
the roughened impressions were left on the others.

Three Alachua sand burial mounds have been investigated by
archaeologists. All date from early in the history of the Alachua
culture and two of them are located apart from any Alachua
village. The earliest mound, the Woodward Mound, 50 feet in
diameter and about 3 feet high, was next to a village. Construction of the mound began with the digging of a circular depression about 18 inches deep and 32 feet in diameter. A mixture of
dark gray sand and charcoal was used to fill in the depression,
forming a base on which the mound was built. Two or three
adults strewn with red ochre were buried in separate graves dug
into this base. A mound was then placed over the graves and the
prepared layer. Later other people were interred in the mound's
eastern side, most lying on their back. Each person was buried
with head toward the northwestern edge of the mound and feet

Figure 1.7 Alachua culture pottery; the top five potsherds were impressed with dried corn cobs; the three pottery discs are thought by some archaeologists to have been made as game counters; others suggest they are expended tools, potsherds used as grinders with all of the edges worn off

toward the mound's edge. After each interment, sand was added to cover the body, a process that added height and diameter to the mound. Three such burials consisted only of the individual's skull and long bones. Two children were interred with shell beads. The people buried in the mound included adults and children of various ages, evenly divided between males and females. They were probably all members of the same lineage or kin group.

This is in contrast to the Henderson Mound, another low sand mound. That mound contained 41 people, 24 of whom were interred lying on their backs. Ten people were represented only by skulls, and five were in flexed positions (two burials were too fragmented to allow archaeologists to ascertain burial form). As with the Woodward Mound, age distribution of the people in the mound was normal for a population. However, of the 16 people whose gender was determined, 15 were female. Perhaps the mound was used to bury the dead of a single matrilineage.

Many of the Woodward burials were interred with red ochre around the person's head, shoulders, and chest. Charred wood, in a few cases actual charred planks, were placed on, beside, or under burials. Apparently the wood was used to line and cover individual shallow graves. Fires were lit on top of the graves, charring the wood, and then sand was used to cover the still smoldering wood and the grave.

Suwannee Valley Culture, AD 750–1539

Unlike north-central Florida where the Cades Pond culture was replaced by ancestors of Timucua-speaking Indians, in north Florida there is continuity through the sequence of post-AD 300 precolumbian cultures. In that region the McKeithen Weeden Island culture is believed to have developed into the Suwannee Valley culture. The appearance of the latter is dated to AD 750, a date when there were sufficient changes in the archaeological assemblage for archaeologists to define a new culture. Timucua-speaking groups living in north Florida in the early colonial period were associated with the Suwannee Valley culture.

The ceramic complex associated with that culture includes check-stamped pottery, as well as cord-marked, cob-marked, punctated/roughened, and brushed wares (Figure 1.8). Some of these surface treatments are the same as those found in the Alachua culture. However, when the total Suwannee Valley assemblage is examined it is distinct from that of the Alachua culture.

Figure 1.8 Suwannee culture pottery; the top three potsherds are check stamped; the middle three roughened or punctated; the bottom three are brushed

Compared to site locations of the McKeithen Weeden Island culture, early Suwannee Valley village sites seem to be less dense and there are more, but smaller, sites. Many sites appear to be single households, small hamlets, or camps rather than villages with many houses. Sites are common in the Middle Florida Hammock Belt as well as in lowland forests.

Compared to the earlier McKeithen Weeden Island culture, the pattern is one of less nucleated villages, more smaller settlements, the presence of many special-use camps, and occupation of localities which were little used in earlier times. These changes may correlate with an increased reliance on agriculture. As yet, however, good evidence for early Suwannee Valley period agriculture has not been found.

By the later Suwannee Valley period nucleation of villages may once again have been common and clusters of village and special-use camps are found. These clusters, similar to those in the Alachua region, may date from the time when maize agriculture was practiced.

Several of the site clusters are associated with sand burial mounds, at least one of which contained glass beads indicating it was in use in the colonial period. Mounds are found next to village sites in both highland and lowland areas.

One Suwannee Valley mound, Leslie Mound, was built and used in the following manner. First, the ground surface was cleaned of humus and a 4-inch thick layer of clean soil was laid down. On top of that a low platform mound 1 foot high and at least 30 feet long a side was constructed. A layer of humic deposit accumulated on the top of this platform. The deposit may have been on the floor of a charnel house erected on the platform mound.

Bundled human long bones and crania were placed on the mound surface on the humic stratum. Previously these may have been stored in the charnel house. The platform mound and the burials were then covered with soil, forming a second platform mound 3.5 feet high. This second platform probably also was used as the base for a charnel house. Later, the building was removed just as the first one had been and more bundled burials were put on the surface of the mound. Then another mantle of soil was used to cover them. Evidence from Carter Mound I, another Suwannee Valley mound, indicates that it too was first constructed as a platform on which bundled burials were deposited and then buried under a mantle of sand. The same process was repeated during a second episode of burial and capping.

There is still much to learn about the Suwannee Valley culture, as well as the other precolumbian cultures that were ancestral to the Timucua Indians. For instance, the archaeology of south-central Georgia south of the Altamaha River is only now being explored in depth. Also, the northern extent of the Suwannee Valley culture into Georgia is unknown.

In the next chapter the colonial period Timucuan groups will be delineated. Where possible, they will be correlated with their respective archaeological manfestation, either the St Johns, Savannah, Alachua, or Suwannee Valley culture.

2

Who Were the Timucua?

Determining who were and who were not Timucua Indians is not as simple a task as one might suppose. Because the Timucua are defined by their language, we must determine who spoke that language to determine who the Timucua Indians were. And, despite the presence of thousands of pages of sixteenth- and seventeenth-century narratives, letters, reports, and religious tracts written by French and Spanish soldiers, colonists, friars, and government officials, remarkably little information was recorded about the language of the native people of northern Florida and southern Georgia.

Indeed, were it not for the writings of Father Francisco Pareja, a missionary friar who lived in La Florida during the first quarter of the seventeenth century, we would know almost nothing about the Timucua language and its regional dialects. Father Pareja, who came to Florida in 1595, served Timucua Indians at the mission of San Juan del Puerto located on the northern portion of Fort George Island north of the mouth of the St Johns River. In order to communicate with the mission villagers, Father Pareja learned Timucua, even turning it into a written language by recording Timucuan words and sentences using his native Spanish alphabet.

Father Pareja soon sought to use his linguistic skills to help other Franciscan friars serving Timucua Indians at missions in La Florida. He wrote several treatises on the Timucua language and translated religious doctrine into Timucua. In those writings, Pareja refers to nine Timucuan dialects, noting that words or pronunciations different from those spoken at his mission could be found in other areas. That information is very important because we can equate each dialect with one or more specific Timucuan groups, important information for mapping the extent of Timucua-speakers.

Unfortunately, the thoroughness with which Father Pareja sought to gather information on the dialects of Timucua is unknown. Were there other dialects beyond those mentioned by him? Are we certain we can accurately map the total range of the Timucua Indians in Georgia and Florida by mapping the known dialects? The answer to both questions is no. And this brings us back to the crux of our problem: how can modern scholars determine who were Timucuan groups?

We have three additional sources of information that are useful in helping to delineate who were and who were not Timucua-speakers. One is place names and other proper nouns. We can use dictionaries of Timucua to try to determine if names recorded in Spanish and French documents are Timucua in origin. Presumably, a Timucua-speaking group used Timucuan words for their towns, their leaders, and the like.

In general that is true. However, it is certain that non-Timucuan words were borrowed into Timucua. For instance, the word *iniha*, a type of chiefly official, is found in Timucua, but it also is widespread in various Muskhogean languages found across the Southeast. It was borrowed from those languages into Timucua, a language very different from the Muskhogean languages.

Place names can be deceptive in another way. For instance, some place names recorded by Europeans from the region of the Apalachee Indians in northwest Florida appear to be Timucua. But the Apalachee spoke a Muskhogean language. Why are the names Timucua? Does their use mean they are old names still in use although a new, different language was spoken in that region? Or is it simply that a native translator better versed in Timucua than in Apalachee gave to the Spaniards the Timucuan word for a place rather than an Apalachee one? Although word analysis is not foolproof, once we recognize its shortcomings and where we have more than a handful of words from a specific group, it is a useful tool for delineating Timucua-speakers.

Another source of information to help map the extent of the Timucua-speakers is to determine who did not speak Timucua. This turns out to be informative. Documentary evidence, for example, leaves no doubt that the Guale Indians north of the Altamaha River on the Georgia coast spoke Guale, a language from the Muskhogean family of languages. As noted above, Muskhogean, also spoken by the ancestors of the Creek Indians in the fall line region and the piedmont of Georgia, is very different from Timucua. From the Aucilla River west into the eastern panhandle of Florida the Apalachee language was spoken, another Muskhogean language. The presence of Muskhogean speakers in those two areas allows us to demarcate the northern and western extent of Timucua-speakers.

The southeast and south-central boundaries of the Timucua-speakers similarly can be delineated. Documents indicate that the Mayaca Indians in the St Johns River drainage south of Lake George spoke a language related to Jororo, the language of a native group who probably lived in Polk and Osceola counties in south-central Florida. Mayaca-Jororo was different from Timucua. Further south in southern Florida Spanish accounts indicate that more than two dozen different mutually unintelligible languages were spoken.

Less certain is the extent of Timucua-speakers to the southwest, towards Tampa Bay. Colonial period Spanish accounts make it clear that several languages were spoken in that region, but it is uncertain if any were related to Timucua. Analysis of place names from around Tampa Bay does provide some basis for thinking that some groups in that locality may have spoken a language related to Timucua. But that evidence has yet to be widely accepted. At this time we are on most solid ground when the southwestern boundary of Timucua-speakers is placed north of Tampa Bay in the Withlacoochee River/Cove of the Withlacoochee wetlands in eastern Citrus and western Marion and Sumter counties, the region of the Ocale Indians. The languages of the native groups who lived north of the Withlacoochee River along the Florida Gulf coast up to the Aucilla River are unknown. That region remains almost a *terra incognita* during the colonial period.

The third additional source of information helpful in mapping the geographical extent of the Timucua-speakers comes from the Spanish colonists, friars, and soldiers who traveled and lived among the native people. In their day-to-day dealings with the native groups the Spaniards knew who were Timucua-speakers. Although they almost never specifically say a person or a group of people spoke Timucua, it often is clear from the context of documents when they were interacting with Timucua Indians. Indeed, as we shall see in chapter 4, the Spaniards used native languages in helping to delineate mission provinces and in referring to other regions. The names the Spaniards used for areas of La Florida are often a reflection of the native groups who lived in those region. The Timucua-speakers living in northern Florida and southern Georgia were one of the three main linguistic groups among whom the Spaniards established missions. The Apalachee- and the Guale-speakers were the other two.

In the sections that follow I will use these sources of information to look at the distributions of Timucuan dialects and the locations of specific Timucuan groups. As much as possible, those groups will be correlated with archaeological assemblages, tying the Timucua Indians to the land and to their precolumbian past. We will see that it is their shared language that allows us to refer to specific groups as Timucua Indians.

Again it should be emphasized that in the colonial period the Timucua were never united politically. The people we call the Timucua were a number of different independent groups who spoke dialects of the same language. Even so, the Timucuan groups, living in close proximity to one another, shared many aspects of their cultures. The differences that did exist most likely resulted from their living in different environmental zones and having different histories.

Dialect Distributions

In the early colonial period native people who spoke Timucua occupied most of the northern third of peninsular Florida, not including the Gulf of Mexico coast. Timucua-speakers were found from the Aucilla River east to the Atlantic Ocean and south perhaps into the central lake district in Lake and Orange counties (but not including the St Johns drainage south of Lake George). Timucua-speakers also lived in southeast and south-central Georgia as far north as the Altamaha River; in Georgia their western boundary was possibly along a line drawn from the Ocmulgee–Oconee intersection southerly through modern Fitzgerald and Tifton down to the Aucilla River in northwest Florida.

For this large region Father Pareja mentions nine Timucuan dialects: Agua Dulce, Icafui, Mocama or Salt Water, Oconi, Potano, Santa Lucia de Acuera, Timucua, Tucururu, and Yufera (Figure 2.1). The Agua Dulce dialect (*agua dulce* is Spanish for "fresh water") was spoken by the groups living along a portion of the lower St Johns River north of Lake George and south of present-day Jacksonville. Archaeological sites in this area are associated with the St Johns culture.

Both the Icafui and Yufera dialects were spoken by Timucuan groups living in southeast Georgia, while Mocama or Salt Water was the dialect found along the coast from the area around the

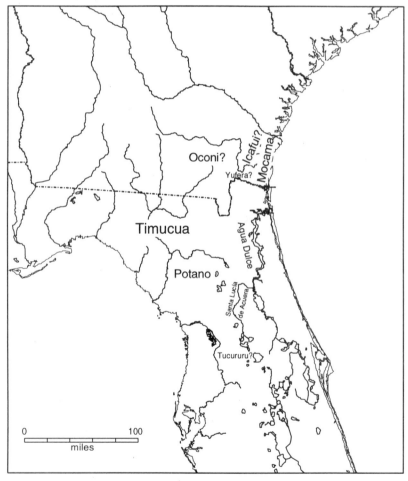

Figure 2.1 Timucuan dialects

mouth of the St Johns River and modern Jacksonville north to the Altamaha River. The Timucua Indians among whom Father Pareja lived on Fort George Island were speakers of the Mocama dialect. In the sixteenth century speakers of the Icafui, Yufera, and Mocama dialects most likely all were associated with the Savannah-related archaeological assemblage described in chapter 1.

Less certain is the location of speakers of the Oconi dialect, said by Father Pareja in 1602 to have been spoken by a group two days' travel from Cumberland Island, Georgia and three days' from Fort George Island. Anthropologist John Worth has suggested the Oconi, a group unrelated to the Oconee Indians of later times who spoke a Muskhogean language, were inland on the eastern edge of the Okefenokee Swamp. Franciscan missionary priests visited the Icafui, Yufera, and Oconi dialect-speakers around the turn of the seventeenth century, traveling north and west from their missions in northeast Florida.

The location of another of the Timucuan dialects, Tucururu, is similarly uncertain. A village called Tucuro is known to have been 40 leagues, about 135 miles, from St Augustine, probably in central Florida. Perhaps Tucururu was the dialect spoken by the people living among the many lakes in Lake and western Orange counties. The distance from St Augustine, measured on trails to the St Johns River and then down the St Johns and/or Oklawaha River to the central lake district is about 40 leagues. Archaeological investigations in that district have shown that the late precolumbian archaeological assemblage in mounds and village sites is related both to the St Johns culture and to the Safety Harbor culture present to the west in Sumter, Citrus, Hernando, and Pasco counties at the same time. John Worth suggests that the people who spoke the Tucururu, such as those at Tucuru, were related to the Acuera dialect-speakers.

The other Timucuan dialects can be correlated with specific Timucuan groups with more certainty. Potano was the dialect spoken by the Potano Indians who lived in what is now Alachua County and northern Marion County. They are represented archaeologically by the Alachua culture. The Santa Lucía de Acuera dialect was spoken by the Acuera Indians who lived along the Oklawaha River perhaps as far south as southern Marion County, near the presumed location of the Tucuru. Santa Lucía also was the name of a mission among the Acuera in the seventeenth century and the dialect most likely was spoken by those mission Timucua. The archaeological assemblage in Acuera territory was the St Johns culture, as it probably was at Tucuru.

Timucua was the dialect spoken by the native groups from the Santa Fe River north into modern Columbia, Hamilton, Suwannee, and eastern Madison counties, probably extending northward into southern Georgia. The Florida portion of this area included the heart of the mission province called Timucua by the Spaniards. The Suwannee Valley archaeological culture was present in those north Florida counties in the late precolumbian period, extending into southern Georgia.

Were there other dialects of Timucua? There may have been, although Father Pareja's classification seems to have encompassed most portions within the large region we know today was occupied by the Timucua, based on evidence from the mission period. One area about which we are not certain is the northern reaches of Timucua territory in southern Georgia. Another is the region of the Yustaga Indians, who were not missionized until after Father Pareja did his linguistic studies.

One thing which is clear is that Father Pareja was familiar with dialectic differences over a wide area, not just those dialects spoken near his mission of San Juan del Puerto. This erudite and energetic Franciscan friar appears to have been systematic in his linguistic survey and the nine dialects he names probably were nearly all there were. Modern scholars owe Father Pareja an enormous debt of gratitude for producing a lasting record of the Timucua language.

Timucuan Groups

During the colonial period all of the speakers of Timucua would become intimately involved with the Spaniards, especially during the seventeenth century, when Franciscan missions were founded in southern Georgia and north peninsular Florida. These interactions generated a very large corpus of written documents and accounts only a few of which contain information about the land and its people. Most comprise the paper trail left behind by colonial bureaucracies. Our knowledge of the Timucua Indians is highly dependent on the snippets of direct information contained in that archival record and the ability of historians to tease pertinent information out of the reams of everyday documentation.

Some of the Timucuan groups are only mentioned in a few accounts; others are cited often and, consequently, are well known. In the next sections the locations of those Timucuan groups as they were when first encountered by people from Europe will be described.

What to Call Them

Before we do that two points need to be cleared up. First is our use of the term "group" to refer to individual Timucuan ethnic units. We deliberately chose this unspecific term, rather than using tribe or chiefdom or another word, because it is indefinite. Exactly what constituted a Timucuan ethnic unit is not always certain. Most seem to have consisted of one main village. Where a new village had budded off in the past and still retained an affiliation with the original village, the two constituted a single group, with the residents recognizing their shared historical identity. Over time several new villages may have been founded and all the villagers shared an identity. In anthropological terminology, groups of these affiliated villages probably formed small-scale chiefdoms (see chapter 6).

In many instances several of these village clusters affiliated with one another. The alliances may have been for mutual defense. This was especially true after European soldiers entered native lands. Other alliances probably existed earlier, such as in northern Florida where groups of Timucua apparently formed an alliance for defense against the Apalachee Indians. Still other alliances may have been for protection against other Timucuan alliances. Alliances might also have been for the purpose of assuring distribution of food among villages. When a poor harvest occurred in one locality, a portion of the shortfall could be made up with maize provided by allied villages.

Alliances were not always friendly. Some were held together by the threat of force. A village chief who gained power could force other villages and their leaders to affiliate with him. These vassals chiefs were forced to pay tribute in the form of homage as well as specific status items, such as hides, feathers, and the like. Chiefs and villages who tried to break away from the alliance were forced back in line with actual or threatened military reprisal.

Alliances could also be cemented by the intermarriage of relatives of village leaders. But even so, alliances did not always persist. They eventually fell apart. In the region of the Timucua there is no archaeological evidence that alliances persisted over long periods, leading to more complex political integration. As we saw in chapter 1, the population growth and political complexity associated with extensive-farming populations in the interior of the Southeast were not present in north peninsular Florida. We will return to this topic in chapter 6.

The second point to be cleared up is this: where did the name Timucua come from and who actually called themselves Timucua? When the French established Fort Caroline near the mouth of the St Johns River in 1564 they interacted with a Timucuan chief named Saturiwa and with a number of the chiefs allied with him. Those people told the French that their enemies, who they called Thimogona or Tymangoua, perhaps from which the word Timucua is taken, lived two or three days' canoe travel up the St Johns River. These enemies were other Timucua-speakers who were part of a second alliance, one headed by Chief Utina. The Utina alliance encompassed a portion of the St Johns River and the lands to the west in modern Clay and Putnam counties. The French adopted the term Thimogona to refer to those people. Later, the Spanish would apply the name Timucua much more widely, using it to refer to much of northern Florida.

Just how the natives did refer to themselves is something of a puzzle. Evidence exists that when asked by a Frenchman or a Spaniard what a place was and who its occupants were, villagers responded "this is our land" and "we are us." For instance, the name Uti-na means "my land" in Timucua.

The French and Spaniards, faced with the problem of designating specific groups, often used whatever name was available, including that of the village chief or leader. The same name might be assigned to the chief's village as well. Thus, to the Spaniards, Chief Potano lived in the village of Potano and his villagers were Potano Indians. Potano also was used to refer to the people and territory within an alliance of villages headed by Chief Potano.

In some instances Spaniards applied Spanish names to a place and to the people who lived at that place. One example from south of the Timucuan region is *Boca Ratón*, Spanish for "rat mouth," the name given to a small inlet on the southeast Florida coast. The Spaniards called the native people who lived there the Boca Ratones. This Spanish practice sometimes led to further confusion in nomenclature. When one group left a place and a new one moved there, the Spaniards might refer to the new group by the same name. The practice, however, was most common in the eighteenth century when only remnants of the indigenous groups were present. Small groups were forced to move between locations to try to escape the Yamasee Indian and other raiders from the north who frequently attacked the remaining Florida Indians (see chapter 8).

Confusing? Somewhat, but despite these shortcomings it is clear that there were separate Timucuan groups who maintained their own identities, identities that were recognized by other groups. Let us now travel to Florida and Georgia and see which Timucuan groups lived there in the sixteenth century.

Groups in East Florida and Southeast Georgia

The archaeological record indicates that native people once lived along much of the upper (northern) St Johns River and the rivers and streams that flow into it, including the Oklawaha River. Sites also are found along the coastal salt marshes and lagoons from St Simons Island southward and in localities in east Florida and southeast Georgia where there are extensive freshwater wetlands. Numerous sites also are distributed around the many lakes in southern Marion County west of Lake George and in adjacent portions of Lake and Orange counties in central Florida father south. Often these village sites contain large quantities of fresh or saltwater shells left as refuse.

A number of these sites were occupied in the colonial period. Archaeologists have found sixteenth- and seventeenth-century glass, ceramic, and metal artifacts from Europe, evidence that the sites were inhabited when the French and Spaniards sought to explore and colonize La Florida. Sites of Spanish Franciscan missions also have been found in this region, including on the St Johns River at Mount Royal (probably the mission of San

Antonio de Enecape), on the northern outskirts of old St Augustine (mission Nombre de Dios), and on Fort George, Amelia, Cumberland, and St Simons islands.

These various sites and the objects they contain are tangible evidence of the Timucuan groups who once lived in east Florida and southeast Georgia. Archaeological investigations and observations, some dating back into the eighteenth century, allow us to pinpoint Timucua Indian sites on the landscape and to determine which are precolumbian and which are from the colonial period. Many date from both periods, having been occupied for many generations.

But that evidence alone is not sufficient for us to determine which specific groups lived where. For that detailed information we must turn again to the documentary record, to archival materials, which, in some instances, prove to be quite informative. For example, in 1564–5 the French collected a great deal of information about a number of eastern Timucuan groups, especially those living on the northern St Johns River. Later, after the founding of St Augustine in 1565, accounts left by the Spaniards provide even more information on the same area.

One Timucuan group encountered in 1564 by the French was the Saturiwa Indians, whose main village was located on the south bank of the St Johns River just inland from its mouth and near the location where the French built a fort in that year (Figure 2.2). A few years later a Spaniard described the village:

One enters the harbor [the river mouth] . . . , and on the left hand there is a pueblo of 25 large houses, where in each one live eight or nine Indians with their wives and children, because [those of] one lineage live together. The pueblo is called Saturiba. (Barrientos, in Solís de Merás, 1964: 159)

The French were told that Chief Saturiwa had thirty other chiefs who were vassal to him, ten of whom were said to be his brothers (Figure 2.3). Most likely this meant they were of the same clan or kin group, or that "brother" was a native term used to designate chiefs who were allied with Saturiwa.

The territory of Saturiwa's alliance, the region of the villages and village chiefs over whom he had authority, was centered near the mouth of the St Johns River, extending up river to present-day Jacksonville and north along the Atlantic coast for a

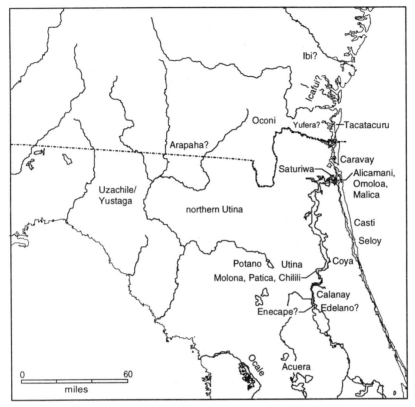

Figure 2.2 Timucuan groups

short distance. The northernmost village and group vassal to Chief Saturiwa was called Caravay, sometimes appearing as Calabay, Sarabay, Saravay, or Serranay. The village was probably located on or near Little Talbot Island.

One allied chief living on or near the St Johns River west and south of Saturiwa's main village was Omoloa, sometimes called Emola; another was Casti, another Malica, and another Alicamani (also called Alimacani in some French accounts). Omoloa, Casti, and Malica marked the westward extent of Saturiwa's political power. Alicamani's village was on Fort George Island north of Saturiwa's own village.

North of Saturiwa's alliance, from Amelia Island, Florida to St Simons Island, Georgia, lived other Timucuan groups. Those along the coast proper were apparently dominated by Chief Tacatacuru, whose main village was on Cumberland Island.

Figure 2.3 Chief Saturiwa (standing) preparing for war. Theodor de
Bry, who first published this illustration, was one of a family of
Flemish engravers working in Germany who published 14 volumes
containing scenes from the Americas in the late sixteenth and early
seventeenth centuries. The illustrations of the Timucua were based
on French narratives and the paintings of Jacques le Moyne. Even so,
they represent a very European view rather than being
ethnographically correct
Source: de Bry (1591).

On the mainland and further in the interior of southeast Georgia were the Cascangue, Icafui, and Ibi, all of whom spoke either
the Yufera or Icafui dialects. The Ibi were said to live 14 leagues,
about 50 miles, from mission San Pedro on Cumberland Island,
Georgia. Their five villages may have been on the Satilla or St
Marys River north or east of the Oconi. The Cascangue and
Icafui lived on the mainland much closer to the San Pedro
mission. The Oconi, as noted above, probably lived on the east
side of the Okefenokee Swamp in southeast Georgia.

Using information from sites on the lower St Johns River north
of Lake George, archaeologist John Goggin plotted site locations
on a modern map of the river. The results showed two dense

regions of sites north of Lake George. One is from Jacksonville east to the mouth of the St Johns River. This locality correlates quite well with the distribution of the late precolumbian Savannah-related archaeological assemblage and the territory controlled by Saturiwa. Farther south along the river is another dense distribution of sites, extending from about Palatka south to Lake George. That area was a part of the territory controlled by another of the powerful eastern Timucuan chiefs, Chief Utina, the enemy of Saturiwa. The sites in the territory of the Utina alliance are associated with the St Johns archaeological culture.

The portion of the river between Palatka and modern Jacksonville contains relatively fewer archaeological sites than do the areas immediately north and south. That portion of the river may have been a buffer zone between the Saturiwa-affiliated villages and those affiliated with Utina.

Archaeologist Kenneth Johnson suggests that Chief Utina's main village, which was visited several times in the mid-1560s by both French and Spanish soldiers, was near George's Lake (not to be confused with the much larger Lake George), which is west of the St Johns River in northwestern Putnam County, near its boundary with Clay County, west-northwest of the modern town of Palatka. Utina's village was located on an east–west trail, called the *camino real* by the Spaniards, leading into interior northern Florida. During the seventeenth century that trail would be the main overland route from St Augustine to the Timucuan and Apalachee missions in northern Florida. The trail led from St Augustine west to the St Johns River at Picolata. Travelers crossed the river by boat or ferry at that point, picking up the trail again on the opposite bank of the river near the mouth of Clarkes Creek. From that point the trail led west to the region of modern Tallahassee and beyond. The distance to Utina's village from the St Johns River along the trail was 5 leagues, about 17 miles.

Utina's name still appears on the landscape today, tied to the George's Lake area. Etoniah Creek, which derives its name from Utina, flows from near George's Lake to the St Johns River. The name Utina/Etoniah appears on nineteenth-century maps of the region in various forms, including It-tun-wah, It-tun-ah, Etinni, Itini, and Itina. The names are used to refer to natural features in the vicinity of Utina's village, including a wooded area of scrub vegetation, a small region of ponds, and the creek called Etoniah today.

Like Saturiwa, Chief Utina had great power and importance. In 1564 one of his vassal chiefs reported to the French that Utina controlled more than 40 chiefs. The names of about a dozen of them are known. As with the chiefs affiliated with Saturiwa, most seem to have been village chiefs.

One village allied with Utina was Coya, near the mouth of Etoniah Creek north of modern Palatka on the St Johns River. The village of Molona was nearby. South of Coya on the river were the villages of Patica, then Chilili, and then Enecape, all vassals of Chief Utina.

Enecape was likely the location of the seventeenth-century Spanish mission San Antonio de Enecape. Exactly where Enecape was is not certain. Most likely it was at the Mount Royal archaeological site just north of Lake George on the east side of the St Johns River. French accounts from the 1560s suggest Enecape was near Edelano, a village on an island which was reached by traveling on the St Johns River. Perhaps Edelano was the archaeological site on Drayton Island at the northernmost end of Lake George, as suggested in chapter 1.

French accounts place the village of Calanay (another village affiliated with Utina, also called Zaravay and Saravai) near Edelano. They also state that a person traveling west from Calanay would reach the native town of Tocobaga known to have been at the northern end of Old Tampa Bay, probably at the Safety Harbor archaeological site. If Calanay were just north of or on Lake George near the Mount Royal site, a south-southwesterly heading would indeed take a traveler to that locale.

Another Timucuan group allied with Chief Utina was the Acuera, who lived on or near the Oklawaha River in a region also known as Ibiniyuti. At least two Spanish missions were established among the Acuera in the seventeenth century. Numerous archaeological sites are known for the Oklawaha River and its environs and a Spanish bell has been recovered from the river.

There also were eastern Timucuan groups allied with Chief Utina which were not located on the St Johns River. The Eclavou, Onachaquara, and Omittagua Indians all probably were east of that river, while the Astina Indians were to the west.

Groups in Northern Peninsular Florida and Southern Georgia

In addition to chiefs Saturiwa and Utina, another powerful chief, one who was an enemy of both those eastern Timucuan leaders, was Chief Potano. The Potano Indians were one of the western Timucuan groups encountered by the Hernando de Soto expedition in 1539 and by subsequent French and Spanish soldiers and explorers later in the sixteenth century.

As was true for chiefs Saturiwa and Utina, Chief Potano may have controlled an alliance of villages and village chiefs, although modern scholars commonly include the allied village groups under the name Potano. The region surrounding those villages is home to the Alachua archaeological culture described in chapter 1.

A scout party from the de Soto expedition marched northward through Potano territory in summer 1539, staying at five villages on five successive nights. Later the rest of the army followed the same route. Today we can provide approximate locations for all five, which were in a roughly north–south line along native trails. Several can be correlated with specific archaeological sites or clusters of sites.

The location of the southernmost of the five Potano-affiliated villages, Itaraholata, probably was in western Marion County, southwest of modern Ocala near Lake Stafford. Chief Potano's town, Potano, was on the western shore of Orange Lake, probably at the Richardson archaeological site north of the small modern town of Evinston in southern Alachua County. Spanish artifacts have been found at that site. Later in the colonial period the town was moved north and west to the vicinity of the Devil's Millhopper, northwest of Gainesville.

Utinamocharra, the third village where de Soto's army stayed, was in the dense and large cluster of archaeological sites immediately east of Moon Lake on the west side of Gainesville. A day's travel from that point brought one to another Potano-affiliated town, one the Spaniards in de Soto's army called *Malapaz*, Bad Peace. Malapaz probably was the large Alachua culture archaeological site on the east side of the modern town of Alachua.

The fifth village, Cholupaha, was within the dense cluster of archaeological sites around Robinson Sinks in northwest Alachua County, just south of the Santa Fe River and farther north along the same trail on which Malapaz was situated. Cholupaha may have been just north of the later, seventeenth century mission of Santa Fé. Spanish artifacts have been found at a number of the Robinson Sinks sites.

South of the Potano Indians were another western Timucuan group, the Ocale. The de Soto expedition camped in the main Ocale town in 1539. Sites on and near that portion of the Withlacoochee River in the Cove of the Withlacoochee River in easternmost Citrus County also may have been associated with the Ocale. Two mound sites have been found in the Cove which contain relatively large amounts of Spanish artifacts and artifacts associated with a variant of the Safety Harbor archaeological culture. Some of the artifacts are from the early sixteenth century and probably are from the de Soto expedition.

Other western Timucuan groups were north and northwest of the Potano. Scholars often refer to those northerly Timucua-speakers as the northern Utina, although that term is a modern designation. In 1539 when the de Soto expedition marched through the area that today is Columbia, Suwannee, and eastern Madison counties north of the Santa Fe River and west of the Aucilla, they came face to face with the northern Utina. The population of the northern Utina was larger and more densely distributed than any native populations the Spaniards had encountered previously on their northward march from Tampa Bay. Like other Timucuan groups, the northern Utina lived in separate villages each of which had its own village chief. Villages and chiefs were organized into alliances dominated by the most powerful chiefs.

Following a trail leading north out of Potano territory de Soto's army first came to the northern Utina village of Aguacaleyquen, probably located on the Ichetucknee River a few miles north of its intersection with the Santa Fe River. The northern Utina villages east of the Suwannee River seem to have been allied with Chief Aguacaleyquen, who lived near the eastern and southern boundary of the northern Utina.

North of Aguacaleyquen de Soto and his entourage stayed at other northern Utina villages. A day's march from that town was a small village whose name is not given in the accounts of the de Soto expedition. It probably was near modern Lake City, perhaps by Alligator Lake. West from that small village on a trail leading toward the Florida panhandle was the town of Uriutina, perhaps one of the cluster of sites near Indian Pond in western

Columbia County between Lake City and Live Oak. Farther west was a village called Many Waters, probably east of Live Oak near Peacock and White lakes in another cluster of sites. A fourth village, Napituca, was still farther west, perhaps near modern Live Oak or to the south of that town.

In the seventeenth century Spanish missions were placed in or near the villages of Aguacalyquen, Uriutina, and Many Waters. Spanish artifacts have been found in the sites clustered around those locations and mission buildings have been identified at Aguacaleyquen and Uriutina.

Certainly there were other northern Utina villages away from the route taken by the de Soto expedition. In a battle at Napituca in 1539 the Spaniards killed at least nine village chiefs and perhaps hundreds of warriors. And during the mission period in the seventeenth century documents indicate that many villages were located throughout the area.

Once they crossed the Suwannee River, de Soto's army entered the territory of the Yustaga Indians, also called the Uzachile, another western Timucuan group. Their territory encompassed eastern Madison County. The Spaniards first traveled past a small native village before entering the main Uzachile town, believed located near modern Lake Sampala. Chief Uzachile was allied with the other northern Utina chiefs living to his east. If the de Soto narratives are correct, the chief was the most powerful of those leaders, even more powerful than Chief Aguacaleyquen. Chief Uzachile or one of his predecessors may have been the chief who met the Panfilo de Narváez expedition when it marched through Florida in 1528 (see chapter 3).

In the seventeenth century Spanish missions were established among the Yustaga, just as they were among other of the western Timucua. If the relative number of missions reflects relative population, then the Uzachile had a larger population than those of the other western Timucuan groups.

The Uzachile were enemies of the Apalachee Indians, whose territory began at the Aucilla River and extended west to the Ocklockonee River in the eastern panhandle. At the time of the de Soto entrada the Uzachile and Apalachee maintained a buffer zone between them, one more than a day's march, about 20 miles, across.

Northward from the Uzachile, perhaps in northern Hamilton County but certainly including modern counties of south-central

Georgia, was still another western Timucuan group, the Arapa-ha. The modern Alapaha River in Georgia, which receives its name from those people, may mark the location of their terri-tory. As was true of their western Timucuan neighbors, missions were established among the Arapaha in the seventeenth century.

Many more Timucuan groups also must have lived in southern Georgia, but as yet they remain little studied. The vast area from the Arapaha up to the Altamaha River also was Timucuan territory and at least one mission was established there, well inland. As more documents are found and as archaeoloical re-search progresses we are certain to learn more about those people as well.

Appearance and Number of the People

The physical appearance of the Timucua was as fascinating to the European explorers, colonists, and friars as the demeanors of the French and Spaniards were to the native people (Figures 2.4 and 2.5). Numerous references provide at least some idea of what the Timucua looked like. Those accounts indicate that to the people from Europe the Timucua were sturdy, muscular, and athletic. Hawked (not flat) noses were frequently mentioned, and the French explorers particularly admired the shapely and well proportioned physiques of the people.

The complexion of the Timucua was probably somewhat ruddy, and was variously described as reddish, olive, and tawny. No doubt a life out of doors in the sun added melanin, darkening their skin tone, especially relative to the much lighter skin of the French and Spanish. Women were noted to have been lighter than the men, a trait European observers attributed to the prac-tice of rubbing bear grease into their skin. Perhaps the ointment protected the skin from the sun to an extent. Women also used various oils and emolliments as cosmetics.

Both women and men wore their hair long. That of the women was allowed to be loose, often flowing to their hips. Men, on the other hand, dressed their hair on the top of their heads, wreathed or entwined with grasses or moss. One account notes that at times men used their dressed hair as a quiver, sticking arrows into it for easy access. When they became Christians, the men cut their hair short in the European style.

Figure 2.4 A Timucuan woman. This painting and the one that
follows, both by John White, may have been copied from Jacques le
Moyne's work
Source: courtesy of the Trustees of the British Museum.

Both men and women wore long pointed fingernails which
could be used as weapons. Both also had pierced ears in which

Figure 2.5 A Timucuan man
Source: courtesy of the Trustees of the British Museum.

inflated fish bladders were worn. Decorative earpins made from *Busycon* shell columellae also were worn in the ears as decora-

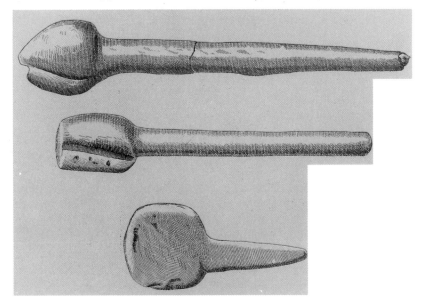

Figure 2.6 Shell earpins from a site east of Palatka on the St Johns River. The largest pin is $5\frac{3}{4}$ inches long
Source: Moore (1894b: 180).

tions (Figure 2.6). Chiefs and members of their families were painted and tattooed with designs in azure, red, and black. Other of the Timucua also decorated themselves with tattooing and paint. Some of these body decorations evidently were a mark of rank. Tattooing is not mentioned in accounts and descriptions of the Timucua from the period of the Spanish missions, suggesting either that the practice was actively discouraged by the mission friars or that the symbolism associated with tattooing was altered.

Chiefly individuals also wore painted deerskin cloaks and painted bird plumes. These latter items were given as symbols of friendship and mutual respect. Round gorgets made of copper probably originally mined in the Appalachian Mountains also were worn by chiefs.

Traditional clothing of the Timucua was minimal. The most frequently noted garment for men was a deerskin loincloth, sometimes painted. Woven palm fronds and fabric made from beaten roots also were used for loincloths. Women wore a short skirt or apron-like garment made from Spanish moss. At times the garment was smoked over an aromatic fire. Leather girdle-like sashes, sometimes painted red and fringed, also were worn by both men and women.

Other than the items worn in one's ears, other personal ornaments included feathers, necklaces and bracelets made of small and large shell beads, bracelets of fish teeth, small copper disks, and freshwater pearls.

Even before the founding of the missions articles of Spanish clothing were introduced to the Timucua. On several occasions Pedro Menéndez de Avilés, the first governor of Spanish Florida, and other Spanish officials gave clothing to Timucuan chiefs whose favor they wished to curry. Some native chiefs received a whole outfit including a shirt, breeches, silk doublet, and hat.

European items – goods salvaged from wrecked ships and items given in trade or as gifts – quickly made their way into native hands after the first Spaniards reached the Florida and Georgia coasts in the early sixteenth century. Glass and metal beads, rings, and necklaces all are mentioned in accounts. Archaeological excavations have recovered examples of all of these items as well as rolled copper beads, amber beads, and even jet beads, the latter probably from rosaries.

How many Timucua were there in 1492 prior to contact with people from Europe? Deriving estimates of precolumbian populations is a difficult and inexact science. Hard numbers on villages and village sizes are simply not available. As a consequence, scholars continue to argue population estimates as well as the merits of the various methods used to derive them. This is certainly true for the Timucua, for whom estimates range from less than 20,000 to as many as 1 million people.

At this time, the best estimate I can come up with is about 200,000 people. That figure is calculated from admittedly slim archaeological and early colonial period information computed county by county in northern Florida and then projected for the entire Timucuan region.

This estimate of 200,000 Timucua is strengthened when compared to data from other regions. The total region occupied by the Timucua was about 19,200 square miles, of which 12,000 square miles are in present-day Florida and 7,200 in Georgia. My population estimate yields a population density of 10.4 people per square mile. This figure is the same as that derived by archaeologist William F. Keegan for the Bahamas at contact. In

The People Who Discovered Columbus (1992: 162–3) Keegan notes such a density is very close to population figures recently calculated for the Caribbean island of Hispaniola and to figures given by scholars for other societies whose level of political complexity was like that of the Timucua (see chapter 6).

Native Neighbors of the Timucua

It is easy to differentiate most of the Timucuan groups from most of their neighbors. Ethnic differences are easy to pluck from the documentary record, and, as noted above, information on linguistic differences also is available from Spanish sources. The native people themselves, as well as the French and Spanish observers, knew who were and who were not Timucua-speakers. Consequently we can delineate their neighbors with some certainty.

North of coastal eastern Timucuan groups, north of St Simons Island on the Georgia coast, were the Guale Indians (Figure 2.7). The Guales, like the Apalachee Indians, spoke a Muskhogean language. Other Muskhogean speakers lived in central and southwest Georgia, north of the Altamaha River and well north and northwest of the Arapaha and the northern Utina. In the late precolumbian period those Georgian Indians were associated with the Lamar archaeological culture. It was the descendants of those Lamar people, as well as other native groups in Georgia and eastern Alabama, who coalesced into the Creek Indians by the early eighteenth century.

Other Lamar groups south of the Altamaha River in southern Georgia probably were Timucua-speakers. Emerging archaeological evidence from that region promises to clarify the extent of these groups.

West of the western Timucua in northwest Florida were the Apalachee Indians who also spoke a Muskhogean language. In the late precolumbian and early colonial periods the Apalachees shared some cultural traits with the Lamar culture to the north.

A number of groups also lived south of the Timucua. Although it seems certain that none of those groups spoke either a Muskhogean language or a dialect of Timucua, almost nothing is known about the languages they did speak. South of Lake George, south of the eastern Timucuan groups on the St Johns

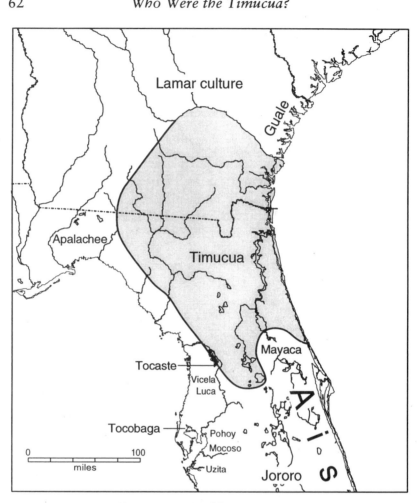

Figure 2.7 Neighboring groups

River, were the Mayaca Indians. Southeast of the Mayaca, south of the eastern Timucuan groups on the Atlantic coast, were the Ais Indians, probably the people referred to as the Costas in some Spanish documents. The territory of the Ais was from Cape Canaveral south to Fort Pierce, encompassing the adjacent mainland probably including a section of the St Johns River in Brevard County, which is very near the coast at that point.

Another group, the Jororo Indians, who were south of the Timucua-speakers, lived among the lakes in Orange and Lake counties south of Orlando. That location places them west of the

Ais, and southwest of the Mayaca Indians. The Jororo probably lived from Orange County south into Osceola County and parts of Polk and Highland counties.

Further west in the region immediately around and near Tampa Bay were the Uzita, Mocoso, Pohoy, Tocobaga, and other non-Timucuan groups. Between those west-central Florida groups and the Ocale Timucua in western Marion and northwestern Sumter counties were other native groups who probably were not Timucua-speakers. In 1539 the de Soto expedition marched through several of their villages, including Luca, Tocaste, and Vicela.

Some of the place names around Tampa Bay do resemble Timucua, as do a few Mayaca place names, suggesting the languages of those regions may have been related to Timucua in some fashion. It may be that the Tampa Bay languages, Mayaca, and Timucua were more similar to one another in the distant past. Like Spanish, Portuguese, and Italian they diverged from one another over time. However, because in every case we have only a handful of words from each of former groups which bordered the Timucua, we cannot be certain of their linguistic relationships.

Linguistic Relationships of the Timucua Language

Hachaqueniqe ponati. Hacha-queni-qe pona-ti: Why-he-(may) be coming-not = "Why isn't he coming?"
Homitala. Ho-mi-tala: Go-I-(present tense) = "I am going."

As we saw earlier in this chapter, the writings and research of Father Francisco Pareja, a Franciscan friar stationed at mission San Juan del Puerto on Fort George Island after 1595, provide most of the recorded information on the Timucua language available to modern scholars. One book, the *Confessionario* published in 1613 in Mexico City, contains sections on religious doctrine in both Timucua and Spanish as well as questions to be asked during the confession, also in both languages. By using the Spanish to decipher the Timucuan version, scholars have been able to learn a great deal about the structure of the Timucua language and to compile dictionaries of Timucuan words.

It is those Pareja texts and a few other primary sources which linguist Julian Granberry used to produce a modern grammar and dictionary of Timucua. Granberry describes the vocabulary of Timucua as very unusual, especially compared to the Muskhogean languages spoken in Apalachee, Guale, and other portions of the Southeast, because it resembles none of those languages. Timucua adds suffixes or affixes to words to form nouns, designate possessives, designate the individual initiating an action, indicate action taking place at a near or far time, and to transmit other information. Although there are some Timucuan words that are borrowed from Muskhogean languages, as well as from Spanish, the basic structure and the vocabulary of Timucua are so different from other southeastern languages that linguists have labeled it an isolate, a language unrelated to all the other southeastern native languages.

Can Timucua be related to any other native languages of the Americas? Granberry's research on Timucua has shown many structural similarities to Warao, a native language once spoken all along the Caribbean coast of northern South America, from west of Lake Maracaibo eastward to the Orinoco River delta. Aspects of Timucua also resemble other native languages found in what are now Venezuela, Colombia, and Panama, including Macro-Chibchan, Tucanoan, Panoan, and Arawakan languages. Granberry suggests one explanation for these similarities may be contact between the Timucua-speakers and the people of northern South America. The nature of Timucua, according to Granberry, also suggests that contacts among the speakers of these related languages continued for some time, accounting for Timucua containing elements of several different languages. One archaeologist has even gone so far as to suggest colonizing expeditions from the latter region reached Florida in the Late Archaic period.

Do the origins of the Timucua-speakers indeed lie well to the south of Florida and Georgia in South America? Was the language brought to Florida and Georgia by people who moved northward through the Caribbean, traveling by sea for purposes of trade or some other reasons, who settled in the coastal areas of Georgia and Florida?

All of the present archaeological evidence says this did not happen. In Florida we can trace the history of the Late Archaic period Orange culture back in time several thousand years.

There is nothing in either the Orange culture or the St Simons culture of coastal Georgia to suggest that either represents new ideas and lifeways brought to the lower Southeast from the circum-Caribbean. Nor is there any evidence from any other culture or period in the region of the Timucua-speakers suggesting contact between the precolumbian inhabitants and contemporary populations in the circum-Caribbean.

How then can we explain the linguistic evidence? Is Granberry's analysis of Timucua and its relationships to other languages incorrect? No, Granberry's analysis certainly appears to be sound. There are similarities between Timucua and Warao and other of the languages from the southern portion of the circum-Caribbean region. Perhaps the answer lies thousands of years in the past. Could Timucua, Warao, and these other languages, all of which are related to some extent, share similar origins in the distant past? Could a proto-Timucua, proto-Waroan language or languages have been spoken by early human societies who settled the entire circum-Caribbean region and, perhaps, adjacent regions? As societies in northern South America, Central America, and the circum-Gulf of Mexico region of the United States developed through time perhaps languages changed in some areas. But similarities continued to exist in some geographically divergent areas, like in northern Florida and southern Georgia and some parts of the circum-Caribbean region.

Another explanation is that Father Pareja learned Timucua and translated it into Spanish with the aid of other texts of Catholic doctrine written by Franciscan friars in Spanish and other native languages from Central and South America. It is certain that such texts were in print by the time Pareja first published his books, beginning in 1612. Indeed, the format of his own Timucua–Spanish texts followed that of texts already printed in Spanish and one or more of the native languages of people in Mexico, Central America, Peru, Chile, and Brazil. By 1600 more than 95 such books were in print.

In 1635 a Florida friar, Gregorio de Movilla, had printed in Timucua a *Forma Breve* or Short Form of certain Catholic sacraments. That treatise was translated from Nahuatl into Timucua, suggesting that texts in other native languages were available in the library in the Franciscan convent in St Augustine, which is said to have housed a very fine collection of books. If

Father Pareja also used one or more books containing a non-Florida language to help in his analysis of Timucua, it may account for Granberry's observation that Timucua contains elements of a number of different languages.

We do not know if either of these explanations is true. The discrepancy between the archaeological evidence and the linguistic evidence remains a puzzle that cannot be explained at this time. It is an intriguing problem which will continue to draw speculation and research in the years to come.

In the next chapter we will return to southern Georgia and northern Florida in the sixteenth century, the time when people from Europe first came to the land of the Timucua Indians. It is ironic that so much of what we know about the Timucua comes from Spanish and French archival materials which document the colonization attempts of those countries. Yet it was those same colonization efforts that ultimately were responsible for the demise of the Saturiwa, Potano, Yustaga, and other Timucuan groups.

3

The Invasion

It started as a drip; in less than a century it was a torrent. The invasion of La Florida by people from Spain, France, and, later, Great Britain was a flood against which the Timucua, despite their best efforts, would not stand.

The story of that invasion begins with the well-known voyage by a Genoese dreamer in 1492. On Christmas Eve of that year, two and a half months after landfall in the Bahamas, Christopher Columbus's ship, the *Santa Maria*, struck a reef as it sailed along the north coast of the Caribbean Island of Hispaniola.

Columbus and his expedition had sailed southward through the Bahamas to the north coast of Cuba before turning east to Hispaniola (Figure 3.1). With the *Santa Maria* aground and beyond repair, Columbus made a decision which would shape the geography of the Spanish conquest of the Americas. He ordered the ship to be salvaged to help supply and fortify a settlement which would be occupied by 42 sailors left behind while Columbus and the remainder of the crew returned to Spain.

The small settlement, christened La Navidad because it was founded at Christmas time, was at a native village near the wreck site. The villagers, whose chief was Guacanacaric, helped Columbus and his men salvage the *Santa Maria*.

In September 1493 Columbus again sailed for the Americas from Spain, this time headed for his small colony at La Navidad. But when the expedition anchored at the settlement in November, Columbus discovered that all the men left there were dead and the outpost destroyed.

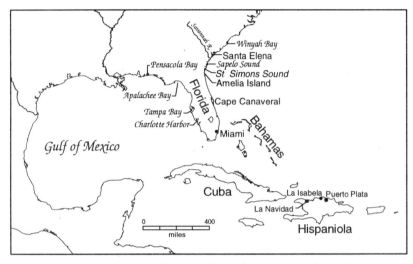

Figure 3.1 Locations of Spanish explorations and settlements
mentioned in the text

In search of a better location to establish what was hoped to be
a permanent settlement the fleet sailed farther eastward along
the Hispaniola coast. Near modern Puerto Plata they landed and
established La Isabela, the first of nearly twenty towns founded
on Hispaniola by Spain in the late fifteenth and early sixteenth
centuries. Because of the 1492 wreck of the *Santa Maria*, Hispaniola had become the base from which Spain's American
empire expanded into the Caribbean, Central and South American, and North America.

Voyages to the Southeast United States

During the early sixteenth century Spanish sailors turned the
Caribbean into a Spanish sea, exploring and mapping while they
searched for wealth and lands suitable for colonization and
exploitation. Spanish influence spread from islands to the main-
lands of the circum-Caribbean region, fueled by the wealth of the
Americas. Gold, silver, and minerals were taken from native
societies or mined with forced native labor. Slaves were bought
and sold; resources such as timber were exported; plantations
established. With the expansion of empire came increased Euro-

pean knowledge of the geography of Central and northern South America and the desire to find, explore, and conquer new lands and their people.

Expeditions were contracted by the Spanish Crown in order to regulate the voyages and expeditions of discovery and conquest and to assure that the monarchy received its share of spoils and future earnings. In reality, however, clandestine voyages not sanctioned by the Crown probably led the way for later, royally contracted ones.

The first contracted expedition to sail northward out of the Caribbean to what is now the southeast United States was led by Juan Ponce de Leon. In March 1513 three ships commanded by this ex-governor of Puerto Rico departed port from that colony on a northwesterly heading. The small fleet sailed through the Bahama Islands, past the Caicos, the Inaguas, Mayaguana, and the island of Guanahani, probably modern San Salvador, where Christopher Columbus had first made landfall in October 1492.

After sailing past Great Abaco Island the fleet took a more westerly heading which brought them to a landfall on the Atlantic coast of Florida, most likely between Matanzas Inlet and Ponce De Leon Inlet, but possibly farther north in Mocama north of the mouth of the St Johns River. The Spaniard's arrival on that coast coincided with Easter Holy Week and the Feast of Flowers (*Pascua Florida*). Drawing on that feast and smitten by the natural bounty of the land before him, Juan Ponce named it La Florida. His arrival must have been watched by Timucua Indians who lived in the area.

To explore the land, which initially was thought to be a large island, Ponce sailed down the Atlantic coast of the Florida peninsula past Cape Canaveral, leaving the realm of the Timucua. He rounded the southern end of the peninsula then sailed along the Florida Keys, which he named the Martyrs. Turning northward he sailed to southwest Florida and landed just below Charlotte Harbor in the territory of the Calusa Indians.

Ponce's expedition remained there for just over three weeks before lifting anchors for the return voyage. On that return they made a landfall on the north coast of Cuba before returning to the southeast Florida coast and the region of the Tequesta Indians near modern Miami. They then sailed eastward to the Bahamas and back to Puerto Rico.

In 1521 Juan Ponce would return to Florida to attempt to establish a colony, probably in southwest Florida. That voyage, well beyond the territory of Timucua-speakers, would end in failure. Warfare with the native people caused fatalities among both the Calusa and the Spaniards. Juan Ponce, wounded by an arrow, ordered a retreat to Cuba, where he died.

Although Juan Ponce's 1513 voyage to Florida may have had little direct impact on the Timucua Indians, it did blaze open sea lanes for more Spanish voyages to the Gulf coast of La Florida. In 1516 Diego Miruelo reached Tampa Bay and in 1517 Francisco Hernández de Cordova sailed to southwest Florida.

The entire Gulf of Mexico coast from Florida all of the way to Yucatan was mapped by a 1519 expedition led by Alonzo Alvarez de Pineda and sponsored by Francisco de Garay, Governor of Jamaica. Pineda's voyage was for the purpose of locating a passage from the Gulf of Mexico to the Pacific Ocean, the presence of which had been determined several years earlier by Vasco Núñez de Balboa's trek across the Isthmus of Panama. None of these voyages had direct contact with the Timucua.

Voyages to explore the Atlantic coast of La Florida also followed in the wake of Juan Ponce's initial voyage. Between late summer 1514 and December 1516, the exact date is uncertain, Pedro de Salazar, a slaver representing interests in Santo Domingo, reached the middle latitudes of what is now the southeast United States. As many as 500 natives were taken as slaves, although most died before the ship returned to Hispaniola. It is likely Salazar's landing site was north of the Georgia coastal Timucuan groups.

In 1521 Pedro de Quejo and Francisco Gordillo, two Spanish slavers, sailed into Winyah Bay just north of the mouth of the South Santee River in South Carolina. One of the sponsors of the earlier Pedro de Salazar expedition and the 1521 Quejo and Gordillo expedition was Lucas Vásquez de Ayllón, a judge in Santo Domingo. Following the 1521 voyage Ayllón quickly moved to secure a royal contract to establish a Spanish settlement on the Atlantic coast. In preparation he sent Quejo back to that coast to reconnoiter in 1525. Quejo made landfall at the mouth of the Savannah River in early May and then sailed northward to Winyah Bay. After sailing farther north to explore, Quejo's two ships reversed course and sailed southward, scouting the coast. The ships put in at St Simons Sound, then sailed as far south as the north end of Amelia Island. At both of these latter landfalls Quejo and his crews may have encountered Timucua Indians.

Based on information gathered by Juan Ponce de Leon, Quejo apparently was aware that below Amelia Island there were no large harbors on the Atlantic coast of La Florida. Instead of continuing farther south, he again reversed course and sailed north along the coast all of the way to Delmarva Peninsula and Chesapeake Bay.

Quejo returned to Santo Domingo and reported what he had found to Ayllón, who readied his colonizing expedition. Six hundred or so people, including 100–150 sailors, women, children, African slaves, and Dominican friars, sailed from Puerto Plata in mid-July 1526 aboard six ships. In early August the fleet reached the mouth of the South Santee River, where one ship ran aground and was lost, along with its supplies.

After scouting the countryside around the landing site, it was determined that the native population in the immediate area was not very large and that a better place to establish the colony was needed. Ships were sent southward along the coast to search for a more suitable site for the colony. One ship ranged as far south as modern Ponce de Leon Inlet south of St Augustine before turning back north and making landfall at St Simons Sound. Two other ships sailed to Amelia Island. These three exploratory voyages all encountered coastal Timucuan groups.

In early September of that same year Ayllón decided to move the colony southward to the Sapelo Sound area. There he established a small settlement which was named San Miguel de Gualdape, Gualdape probably referring to the Guale Indians of that region.

But this Spanish attempt at settlement would be short-lived. The colonists suffered from hunger, disease, and cold; many died. In mid-November San Miguel was abandoned. Later Spanish expeditions to La Florida would suffer similar failures. The Timucua and other native observers must have been bemused at the inability of the invaders to live off the land.

Despite the failure of Ayllón's colony, Spanish interests were still drawn to La Florida and its promise of wealth. It was clear that the Florida peninsula was only the tip of a huge landmass. Who knew what wealth lay within?

The Expeditions of Pánfilo de Narváez and Hernando de Soto

To successfully exploit La Florida, at that time the Spanish name for all of the region north and east of modern Mexico, Spain first needed to conquer the lands around the Gulf of Mexico and establish an overland trail from the Atlantic coast to Mexico. Hernán Cortés (1519), Francisco de Garay (1523), and Nuño de Guzmán (1527) had brought Spanish settlements to the Gulf coast of Mexico, first at Veracruz then farther north. Yucatan, to the south, had already felt the might of the invading Spanish conquistadors. What remained was exploration and settlement of La Florida. Conquering that region would secure the northern edge of Spain's American empire and provide a frontier for further northward expansion.

In 1526 a royal contract to explore those Gulf lands was given to Pánfilo de Narváez, a conquistador who had helped sack Cuba and who had been in Veracruz. His contract instructed him to colonize the region from Florida around the Gulf coast to the Rio de las Palmas (modern Rio Soto la Marina).

Narváez's expedition, which sailed from Spain in June 1527, included five ships, 80 horses, and 600 people, including ten women and African servants. The ships first landed in Santo Domingo, where supplies were loaded and 140 people deserted. The ships next sailed west to Cuba, where more supplies were acquired. While there, a storm struck killing 60 members of the expedition and 20 of their horses.

The remaining 400 soldiers, including the women, left Cuba in February 1528 headed toward the Gulf coast of La Florida, but the fleet ran aground almost immediately, causing further delay. It was not until April 12, ten months after setting sail from Spain, that the coast of La Florida was sighted.

Narváez originally had planned to sail along the Gulf coast toward Mexico, but the delays, especially the long voyage from Cuba to Florida, had depleted his supplies. The expedition probably needed fresh water and the horses must have been suffering after being transported below deck for so long. At sea two months, the expedition could go no further. Narváez instead opted to try to find a large harbor on the Gulf coast known to Spanish sailors and navigators, the harbor today called Tampa Bay.

But the expedition sailed past the mouth of Tampa Bay without seeing it, apparently in part because the latitudes the pilot had were erroneous. Facing dire conditions aboard his ships, Narváez ordered the ships to anchor just off the coast and he went ashore to scout the area. As fate would have it, the anchorage was off Pinellas Peninsula, just west of the northern end of Tampa Bay. Supplies and the 42 horses that had not died on the sea voyage were off-loaded and a camp established.

After several days a scouting party of 45 men went inland to explore. By evening they came to a large bay, probably the western side of Old Tampa Bay north of modern St Petersburg. Because the bay's latitude was well south of the erroneous latitude Narváez's pilot had for Tampa Bay, it was thought that the harbor they sought still was farther north. It would be a fatal mistake.

One ship was sent north along the coast to search for the nonexistent northern harbor. If it were not located, the ship was to return to Cuba for supplies and then return to the camp. The ship did just that, but by the time it returned to Tampa Bay the expedition had left. Four men from the ship went ashore to look for some sign of Narváez or his men, but they were captured by Indians. With no chance of rescuing their comrades, the rest of the crew lifted anchor and sailed for Cuba. One of the four captive Spaniards, Juan Ortiz, would be encountered by Hernando de Soto's men in 1539, 11 years later.

Shortly after the first ship had raised anchor and departed to find the non-existent northern harbor a second scouting party was sent by land from the camp to Tampa Bay. Several natives were captured and forced to take the soldiers to their village. There the Spaniards saw unripened corn and boxes and other items, including gold, salvaged from wrecked Spanish ships. The villagers indicated more gold could be found to the north in the territory of the Apalachee Indians.

The captive guides took the soldiers 35 to 40 miles north to another village where there were corn fields. Narváez must have been planning to take food from native villagers to feed his army on the march.

Satisfied his army could be fed, Narváez sent his remaining ships north to find the non-existent harbor. He would march his army overland and rendezvous with the ships at the harbor. Aboard the ships were the ten Spanish women.

While the ships searched for the harbor Narváez and his army marched northward toward the rendezvous. But because no

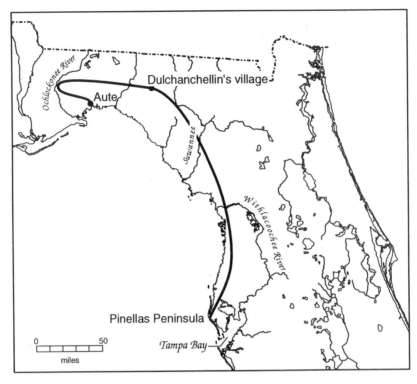

Figure 3.2 Route of the Pánfilo de Narváez expedition in Florida

harbor existed, the ships and the land army never met. The ships would spend nearly a year searching in vain for Narváez and his army. The people aboard soon realized the mistake in geography that had been made. The harbor they were seeking was the one they had already found. But by then it would be too late for Narváez and the army.

After the army, then about 300 men including 40 cavalry, broke camp, they had marched north paralleling the Florida Gulf coast (Figure 3.2). They first crossed the Withlacoochee River and then marched into modern Dixie County where they were met by a native chief who, having heard about the expedition, had traveled from his village.

The chief, carried in a litter and wearing a painted deerskin, symbols of his importance, was accompanied by villagers, some of whom played reed flutes. This imposing leader, whose name was Dulchanchellin, led the Spaniards north to his village in modern Madison County. On that journey the party of Indians and Spaniards crossed the Suwannee River.

Dulchanchellin and his people, who indicated they were enemies of the Apalachee Indians who lived to the west, were Timucua-speakers, probably from the group known as the Uzachile (also called the Yustaga). The chief tried to convince Narváez to aid him in a raid against the Apalachee Indians, but Narváez chose not to do so.

Leaving Dulchanchellin's village and again led by captive native guides the Spanish army marched westward toward Apalachee. The guides deliberately led the army through rough terrain, tiring the Spaniards and keeping them away from the main Apalachee population. Ultimately the Spaniards came to a small village of 40 houses where they set up a camp. But attacks by the Apalachee and the failure of scout parties to locate villages that could be sacked caused Narváez to lead the army to a town called Aute (Ochete) nearer the Gulf of Mexico where captives told him he would find food.

But Aute brought little solace. Hungry, sick, and suffering from native attacks the army moved to an inlet on the Gulf where they set about constructing rafts, intending to pole along the Gulf coast to Mexico. The Spaniards labored for six weeks to reshape weapons and tack into hardware. Their butchered horses provided food, as well as tails and manes for ropes and hides for water bags.

On September 22, 1528 the 250 men who were still alive boarded five newly constructed rafts. But these were soldiers, not sailors. None of the rafts ever reached Mexico. Most either were lost at sea or washed ashore; the Spaniards died or were captured by native people. By fall 1532 only four of the 400-man army may have been alive. One was Alvar Núñez Cabeza de Vaca, who later wrote an account of the expedition.

In September 1534 the four ran away from their captors and marched west. Nearly two years later they were found in northwest Mexico by slavers from New Galicia who were raiding native groups. So ended the incredible story of the Narváez expedition.

The people in Narváez's army were the first Europeans that any of the Uzachile Timucua had ever seen. The native people must have quickly learned about the cruelty that could be administered by the soldiers and their fierce weapons. The Timucua also may have suffered from diseases brought by the invaders. But as horrible as Narváez's *entrada* may have been, the expedition of Hernando de Soto 11 years later would be even worse.

De Soto, like Narváez, was a veteran of Spain's conquests in the Americas, a conquistador who had participated in military campaigns in Central America and in highland South America. He had gained wealth in the slave trade and other mercenary endeavors, including serving as an officer in the invasion and sacking of the Inca empire in the early 1530s, an initiative led by the Pizarro brothers.

In November 1536 de Soto obtained a royal contract directing him to colonize La Florida. The contract negated the previous land claims of Ayllón and Narváez, both of whom had died in their own attempts at colonization.

De Soto was well aware of the fate of Narváez's expedition, but he also heard the embellished stories told by Cabeza de Vaca, one of the survivors. In fall 1537 Cabeza de Vaca arrived in Spain to relate first hand tales which one observer said led people "to understand that it [La Florida] was the richest country in the world" (Smith, 1866: 8).

The result of these stories was that soldiers, craftsmen, and other people were eager to join de Soto's expedition, which was organized both as a military expedition and a colonization endeavor. Forts and settlements were to be established as the land was conquered.

The well-supplied expedition sailed from Spain in April 1538, bound first for Cuba. De Soto's *caballeros* (knights) were accompanied by servants and they took extra arms and armor and spare horses. De Soto and other high-ranking officers brought all the gear – including tents and furnishings – they would need to live reasonably comfortably in the field. By any measure, the de Soto *entrada* would be the largest and best-equipped effort which Spain had mounted thus far to conquer La Florida and its people.

Once in Cuba, de Soto, who had been awarded the governorship of the colony as a part of his contract, finalized plans for the invasion. Scout ships were sent to reconnoiter the landing site, which was to be at Bahía Honda (Tampa Bay), the same harbor Narváez's pilot had sought in 1528. On May 18, 1539 de Soto and his fleet of five large and four smaller ships sailed. On board were 725 people, including two women, tailors, shoemakers, stocking-makers, a notary, a farrier, a trumpeter, servants, friars, cavalry, and infantry. Two hundred and twenty horses, war dogs, and a drove of pigs – meat on the hoof – also were aboard.

One week later the fleet sighted land and dropped anchor just south of the mouth of Tampa Bay, south of Narváez's landfall. Over the next few days the Spaniards located the passage into the harbor and unloaded men, supplies, and livestock and set up camp. The fortified camp, in an Indian village located near the mouth of the Little Manatee River, provided a base of operations for many months.

Almost immediately after landing the army met Juan Ortiz, the Spaniard who had been abandoned at Tampa Bay by the ship looking for Narváez 11 years previously. Ortiz, who had lived as a captive among Tampa Bay Indians, would serve de Soto as an interpreter.

Six weeks later an army of 500 Spaniards accompanied by hundreds of native people forced to serve as bearers marched out of the camp. The rest of the expedition remained at the camp with a large quantity of supplies and the ships, a strategic reserve force. Their route took the expedition from the southeast side of Tampa Bay northward through modern Hillsborough, Pasco, Hernando, and Citrus counties to the Cove of the Withlacoochee, the large freshwater wetland bounded on the eastern side by the Withlacoochee River (Figure 3.3). Along the way infantry and cavalry were sent to scout the territory and determine what routes would bring the army to native villages that could be commandeered for shelter and food. Accounts written by participants make it clear that, as much as possible, the army followed existing native trails. At times, however, captive guides misled the Spaniards or tried to take them through rough terrain, just as Narváez's guides had done.

De Soto's immediate goal was the land of the Ocale Indians, where he initially planned to spend the winter. Native informants had led him to believe there was sufficient food there to feed his army. The Ocale were the Timucuan group living from the Withlacoochee River east into modern Marion and Sumter counties.

The main town of the Ocale, however, was on the eastern side of the Cove of the Withlacoochee, while de Soto's route had brought his army to the western side. After considerable trouble

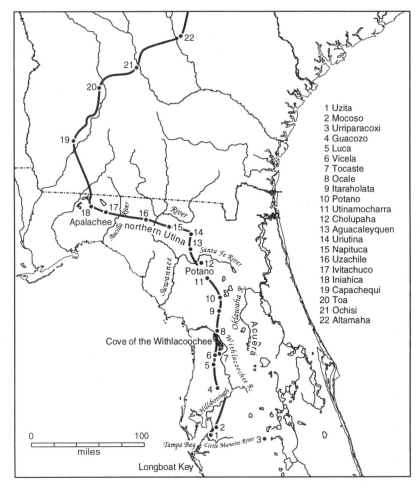

1 Uzita
2 Mocoso
3 Urriparacoxi
4 Guacozo
5 Luca
6 Vicela
7 Tocaste
8 Ocale
9 Itaraholata
10 Potano
11 Utinamocharra
12 Cholupaha
13 Aguacaleyquen
14 Uriutina
15 Napituca
16 Uzachile
17 Ivitachuco
18 Iniahica
19 Capachequi
20 Toa
21 Ochisi
22 Altamaha

Figure 3.3 Route of the Hernando de Soto expedition in Florida and
Georgia

a way through the wetlands of the Cove was found and the army
reached the town just east of the river.

The journey through the swamps of the Cove was especially
hard on the people who were on foot. It took them several days
and they arrived starving. But Ocale did not have the reserves of
food that de Soto had been told were there. The people were not
extensive agriculturists. To feed the soldiers and colonists a
raiding party was sent east to take corn from the Acuera Indians,
the western Timucuan group who lived around the headwaters

of the Oklawaha River. It was clear that the army could not winter at Ocale. It also must have been obvious that winter was yet far off – it was only early August; perhaps the army could find a better place farther north to spend the winter, a place like Apalachee.

De Soto, accompanied by 50 calvary and 60 infantry, decided to push forward to explore, leaving the main body of the expedition at Ocale. During the several weeks the army was at Ocale, the soldiers would have ravaged the countryside for a considerable distance in order to find food. The immediate impact on the native people of the area must have been devastating.

De Soto and his soldiers marched rapidly due north through modern Marion and Alachua counties, the territory of the Potano Indians. On five successive nights they stayed at the five different native villages recounted in chapter 2. After crossing the Santa Fe River they marched into the main village of the Aguacaleyquen, the northern Utinan group living in southern Columbia County.

De Soto and the advance party soon realized the northern Utina were more numerous than any of the native groups they had encountered thus far on their journey from Tampa Bay. Though better armed, the Spaniards were badly outnumbered. To counter this threat de Soto took Chief Aguacaleyquen's daughter hostage. Later the chief also would be made captive. Seeking reinforcements, de Soto sent a horseman back to Ocale to tell the remainder of his army to break camp and join him at Aguacaleyquen. The Potano towns through which de Soto and his advance party had marched must again have been heavily impacted by the passage of the remainder of the army as it hurried north along the same route the advance party had taken.

Once reinforced, de Soto and his army moved out with the hostages, heading westward through northern Utina territory toward Apalachee across modern Columbia and Suwannee counties. At the town of Napituca, probably near modern Live Oak, the Spaniards fought two fierce battles with natives, inflicting huge numbers of fatalities, including the execution of six captive chiefs and several hundred other Timucua Indians. Refusing to tolerate military opposition, de Soto was especially cruel. The late summer of 1539 must have been a terrible time for the northern Utina.

De Soto's army crossed the Suwannee River into modern Madison County and the territory of the Uzachile Indians, the same western Timucuan group whose chief Dulchanchellin had befriended Narváez. Emissaries from Chief Uzachile had taken venison to de Soto – a sign of friendship – even before the army had crossed the Suwannee River. Like the native people who had accompanied Chief Dulchanchellin those emissaries played flutes.

De Soto's army marched into Chief Uzachile's main town, which its inhabitants had burned and abandoned. They had learned in 1528 the harm an invading army from Europe could do to them. The town was probably near modern Lake Sampala.

From Uzachile's town the army marched west to the Aucilla River through an uninhabited forest, a geographical buffer between the western Timucuan groups and the Apalachee Indians whose territory began at that river. Reaching the main Apalachee town of Iniahica in early October de Soto set up camp and sent orders to Tampa Bay for the remainder of his army camped there to join him. Most would march overland, following the route he had taken north and west through Timucuan territory. Timucua Indians who had been relieved to have seen what they thought was the last of de Soto's army must have been dismayed when the hundred or so soldiers from the Tampa Bay camp raided their villages when the reserve army marched north to join de Soto at Apalachee. The horrors of the summer continued into the fall.

The ships previously anchored at the Tampa Bay camp also went north, sailing up the coast to Apalachee Bay, just south of Iniahica, where they were off-loaded. In the early spring of 1540 – resupplied and having withstood the winter – de Soto's army broke camp and headed northeasterly across Georgia toward the Carolinas and the mythical land of Chicora. Their route across Georgia took them north of the Timucuan groups in the southern part of that state. Once in South Carolina the army turned north, crossing the Appalachian Mountains into Tennessee. Next the Spaniards traced the Tennessee River Valley southwesterly into eastern and central Alabama.

Opting not to continue on to the Gulf coast where he might have been able to rendezvous with his ships and leave La Florida, de Soto ordered his army to march northwest, a heading that took the Spaniards across Alabama into Mississippi where the expedition spent the winter of 1540–1. In May 1541 the army would cross the Mississippi River into Arkansas, still searching for the wealth they would never find. A year later the expedition returned to the banks of the Mississippi River where de Soto became ill and died in June 1542.

An attempt to march overland to Mexico failed and the army returned to the Mississippi River a third time. During the first six months of 1543 the Spaniards built boats. In June the expedition survivors, then totalling just over three hundred, floated down river to the Gulf of Mexico and made their way along the coast to a Spanish settlement near present-day Tampico, Mexico. Their odyssey was over.

The overall military impact of the de Soto expedition on the Timucua-speakers of north Florida must have been horrendous. Even worse may have been the effects of diseases introduced by the Spaniards. Evidence excavated by archaeologists and biological anthropologists from Tatham Mound, an early sixteenth-century Ocale Indian site near the Withlacoochee River, suggests that epidemics followed in the path of the invading Spanish armies. The double-edged sword of warfare and disease dealt the western Timucua a devastating blow.

Although the Ayllón, Narváez, and de Soto expeditions all were failures, the strategic position of La Florida on the northern rim of the Spanish empire would continue to draw the interest of Spain as well as that of other European colonial powers. Settlements in La Florida could provide protection for shipping lanes in the Gulf of Mexico and the straits of Florida and those lanes off the Atlantic coast. Settlements also could be used as bases for mission efforts among the native people. Cooperative Christian Indians would be inclined to save shipwrecked Spanish sailors. Still another role for settlements was to serve as bases from which the cargoes of ships wrecked on the coasts could be salvaged. Ships bound for Spain from Veracruz often carried great wealth taken from the Americas.

The planned La Florida settlements were to be connected by overland trails. One trail would tie the settlements to Spanish towns and mines in New Spain. It would lead from northern Mexico across the Gulf of Mexico coastal plain to the South Carolina coast at Santa Elena, where Ayllón had been in 1526. That trail could be used to transport goods from New Spain to Santa Elena, where they could be loaded aboard ships for Spain, thus avoiding the more dangerous shipping lanes along the coasts of Florida.

To begin to carry out these plans a first colony was to be established at Ochuse on modern Pensacola Bay. Ochuse had been surveyed by boats sent by de Soto while his army wintered in Apalachee. Future settlements were to be in interior La Florida and at Santa Elena.

The expedition to Ochuse, supported by the viceroy of Mexico, Luís de Velasco, and led by Tristán de Luna y Arellano, sailed from Mexico in June 1559. It took the expedition more than two months to find Ochuse, which created considerable hardships for the colonists aboard the expedition's ships. Finally the fleet of 13 ships and 1,500 people arrived at Ochuse, which was renamed Bahía Filipina del Puerto de Santa María.

Almost immediately a hurricane struck, sinking nine ships. The loss of supplies meant that Luna would have to try to secure food from local native groups in order to ensure the survival of his colonists. Scouting parties were sent well into the interior of modern Alabama north of Pensacola Bay, but native towns from which food could be taken were few and far between. In a few instances villagers withdrew at the approach of the Spaniards, taking their food stores with them or destroying them so they could not be used. The native people of interior La Florida had learned from the invasion of de Soto's army.

Things went from bad to worse and, in April 1561, the colony was abandoned. Some of the survivors were boarded on ships bound for Santa Elena, where another try at establishing a settlement was to take place. But storms sank several of those vessels, ending the attempt almost before it began. Spanish attempts to colonize La Florida had failed.

Fort Caroline and the French

Another European colonial power also had designs on La Florida. As early as the late 1550s rumors of French expeditions to La Florida had reached Spain. Those rumors became reality in 1562 when the Frenchman Jean Ribault and a crew of 150 sailed for the Atlantic coast. Making landfall about St Augustine, Ribault sailed north to the mouth of the St Johns River, claiming the land for France. Like the western Timucuan groups in interior Flori-

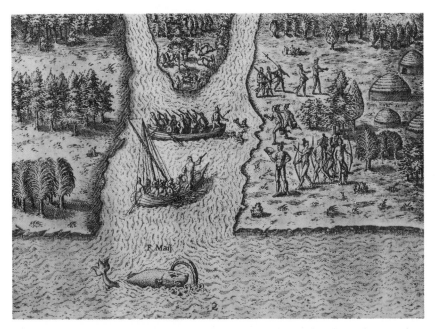

Figure 3.4 Boats from Ribault's 1562 expedition land on the north
side of the mouth of the St Johns River
Source: de Bry (1591).

da, the eastern Timucua living along the Atlantic coast and along
the St Johns River were soon to experience firsthand of the
invasion from Europe.

While exploring the region around the mouth of the St Johns
River Ribault and his men encountered three different native
groups, all Timucua (Figure 3.4). One group gave him tanned
animal skins as a sign of friendship. The chief of another group
presented Ribault with an egret plume dyed red, a basket, and an
animal hide painted with depictions of various animals. Still
another group brought baskets of berries and corn. In return the
French gave the native people metal bracelets, tools, mirrors,
and knives.

Ribault continued northward along the coasts of Georgia and
southern South Carolina, reaching the harbor near Santa Elena
which he named Port Royal. Along the way he probably was in
contact with the Timucuan groups of the Mocama region living
along the Atlantic coast. At Port Royal the French built Charlesfort and Ribault staffed it with 30 French soldiers. Having

accomplished his mission, Ribault returned to France, planning to return with more people and supplies.

Word that France had successfully placed an outpost in La Florida brought Spanish retaliation. A Spanish ship sent to destroy the fort reached Port Royal in summer 1564, only to find the French had already abandoned it, apparently unable to live off the land. The soldiers left by Ribault had taken a small boat and sailed to France. On the voyage they were forced to eat their dead to survive.

Meanwhile, plans for a second expedition to La Florida were being laid by the French. René de Laudonnière, who had been with Ribault on the 1562 voyage, sailed for the Americas in April 1564, with three ships and 300 people. Laudonnière's expedition, which included women, children, and craftspersons, made landfall on the Atlantic coast of Florida in July. Two days later the fleet found the mouth of the St Johns River and sailed up it to St Johns Bluff where they went ashore. Returning to the coast Laudonnière sailed northward, exploring further, before deciding to return to the St Johns River where he would found a

Figure 3.5 The French under Laudonnière begin construction of Fort Caroline
Source: de Bry (1591).

settlement. There, in late July, construction of Fort Caroline began (Figure 3.5).

But the same supply problems that had beset Spanish attempts at colonization also vexed the French. To avoid the hardships some of the soldiers deserted, stealing boats and sailing for the Caribbean. From fall 1564 into spring of the next year the colonists, suffering from hunger, tried to wrest food from various eastern Timucuan groups. The French traded axes, knives, glass beads, combs, mirrors, and even their clothes for maize, beans, acorns, fish, turkeys, deer, and other game brought by native people. Some of the Indians came from far away to take advantage of the colonists' plight. Realizing the French were at their mercy, the Timucua struck hard bargains.

During the 15 months they occupied Fort Caroline the French traveled far and wide through the Timucuan region in northern Florida. One goal was to find mineral wealth. They also sought to form alliances with native groups for protection and to obtain badly needed food. Their most intensive interactions were with the Timucua living close to the fort on the St Johns River. That area was a part of the region where Chief Saturiwa held together his alliance of villages and chiefs. The French also had numerous dealings with Chief Utina, Saturiwa's enemy. Because Utina controlled agricultural fields and the main trail into northern Florida west from the St Johns River, the French sought his favor.

The French first had met Chief Utina in September 1564, when a group of French soldiers had boated up the St Johns River and then marched overland to Utina's village. Utina, who sought to manipulate the French just as they wished to use him, convinced the French to send six or seven soldiers on a raid he was planning against Chief Potano. With the French *arquebusiers* in the lead Utina and 200 warriors easily carried the day. A number of Potano's villagers – men, women, and children – were taken prisoner; others were killed.

Early in 1565 Chief Utina again convinced the French to send soldiers for another raid on Potano. The war party of 30 French soldiers and 300 native warriors was about 10 miles from Potano's village when scouts saw three of Potano's villagers fishing in a canoe. The scouts attempted to kill the fishermen so they could not warn Potano, but two escaped. The third was captured, killed, scalped, and dismembered.

With the element of surprise lost, Chief Utina camped so his *jarva*, a diviner or shaman, could foretell the outcome of the approaching battle. When the *jarva* predicted defeat for Utina because Potano had 2,000 warriors, Utina expressed a desire to withdraw. But the French – irate at having marched so far, and not believing in divination – convinced the chief to attack anyway. In the ensuing battle French powder and shot again proved decisive and the Potano suffered greatly (Figure 3.6). Even so Utina did not press his military advantage, instead returning to his own village where he prepared for retaliatory raids. Utina had wanted to take prisoners and embarrass and insult Chief Potano; the French wanted to inflict heavy casualties on Potano and his people.

By late spring 1565 the French colonists at Fort Caroline were close to famine. Nearby native people refused to provide them with corn, saying it was not yet ripe. Laudonnière ordered Chief Utina to be taken hostage and held for a ransom of food. But

Figure 3.6 Chief Utina and his warriors, with the French *arquebusiers* in the lead, attack Chief Potano and his men. This very European-like battle scene probably was nothing like the actual raid that took place, unless the Timucua had begun to adopt French battle tactics
Source: de Bry (1591).

several weeks of negotiations brought nothing and Utina was released.

During the time they occupied Fort Caroline, the French explored much of the Timucuan region. Laudonnière sent expeditions north along the coastline into northern Mocama and he sent boats to explore the St Johns River. The boats apparently got as far as Lake George and Drayton Island.

French soldiers also traveled into the interior of northern Florida, well west of the territory of the Potano. Two of Laudonnière's men went as far west as the Yustaga/Uzachile Indians, the same western Timucuan group visited by Narváez and de Soto. The soldiers reported that the chief of that region had three to four thousand warriors. Later another of Laudonnière's men would again visit the Yustaga during a five- or six-month-long excursion into interior La Florida.

In early August 1565 French spirits lifted when four English ships were sighted on the coast. The ships' crews traded badly needed supplies to the French for arms and artillery. Resupplied, the French quickly set about preparing for a return to France. They had had enough of La Florida. By mid-month ships were loaded and the French waited only for favorable winds to set sail. At the month's end the right combination of tides and winds was present. But as luck would have it an approaching fleet came into view before Laudonnière and his colonists sailed. The fleet was commanded by Jean Ribault, who was bringing more supplies along with orders to assume command of the colony. Fort Caroline was to be reinforced and maintained.

But it was not to be. The Spanish Crown was well aware of Laudonnière and Ribault and the probability that a French colony was somewhere on the Atlantic coast of La Florida. A contract had been awarded to Pedro Menéndez de Avilés, commander of Spain's Caribbean fleet, ordering him to sail from Spain, locate the French colony, destroy it, and establish a Spanish colony in its place.

On September 4, 1565, only a week after Ribault's fleet had landed at Fort Caroline, Menéndez arrived on the scene. He had received information about the location of the fort from French deserters questioned in the Caribbean. Ribault's four ships, anchored just inside the mouth of the St Johns River when Menéndez arrived, cut anchors and sailed beyond the reach of the Spanish fleet. Menéndez then sailed his ships southward. He took refuge at a small harbor where he had landed several days earlier. At that location, in the village of a Timucuan chief named Seloy, Menéndez began to set up a fortified camp. The small settlement was named San Agustín.

Several days later, just as Ribault was mounting a sea attack on St Augustine, a fierce storm struck the coast. The attacking French ships were blown ashore south along the coast. Three were wrecked south of modern Daytona Beach near Ponce de Leon Inlet. The fourth, the *Trinité* with Jean Ribault aboard, was wrecked near Cape Canaveral.

Just over a week later Menéndez and 500 soldiers counterattacked at dawn, marching overland to Fort Caroline where they caught the French flat-footed during a driving rainstorm. The fort was quickly taken. In the ensuing months Menéndez proceeded to wipe out any trace of French resistance. The infamous slaughters of two groups of survivors from Ribault's wrecked fleet occurred at Matanzas Inlet south of St Augustine in late September and mid-October. Later in October Menéndez learned that others of the shipwrecked French were fortifying an encampment just north of Cape Canaveral. He raided it, capturing or scattering the French. La Florida was under Spanish control.

Pedro Menéndez de Avilés and the Conquest of Florida

Menéndez quickly set about securing the colony and fulfilling the conditions of his royal contract. That contract required that he explore the coast of La Florida, establish two or three towns, and provide for the Christian conversion of the native peoples. The latter would be accomplished by using Jesuit missionary priests.

Although the colony's initial settlement was St Augustine, Menéndez intended to place his main town at Santa Elena, the same location where Ribault's 1562 expedition had built Charlesfort. Santa Elena was first occupied in 1566, but it was abandoned in 1587 due to supply problems and raids by native people.

Another of Menéndez's plans was to use naval strength to control the coasts, providing some measure of safety for Spanish shipping interests. To expedite transportation in the interior of

Florida he intended to use the rivers that traversed the interior of the peninsula, which he thought were interconnected. Missions and/or garrisons were placed near the mouths of several of the rivers in order to protect access to the river system.

The largest river, the St Johns, was protected by Fort San Mateo – formerly the French Fort Caroline – near its mouth. That river was thought to flow southward to Lake Okeechobee (Figure 3.7). Along its course it was thought to connect with the Hillsborough River, or perhaps the Alafia River, both of which flowed into Tampa Bay. Menéndez placed a garrison at the native town of Tocobaga near the modern town of Safety Harbor in Old Tampa Bay. Tocobaga probably was one of the towns which Narváez had been in in 1528.

It also was thought that the Miami River flowed into Lake Okeechobee and was thus connected with the St Johns River. A settlement was placed at the mouth of the Miami River at the native town of Tequesta which had been visited by Juan Ponce de Leon on his 1513 voyage. Still another mission–garrison, one named San Antonio, was on Mound Key in Estero Bay just south of modern Fort Myers. Mound Key was the site of the Calusa Indian town of Calos at or near Juan Ponce de Leon's landing site and it was just south of the mouth of the Caloosahatchee River, thought to flow from Lake Okeechobee.

To the north the lagoon system which today is the Inland Waterway provided passage between St Augustine and Santa Elena. That saltwater route was protected by the forts at the two towns and by a third fort, Fort San Pedro, on Cumberland Island, Georgia. Still another garrison was at Santa Lucía, modern Saint Lucie Inlet, on the lower Atlantic coast. Together these fortified settlements, rivers, and coastal waterways were intended to provide the Spaniards with a protected shipping network tying Santa Elena and St Augustine with strategic points on the coasts of La Florida, points relatively near Spanish colonies in Cuba and Mexico.

Because of supply problems and raids by native peoples Menéndez's three coastal settlements at Miami, near Fort Myers, and at Tampa Bay all soon disappeared; none lasted more than a year or two. What Menéndez planned was never realized; the river transportation system he envisioned did not exist. Although native dugout canoes might have been able to travel widely within and across Florida, Spanish boats could never do

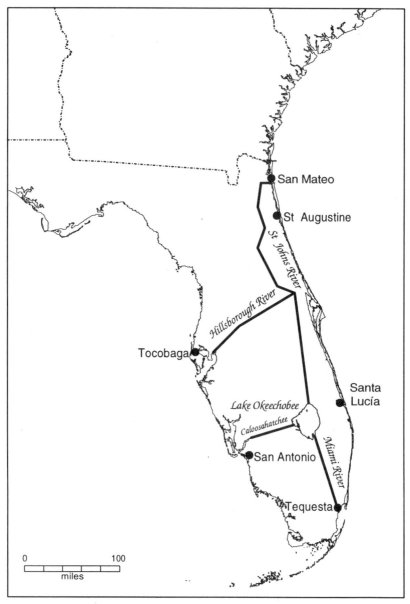

Figure 3.7 Location of the early Spanish outposts established by
Pedro Menéndez de Avilés and his erroneous conception of the river
system within Florida

so. Even today a water route across Florida from the Gulf to the
Atlantic remains only an unfulfilled dream.

Erroneous information regarding the geography of North America also thwarted other of Menéndez's plans for his colony. For instance, it was believed there was a sea route, a northwest passage, leading from the Atlantic coast to the Pacific across northern North America. An arm of the Pacific Ocean was thought to extend eastward to Chesapeake Bay or to another east coast location. In 1566 Menéndez sent a Spanish expedition to the Chesapeake Bay, called Bahía Santa María by the Spanish, to establish a settlement here, but it was unsuccessful.

Another geographical error made by the Spaniards was their belief that the distance from Santa Elena to northern Mexico and the silver mines of Zacatecas was much less than it actually was. The latter mistake was at least partly responsible for Menéndez's failure to successfully establish the long-sought overland route from Santa Elena to Mexico.

To try to establish that route Menéndez twice sent an expedition commanded by Juan Pardo into the interior of La Florida. On the first attempt, in December 1566, Pardo and more than 100 soldiers marched from Santa Elena into western North Carolina. On the second the expedition followed the same route, continuing across the Appalachian Mountains into Tennessee near the modern town of Newport. But Pardo went no further and the forts he left behind were quickly abandoned.

Menéndez did explore portions of the Timucuan region in northern Florida. In summer 1566 he met a number of eastern Timucuan chiefs along the St Johns River. Many were allied with Chief Utina. The Spaniards also interacted with the Timucuan groups in the vicinity of St Augustine and those living in the coastal Mocama region in northeast Florida and southeast Georgia.

One way to control the Timucua and other native groups and to assure they remained peaceful was to put Jesuit missions among them and form alliances with the chiefs. Jesuit missions were established along the Georgia and South Carolina coasts as well as at the small coastal garrisons mentioned above. But these early missions never were very successful. Several Jesuits were killed by native people, and there were frequent disagreements between soldiers and friars. In 1572 the Jesuits withdrew from La Florida.

With Menéndez's death in 1574, the plan for a Spanish colony encompassing much of La Florida was scaled back. Abandonment of Santa Elena and the failure of the coastal garrison–missions in peninsular Florida would cause the new leaders of the colony to focus more on coastal Georgia and northern Florida, in large part the region of the Timucua, to garner colonial success.

4

Spanish Missions

The founding of St Augustine would assure that life would never again be the same for the Timucua Indians. Invading armored conquistadors would be replaced by robed missionary friars and gift-bearing governmental officials who would seek to make the Timucua a part of Spain's Catholic empire.

Establishing missions among the Timucua and other native peoples of La Florida in order to convert them to Catholicism was one of the requirements of the contract negotiated between Pedro Menéndez and the Spanish Crown. That process of conversion not only included teaching religious doctrine, it also was intended to bring aspects of the Hispanic way of life to the Timucua, to make them loyal subjects of the Spanish monarchy.

Loyal native subjects were thought less likely to take up arms against the Spaniards. On several occasions in the 1570s prior to the establishment of Franciscan missions, St Augustine itself was attacked by Timucua Indians who burned and destroyed houses of the Spanish colonists. Relations between the Spaniards and Timucua remained someone tenuous through the 1580s as well. When the Englishman Francis Drake raided St Augustine in 1586 native people looted the town.

The establishment of a system of missions thus was an important part of Menéndez's plan for his colony. Missions not only provided a means of pacifying the Timucua and other native groups and making them allies, they also were a means of organizing the native population for administrative and other purposes, including for labor. Free or lowly paid labor was needed if the colony was to produce profits and assure a reasonably comfortable life for Menéndez and his family and the other colonists. And native agriculturists could supply corn and other foods to help fill the stomachs of the Spaniards in St Augustine. Missions and colonization were parts of the same process.

Was the use of native people as laborers legal? Was forced labor a form of slavery? To the Spaniards labor drafts were perfectly legal, an accepted benefit of colonization. For instance, Menéndez and other colonists could point to the *Ordenanzas* of 1563 which permitted the founders of colonies to use native labor. Those laws allowed founding governors of colonies, people like Menéndez, to receive land and the labor of the native residents living on that land. Also, land and labor could be granted to other colonists.

The contract awarded Menéndez stated he could take *repartimientos* in each town he founded. *Repartimientos*, common in Spain's American empire, included the ownership of specific lands and the right to use the labor of the native people living on those lands. Along with the land came the responsibility to protect its native inhabitants and to instruct them in the Catholic faith. Menéndez's contract also permitted him to grant three *encomiendas* to other colonists. An *encomienda*, a block of land, also included the right to use resident native labor in exchange for the holder of the *encomienda* accepting responsibility for the religious education of the laborers.

Missions, *repartimientos*, and *encomiendas* were methods for assuring the religious education of the colony's native people, those living on lands granted to Spaniards as well as those living in the mission provinces. Education also meant obedience to the Spanish Crown. Religious instruction brought the Timucua to Catholicism and it made native people members of the Spanish empire.

Despite the best intentions of individual missionary friars and some Spanish colonists, those same missions, *repartimientos*, and *encomiendas* all were ways in which native people could be harnessed for the economic good of the colony. Profits were derived from the export of produce and goods obtained from or transported by native people. Using native labor for construction and maintenance projects reduced the costs of those endeavors to the colony. Without mineral wealth to be mined, the Spaniards of La Florida sought a profit wherever it could be found.

A 1598 document indicates one bizarre way in which the townspeople of St Augustine secured labor. A native war party was sent against the Surruque Indians who lived north of Cape Canaveral. Fifty-four men, women, and children were taken prisoner and brought to St Augustine where they were distributed to families and to the military. In large part the success of St Augustine would be built on the backs of the land's native inhabitants.

For all of these religious and economic reasons the Spanish missions would be an important arena of Timucua–Spaniard interaction beginning in the late sixteenth century and continuing through the seventeenth. And much of what is known about the Timucua during that period comes from documents surrounding the founding and operation of those missions.

Early Missions

On the heels of the withdrawal of the Jesuit missionary friars from La Florida in 1572 the colony was faced with finding another religious order to assume the responsibility for conversion of the Timucua and other native people. Pedro Menéndez, with the permission of the Spanish Crown which provided subsidies for the support of friars, quickly arranged for the Franciscan order to provide missionaries to the colony. In 1573 the first Franciscan friar, Father Francisco del Castillo, landed in Santa Elena. He was followed by Father Alonso Cavezas, who was assigned to St Augustine. Fathers Castillo and Cavezas both served as chaplains to the soldiers stationed in those Spanish towns; it is uncertain if they also did missionary work among the Indian who lived nearby. In that same year three other friars began to administer to the native people of Guale and Orista, an area north of Guale.

Soon *doctrinas* were established in native villages. *Doctrinas*, missions with churches and resident friars who instructed native people in religious doctrine, were first established in the 1580s along the coast from Santa Elena to St Augustine, including in the Mocama region. The St Augustine to Santa Elena missions were intended to pacify the Guale and Timucua Indians who lived along the coastal region between the two towns. The presence of native people who were friendly to the Spaniards helped to assure safe transportation and communication between the colonial towns.

The missions in Mocama and Guale were on the barrier islands and on the adjacent mainland, most often in locales that could be reached by water. Because Santa Elena was abandoned in 1587, just about the time Franciscan mission efforts began in earnest, the chain of coastal missions stopped short of present-day South Carolina. The northernmost mission was San Diego de Satuache located near the mouth of the Ogeechee River. It served the Guale Indians, northerly neighbors of the Timucua living in southeast Georgia.

The first large group of Franciscans – eight friars – left Spain in May 1584, for the Florida mission field. But only three actually arrived. One friar was left in the Canary Islands, a port of call for the ships the friars had sailed on; two friars remained in Hispaniola, another stopover on the journey; and a fourth simply deserted. After arriving in Florida a fifth friar quickly left for Havana and then Mexico. Evidently the friars heard stories about La Florida which painted a bleak picture of what awaited them in the mission field.

In 1587, 12 more Franciscan friars sailed for La Florida, followed in 1590 by another eight. But the trials and tribulations of establishing missions in La Florida apparently were as daunting as the stories suggested. In 1592 only two friars and one lay brother remained at work in the field.

Despite these early problems, recruitment of Franciscan friars for missionary work in La Florida continued. Twelve more friars arrived in 1595 and missionary efforts among the Guale and the Timucua began in earnest. The superior of the Florida Franciscans, Father Francisco Marrón, consulted with the governor of La Florida, Domingo Martínez de Avendaño, to select sites for the missions. At least some of the missionaries went to their new posts accompanied by the governor and a detachment of soldiers, a display of pomp meant to impress upon the native people that the Franciscans were protected by Spanish military might.

The Franciscan order maintained their La Florida headquarters in St Augustine at the south end of town. Portions of the Convento of San Francisco, rebuilt many times during the colonial period, still exist today incorporated into the buildings of what until a few years ago were the headquarters of the Florida National Guard.

As the number of *doctrinas* grew, first along the coast and then among the Timucua living in the interior, the Spaniards would divide the region of missionary activity into provinces or districts correlated with native languages and dialects (Figure 4.1). There were flexibility and changes in the use of the names as the mission system grew in some areas and declined in others. And through time various of the province names were used differently by different people.

The Georgia coast north of the mouth of the Altamaha River was Guale. That, of course, was the region of the Guale Indians.

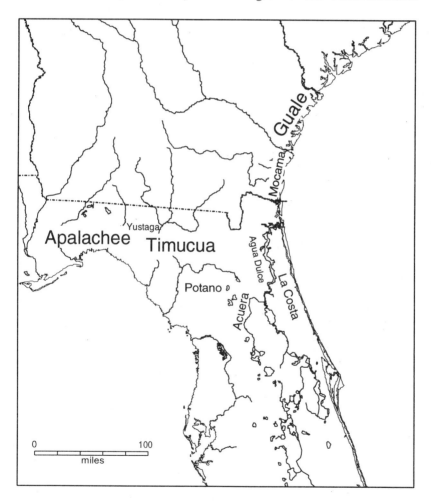

Figure 4.1 Mission provinces

Just to the south of the Guale missions was Mocama, the district encompassing the coast and adjacent mainland from St Simons Island south to St Augustine. During the seventeenth century Mocama, which was occupied by Timucua-speaking groups, would sometimes be included in the province of Guale. It was in Mocama that the French established Fort Caroline in 1564 and where they interacted with the Timucuan groups allied with Chief Saturiwa.

The coastal region south of St Augustine for an uncertain distance was sometimes referred to as La Costa, the coast, although that term was more used late in the mission period. At least some of the native groups, those between St Augustine and the territory of the Ais Indians which began around Cape Canaveral, were Timucua-speakers. La Costa was never a major focus of Franciscan mission efforts, perhaps because native populations were less dense than those of interior northern Florida, or because they suffered population losses very early in the colonial period.

Following the initial conversions in Guale and Mocama, missions were also established among the eastern Timucua living on the St Johns River north of Lake George, a region the Spaniards referred to as Agua Dulce. One mission was even farther south on the St Johns River in the territory of the Mayaca Indians, south of the Timucua Indians.

The mission province of Timucua was the largest, encompassing all northern Florida and south-central Georgia east of the Aucilla River to Mocama and Agua Dulce. This was the territory of the western Timucuan groups. Sometimes that portion of Timucua province between the Aucilla and Suwannee rivers was treated as a separate region called Yustaga. The name, of course, was derived from the Yustaga (Uzachile) Indians, the western Timucuan group through which both the Narváez and de Soto expeditions had marched. Occasionally Yustaga was called Cotocochoni, perhaps a Muskhogean word used to refer to the Indians of that area.

Early in the mission period the region of Potano, roughly modern-day Alachua County, at times also was treated as a separate province within Timucua. Later, as its population dwindled in number, it most often was included in Timucua province. It may have been for that same reason that Mocama district came to be included in Guale.

The upper Oklawaha River drainage was referred to as Acuera, a name taken from the Acuera Indians. In some accounts Acuera is called Ibiniyuti. Early in the mission period Acuera towns may have been relocated northward, causing Acuera to be included in the Timucua province.

Just as the Guale Indians were treated as a separate mission province, so was Apalachee a separate mission district, one correlating with the territory of the Apalachee Indians. During the seventeenth century a few missions were established west and north of Apalachee in the lower Flint River and Apalachicola–Flint River drainages.

A few attempts were made to establish missions elsewhere in Florida. Most, however, never lasted more than a short time or they were completely unsuccessful. The mission provinces of Mocama, Timucua (including Agua Dulce, Yustaga, Potano, and Acuera), Apalachee, and Guale would be the major arena for Spanish–native American interaction throughout the seventeenth century.

Growth of the Timucuan Missions

By 1596 nine *doctrinas* were in operation in Guale and Mocama, administered in large part by the 12 Franciscan friars who had arrived the previous year. Over the next six years additional missions were established in those same provinces. The southernmost Timucuan missions were Nombre de Dios, on the north side of St Augustine just north of the old city gates, and San Sebastián, located nearby. San Juan de Puerto, also serving Timucua-speakers, was on Fort George Island just north of the mouth of the St Johns River. San Pedro, sometimes called San Pedro de Mocama, was on the southern end of Cumberland Island, Georgia. That mission was about halfway between St Augustine and the mission on Saint Catherines Island in Guale, the northernmost coastal mission.

On the mainland (after 1616) in southeast Georgia a mission served the Ibi. Along the coast the northernmost Mocama mission was San Buenaventura de Guadalquini, on the southern end of St Simons Island.

Most commonly each mission was named for the saint's day at which Mass was first conducted at the mission. Often the name of the native village where the mission was built was incorporated in the name. Thus, San Buenaventura de Guadalquini was named for the day of San Buenaventura and it was located at the native village of Guadalquini.

By the early seventeenth century additional missions were founded among the eastern Timucuan groups. San Antonio de Enacape (Antonico) was on the St Johns River, probably at the Mount Royal site, as related in chapter 2. Several other Timucuan villages along that portion of the river also were served by Franciscans. At least one mission was placed near Surroque, possibly near Spruce Creek in Volusia County near the coast.

The continued growth of the missions had been interrupted in September 1597, when some of the Guale Indians revolted against the Franciscans. During the short-lived rebellion five friars were killed and most of the missions in Guale were destroyed. In October and early November of that year Spanish soldiers sailed northward from St Augustine to put down the rebellion and restore order. Some of the Timucuan villagers from mission San Pedro on Cumberland Island were moved to the mission of San Juan del Puerto on Fort George Island, apparently to prevent their joining the rebellion.

Missions were returned to Guale during the two decades following the rebellion, a time when the Franciscans also began to look inland toward the western Timucua for new converts. Initially friars from the coastal missions in Mocama visited the western Timucuan groups to lay the groundwork for future *doctrinas*. Father Baltasar Lopéz made several trips in the late 1590s, traveling 50 leagues, more than 160 miles, from his mission on Cumberland Island into northern Florida. One town Father Lopéz visited he called Timucua, the name that later was given to the same province. The town of Timucua probably was Aguacaleyquen, the town where de Soto had been in the summer 1539.

Father Lopéz, who spoke a dialect of Timucua, established a *visita* at the town. He also founded at least two additional *visitas* among the Potano Indians in the general vicinity of Gainesville. *Visitas* were mission stations which, unlike *doctrinas*, did not have a resident friar. They were served by friars who visited them irregularly because distances were so great. Each *visita* probably had a small church or chapel where Mass and other rites were conducted.

Historian John Hann discovered a Spanish document describing how, in 1597, the small church or chapel at the town of Timucua was built with tools given to the village chief. Perhaps prompted by Father Lopéz, the chief had gone to St Augustine and requested that a friar be sent to serve his people. The tools were sent to the northern Utina chief and he was instructed to build a church and a house for a friar.

Archaeologists have found the site thought to be the location of the *visita* administered by Father Lopéz. That same native village is the site of the later mission San Martín de Ayacuto, sometimes called San Martín de Timucua, founded by Father Martín Prieto in 1608. Excavations by archaeologist Brent Weisman at the site just east of the Ichetucknee River in Columbia County uncovered a small church or chapel, perhaps the very structure built in the late sixteenth century. Excavations at the same site also have located a large church, probably the church of San Martín.

As they were intended to do, Father Lopéz's initial missionary activities among the western Timucua led to establishment of *doctrinas*. The first *doctrina* in Timucua province west of the St Johns River was San Francisco de Potano, founded by Father Martín Prieto in 1606. That mission was south of the prairie today called San Felasco Hammock – Felasco is a Muskhogean (Seminole) pronunciation of Francisco. The archaeological site corresponding to the mission was found in the 1950s and excavated in the early 1960s. The site is not the location of the village of Potano raided by Chief Utina and French soldiers in 1564. That village was abandoned in 1585, when it was probably decimated and destroyed by a contingent of Spanish soldiers from St Augustine in retaliation for a 1567 attack by the Potano Indians on a detachment of Spanish soldiers sent to the area by Menéndez and led by Captain Pedro de Andrade.

Father Prieto, who had arrived in Florida in 1605, and a second friar, Father Alonso Serrano, also served several Potano villages near San Francisco de Potano. They christened the towns Santa Ana, San Miguel, and San Buenaventura, each named for the saint's day Mass was first said in each. The first two could be reached in a day's walk from San Francisco.

San Francisco de Potano would continue to exist for nearly a century, although it was abandoned for short periods of time, possibly due to population fluctuations. Today, like all the

Timucuan missions discovered thus far, nothing of the former mission buildings can be seen above ground. It is only through archaeological investigations which uncover hardware, burned posts, and other elements of building construction that the missions can be pinpointed.

Other western Timucuan missions soon followed San Francisco, as the Franciscans began to establish a chain of missions westward across northern Florida through the Potano, northern

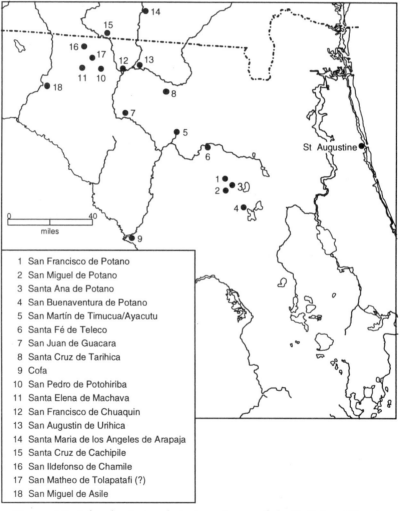

1 San Francisco de Potano
2 San Miguel de Potano
3 Santa Ana de Potano
4 San Buenaventura de Potano
5 San Martín de Timucua/Ayacutu
6 Santa Fé de Teleco
7 San Juan de Guacara
8 Santa Cruz de Tarihica
9 Cofa
10 San Pedro de Potohiriba
11 Santa Elena de Machava
12 San Francisco de Chuaquin
13 San Augustin de Urihica
14 Santa Maria de los Angeles de Arapaja
15 Santa Cruz de Cachipile
16 San Ildefonso de Chamile
17 San Matheo de Tolapatafi (?)
18 San Miguel de Asile

Figure 4.2 Inland mission locations (west of the St Johns River) prior to 1633 and the founding of the Apalachee missions

Utina groups, the Yustaga, and the Arapaha (Figure 4.2). Next after San Francisco was San Martín, the *doctrina* built at the village Father Lopéz called Timucua. Next was mission Santa Fé (Holy Faith) located between San Francisco and San Martín in northwest Alachua County. The archaeological site corresponding to Santa Fé also has been found by archaeologists and partly excavated. It is adjacent to an earlier site which may be the town of Cholupaha visited by Hernando de Soto in 1539. The name of the modern Santa Fe River is derived from the mission, which was just south of the river.

Other missions established in western Timucua during the first two decades of the seventeenth century were San Juan, probably the archaeological site at Baptizing Spring in southern Suwannee County, and Santa Cruz, probably the Indian Pond site in western Columbia County west of Lake City. After 1623 new missions continued to be founded farther west and north among the Yustaga and Arapaha Indians. Missions in that western Timucuan region were San Pedro y San Pablo de Potohiriba (usually shortened to San Pedro de Potohiriba) near modern Lake Sampala in Madison County, Santa Elena de Machava, San Miguel de Asile near the Aucilla River, San Matheo de Tolapatafi, San Augustín de Urihica, Santa Cruz de Cachipile, San Ildefonso de Chamile, San Francisco de Chuaquin, and Santa María de los Angeles de Arapaja, the latter presumably on the modern Alapaha River in southern Georgia. Most commonly, modern scholars call the people from the Arapaja mission the Arapaha, the name used here. A 1655 Spanish document giving the distance of that mission from St Augustine suggests the mission could have been as far north as Tift County. Still another mission was established at Cofa at the mouth of the Suwannee River. It may have been put there specifically to provide native labor for river transportation on the Suwannee. Far to the north in Georgia near the forks of the Oconee and Ocmulgee rivers was Santa Isabel de Utinahica, which also served Timucua-speakers.

More Timucuan missions were established in northern Florida than in southern or coastal Georgia. The reason for this may have been simple: it was easier to gain access to locales in northern Florida than in south-central Georgia. The former region was closer to St Augustine and could be reached by relatively convenient trails. Even so, a few missions were placed among some of the Timucuan groups living to the north in southern Georgia.

Two missions, San Luís de Acuera and Santa Lucía de Acuera, were among the Acuera Indians in modern Marion County. San Luís de Eloquale served the Ocale Indians; it probably was in Marion County also. Following the establishment of missions among the Timucuan groups in Georgia and northern Florida, the Franciscans moved farther west into Apalachee province. Between 1633 and 1635 a number of missions were founded there.

The impact of the missions went well beyond the mission villages themselves. Most if not all of the *doctrinas* served not only the resident population, but nearby villages as well. In 1620 there were 32 missions and 27 friars in the provinces of Guale and Timucua serving more than 200 villages. It is likely that by the third decade of the seventeenth century, a time of declining Timucua population numbers and fewer native villages, almost all of the Timucuan villages were associated with missions. Documents only rarely mention non-Christian villages.

Early Mission Period Population Movements

Archaeologists investigating Franciscan mission sites in interior northern Florida in Alachua, Columbia, Suwannee, and Madison counties all have noticed that much of the native pottery found at the missions is quite different from the pottery found in late precolumbian and early colonial period sites in the same region. During the period of the missions the latter pottery – assemblages associated with the Alachua and Suwannee Valley cultures – apparently existed along with and then was replaced by a new ceramic assemblage. In that region this new assemblage, called Leon-Jefferson, is typified by Jefferson Ware ceramics, pottery which often is decorated with concentric circle designs which were carved in negative on wooden paddles and then applied to the surfaces of clay vessels before they were fired (Figure 4.3). This Jefferson Ware pottery is very similar to the Square Ground Lamar complicated stamped pottery found by archaeologist Frankie Snow at Lamar culture sites in the upper Satilla river drainage.

The differences between Alachua and Suwannee Valley pottery on the one hand and Leon-Jefferson pottery, especially Jefferson Ware, on the other, are striking. Not only are surface decorations different, but vessel shapes and the pastes of the ceramics

Figure 4.3 Leon-Jefferson pottery; compare with the precolumbian
types of pottery illustrated in chapter 1

are clearly unlike each other. The differences are so great that
several generations of mission archaeologists have stated that
the appearance of Leon-Jefferson pottery at western Timucuan
missions signals the presence of new people at the missions,

people who brought their own ceramic tradition with them. Previously the best explanation was that the new arrivals were from Apalachee, where Leon-Jefferson pottery is also found during the mission period. It was thought that to satisfy the labor needs of the Spaniards, Apalachee families were moved to Timucuan missions.

But, as historian John Hann has emphatically noted, there is no documentary evidence for such movements. Apalachee Indians were not moved to western Timucua to repopulate Franciscan missions in the seventeenth century. The western Timucuan missions continued to be occupied by Timucua-speakers throughout their histories.

With the recognition that the region of the Timucua extends to the Altamaha River and apparently includes groups who made Lamar pottery this puzzle may be on the way to being solved. It is likely that it was Timucua-speakers from Georgia who moved to the western Timucuan missions in north Florida and brought the Leon-Jefferson, Lamar-like pottery.

Archaeological evidence from north Florida indicates that Leon- Jefferson ceramics appear at the western Timucuan missions from the time those missions were first founded. At San Francisco de Potano, Santa Fé, and other sites the appearance of Leon-Jefferson pottery types is coterminous with the founding of the missions. That suggests that the movement of Timucua from Georgia into Florida took place at the time the missions were founded.

Why might such movements have occurred? One reason is that the Georgia Timucua wanted access to the goods – metal tools, clothing, beads, and other trinkets – proffered by the Spaniards. The missions were places where these goods were available to the native people. Missions in Georgia also would have attracted non-mission Timucua, but there were many fewer missions in south-central Georgia – only a handful – compared to more than a dozen founded across north Florida in the early seventeenth century.

The Spaniards probably encouraged the Georgia Timucua to move to the Florida missions, since missions built in Georgia would have been relatively difficult for the friars to travel back and forth to from St Augustine. There also are hints in documents that the Spaniards wished to consolidate populations, to reduce them, in order to make their missions' efforts more efficient.

As yet definitive documentary evidence for the widespread movement of Timucua from Georgia into Florida is lacking. But it is known that when Father Luís Gerónimo de Oré, who was reviewing the Florida missions in 1616, made his way from Timucua up to the Altamaha River passing through southern Georgia, the land in between was little populated. Perhaps this is a reflection of the movement of people out of that region to the Florida missions. The fact that the names of de Soto-era, northern Utina villages – for example, Aguacaleyquen, Napituca, and Uzachile – do not appear in mission period documents further hints at new populations in that western Timucuan region. In the coming years archaeologists and historians hopefully will have much to say about this problem.

The Western Timucuan Rebellion and Mission Reorganization

In 1674–5 the Bishop of Cuba, Gabriel Díaz Vara Calderón, visited the Florida missions to see firsthand what the Franciscan missionaries had accomplished and to assess the state of the missions. His report on the months he spent in Florida lists names of the western Timucuan missions and gives their locations relative to one another as well as the number of leagues between missions. It is obvious from Calderón's report and other documents that at that time the Timucuan missions in northern Florida, those west of the St Johns River, were arranged along the main trail that led from St Augustine to the mission province of Apalachee (Figure 4.4). Modern scholars often refer to this trail, mapped by the British in 1778, as the *camino real*, the royal road. The road, probably little more than a trail in the early seventeenth century, continued to be used into the nineteenth century when Florida became a territory of the United States. In 1824 federal dollars were used to improve the road, then the major territorial link between Tallahassee and St Augustine. At that time it became known as the Bellamy Road.

Today, using the 1778 British map, Bishop Calderón's account, and other sources of information as guides, scholars can trace the *camino real* across the modern landscape and begin to locate the Timucuan missions that were located along it. Archaeological sites corresponding to the missions of San Miguel de

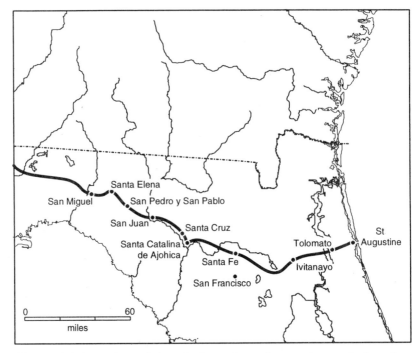

Figure 4.4 Location of the missions along the *camino real* after the
Timucuan rebellion

Asile, San Pedro de Potohiriba, San Juan de Guacara, San Martín
de Ayacuto, and Santa Fé all have been identified on the road.
The site of San Francisco de Potano was just south of the *camino
real* on a connecting trail.

In the 1980s archaeological surveys carried out by Kenneth
Johnson in north Florida in the territory of the northern Utina
identified two missions well north of the *camino real*. Earlier a
third mission, one directly on the road, also had been found, but
it was not at a location specified in Bishop Calderón's account.
Other documents from the first half of the seventeenth century
indicated that once missions had existed north of the trail. These
sources of information seemed to suggest that the well-known
linear arrangement of Timucuan missions along the *camino real*
was not necessarily true.

This mystery was solved when archaeologist/historian John
Worth, carrying out research in the Archives of the Indies in
Seville, Spain, found documents indicating that, following a

rebellion in 1656, the geography of the Timucuan missions was rearranged. The linear arrangement of the missions along the *camino real* proved to be an artifact of the outcome of the rebellion. Prior to the rebellion, a number of the missions were located on other trails farther north in northern Florida and southern Georgia. One Spanish observer at the time noted that reaching the missions in Timucua was difficult because they were scattered, connecting with one another not by direct trails but by trails leading only to the *camino real*.

The rebellion began in the spring 1656, when Lúcas Menéndez, one of the major chiefs in Timucua, and other Timucuan chiefs decided to defy orders from the governor of Spanish Florida, Diego de Rebolledo. The governor had commanded the chiefs of both Apalachee and Timucua to assemble 500 of their principal men and warriors and march to St Augustine. The people were ordered to carry on their backs the corn and other food they needed for a sojourn of at least a month in St Augustine.

Rebolledo's decree followed on the heels of intelligence indicating that the British were planning a raid on St Augustine. At that time the town was poorly prepared to withstand an attack. Construction of fortifications was still underway and the number of soldiers stationed in the colony was well below its full complement. Worse, the stores of food that would be needed to sustain the Spanish during a siege were depleted. Faced with these problems and the likelihood of a military attack, the governor decided to call up the native militia from the mission provinces in the defense of St Augustine and the La Florida colony.

But the chiefs of Timucua, led by Lúcas Menéndez, refused to go to St Augustine. Their refusal grew out of dissatisfaction with treatment they had previously received from the governor. On their visits to St Augustine Rebolledo had not properly feasted the chiefs and he had not provided them gifts, both of which were customary. Nor were the leaders inclined to carry their own food and supplies or to provide villagers to St Augustine without compensation.

In the context of the times these were not insignificant slurs. The power of the traditional native leaders in Timucua already was being threatened as a result of nearly a century of Spanish colonization. Epidemics continued to severely deplete populations, reducing the importance of the chiefs. The continued labor drafts further took adult males away from chiefly authority to St Augustine, often leaving the mission villages inhabited largely by women and children and the native leaders who themselves normally did not perform the labor demanded by the military government of St Augustine.

For these reasons, Rebolledo's 1656 order was viewed by the Timucuan chiefs as a direct blow at their status as leaders and an attempt to reduce their authority. Chiefs did not wish to be treated as ordinary people and should not have been ordered to be burden carriers. Governor Rebolledo's demands were the final straw.

When Chief Lúcas Menéndez told his followers and the other Timucuan chiefs to kill Spaniards it was clear that the Franciscan friars living at the Timucuan missions were not included in the death threat. The disenchantment of the Timucua was with the military government, not the friars. At the time of the rebellion the Timucua had been missionized for half a century and the missions were an integral part of their lives. Indeed, during the rebellion some of the Timucuan chiefs communicated by writing letters to one another in their native language, a skill taught them at the missions. The Timucua also intercepted letters written by the Spaniards and read them as well.

The first deaths in the rebellion occurred at Asile, where there were both a Spanish farm and a mission (San Miguel de Asile), and at San Pedro de Potohiriba, both in Yustaga. At each location a Spanish soldier, part of the small military presence in the province of Timucua, was slain. A Spanish servant and a Mexican Indian who had camped on the west of the Suwannee River on a journey to the hacienda in Potano known as La Chua were the next to die. A large group of Timucua, led by Chief Lúcas Menéndez, next raided La Chua on the north side of Paynes Prairie, southeast of modern Gainesville. A third Spanish soldier and two African slaves were slain in the raid. The Spanish owner of the ranch, the patron of Lúcas Menéndez, was spared.

Although the killing halted with the La Chua deaths, the rebellion continued. Timucuan villagers all across northern Florida abandoned the missions. Crops they needed to feed themselves and the populace of St Augustine were not sown. Most of the province was in disarray. However, not a single friar had been harmed.

Knowing the governor would retaliate, some of the rebellious Timucua congregated at Santa Elena de Machava in Yustaga. Perhaps they hoped to draw the Apalachee Indians into the rebellion. But the Apalachee, along with some of the more northerly Timucua, such as the Arapaha, did not join in the rebellion.

Near Santa Elena de Machava the Timucua fortified themselves inside a palisaded fort they had constructed, perhaps using techniques they had learned from working on forts in St Augustine. There they waited for the Spanish response they knew would come.

It was not until September that Governor Rebolledo, who first had to make sure the mission villagers of Guale remained loyal to his cause and that a British attack was not imminent, planned his military countermoves. Initially he sent 60 Spanish infantry and as many as 200 Apalachee Indians who had been in St Augustine, into the interior. This large force marched across Timucua to a town in eastern Apalachee, avoiding the main trails in an effort to avoid encountering Timucuan rebels.

In Apalachee the Spaniards were reinforced with a double handful of other Spaniards recruited out of Apalachee. They soon learned about the native fort near Santa Elena de Machava. After extended negotiations the rebellious Timucua in the fort were persuaded to come out. Their leaders were seized along with several natives who had participated in the murders. One Timucuan man confessed almost immediately and was executed. The other prisoners were taken to Apalachee and held while word was sent to the governor.

In late November Rebolledo and a small entourage marched from St Augustine across Timucua, capturing several chiefs along the way and taking them to Apalachee. There a trial was held and the fates of the captured Timucua were adjudicated. Ten or so individuals were sentenced to forced labor in St Augustine, while six chiefs and four other Indians were given death sentences. Rebolledo ordered the latter to be hanged at strategic places in Timucua, grim reminders of the power of the Spaniards and the fate which awaited those who rebelled against the Crown. Timucua would never be the same again.

The leadership of Timucua was decimated and many missions had been abandoned. Rebolledo seized the opportunity to reorganize the province and its missions so they could better serve the needs of the colony and its Spanish overlords. He ordered the abandonment of some of the missions and had others moved to the *camino real*. The Timucuan missions were placed roughly a day's travel apart along the road, as well as at river crossings where ferries were needed. They no longer would be located crosswise from one another, with some far to the north of the road in southern Georgia. Even some of the Timucuan missions already on the *camino real* were moved east or west so their new locations fit with the governor's reorganization plan.

As a result of the rebellion the Timucuan missions would become way stations supporting the major overland route between Apalachee province and St Augustine. Food from Spanish-owned farms and ranches in Apalachee, and to a lesser extent in Timucua, was transported along that road to St Augustine. As Bishop Calderón noted in the report of his 1674–5 visit to Florida, the population of St Augustine were dependent on Apalachee for their sustenance.

Following the reorganization, mission villages in northern Florida would be used to supply labor to transport corn, keep the road in repair, and staff the ferries on the Aucilla, Suwannee, and St Johns rivers. By the time of Calderón's visit the bulk of the western Timucuan population lived in 11 missions stretching from mission Santa Fé in northwest Alachua County west to the Aucilla River. Nearly all were on the *camino real*. Other Timucua lived at Nombre de Dios next to St Augustine and at other missions around that town and in Mocama. It is doubtful that any significant Timucuan populations remained in interior southern Georgia.

By the time of the rebellion epidemics and more than a century of interaction with colonial powers from Europe had severely reduced the Timucuan population (see chapter 8). Timucua could no longer provide significant laborers for Spanish needs. This may have been a major reason why the reorganization was ordered. A demographic collapse in Timucua might also have been one of the reasons the Spaniards welcomed Timucua from Georgia to the north Florida missions.

The results of the demographic catastrophe in Timucua were dramatically evident to Bishop Calderón. By the time of his visit a 20-league – about 70-mile – portion of the *camino real* between the St Johns River and mission Santa Fé was uninhabited. Timucua and Apalachee had been fully integrated into colonial Florida as a result of the rebellion. But the cost had been heavy.

Haciendas

Even before the Timucuan rebellion the Spaniards sought to take advantage of native labor and the land in interior northern Florida to profit the colony. Two haciendas – farms – were established in Timucua by 1656, the one called La Chua on the north side of Paynes Prairie and another at Asile just east of the Aucilla River. As related above, Spanish soldiers stationed at both places were killed during the rebellion. The farms produced wheat, corn, cattle, and cattle byproducts, such as hides, for use in St Augustine and for export. Following the rebellion, haciendas were established in Apalachee and in eastern Florida east of the St Johns River. Additional haciendas would also dot the countryside in Timucua. As the native population in the region of the Timucua-speakers diminished in number, more lands were open to Spanish use. During the latter half of the seventeenth century at least 25 ranches existed in what had been Timucuan territory, most east of the St Johns River.

The earliest farm in Timucua, La Chua, was owned by the royal treasurer for the colony, Francisco Menéndez Márquez, a relative of Pedro Menéndez de Avilés. Archaeologist Henry Baker has located the site of the ranch's main buildings on the northern rim of Paynes Prairie. The hacienda, in operation by 1630, encompassed a large amount of land. One account states it was five leagues on a side – about 17 miles. Menéndez Márquez was given permission to use the land by the Timucuan chief Lúcas Menéndez, the same chief who was involved in the raid on La Chua during the rebellion. Menéndez Márquez's son Tomás owned the ranch at that time and it was his life that Lúcas Menéndez spared. The Timucuan chief's close ties to the family are reflected in his taking the name Menéndez as his Christian surname.

Menéndez Márquez, and later his sons Antonio, Juan, and Tomás, served as Lúcas Menéndez's patrons, providing him with gifts, perhaps including livestock, in exchange for the right to ranch on the lands legally controlled by the Timucua. After Menéndez Márquez died in 1649, Lúcas Menéndez complained that things were not the same. The gifts and his association with Menéndez Márquez must have been important to maintaining his chief's status and authority among the Timucua. Menéndez Márquez's sons, the chief's new patrons, evidently were not disposed to offer the chief the same courtesies.

An inventory of the ranch made after Menéndez Márquez's death lists cattle, pigs, and two African slaves among the assets. The Africans were most likely the same two individuals killed in the 1656 La Chua raid. Several native laborers also worked the ranch, which was a valuable business venture. After his death an audit discovered that Menéndez Márquez's business acumen may have been superseded by his corruption; while serving as a colonial official he had embezzled 16,165 pesos from St Augustine's treasury. Some of those funds may have been used to set up and maintain the ranch, which was mainly for raising cattle.

La Chua would continue to operate throughout the remainder of the seventeenth century following the rebellion, when it was a major source of beef for St Augustine. Cattle from the ranch were driven to St Augustine, probably along the *camino real*, and then slaughtered in the town slaughterhouse. The beef was sold and the cowhides and tallow exported. Cattle from Timucua could also be driven to San Martín, a small village on the lower Suwannee River that served as a port, loaded on ships or boats, and shipped out. Tomás Menéndez Márquez, Francisco's son, is known to have carried on a thriving trade between Florida and Cuba. Cattle products were sent to Havana in exchange for rum, which was traded in Apalachee province for furs that could be sold.

The other pre-rebellion Spanish hacienda in Timucua that used native labor was the farm at Asile. Begun about 1645 by then governor Benito Ruíz de Salazar Vallecilla, the farm was close to San Miguel de Asile in western Madison County, Florida on the east side of the Aucilla River. The site of that mission has been found near the present-day highway US 27 river crossing. That modern bridge is near where the *camino real* crossed the river in the seventeenth century.

Asile was a farm rather than a cattle ranch. Wheat and corn were grown and pigs were raised for export. Because fields had to be tended and crops harvested, Asile used larger numbers of native laborers than did La Chua. But like that ranch, Asile operated with the consent of the chief of the mission village of Asile, who controlled the land. When Governor Salazar died, the farm was sold to the acting governor who succeeded him, but it was soon closed down, probably just after the Timucuan rebellion.

The farm, which encompassed six square leagues, more than 60 square miles, had extensive planted fields cultivated with the help of horses, mules, and oxen. Several documents, including an inventory taken after Salazar's death, provide a limited view of what the farm may have been like. The farm buildings included a large wooden house, a separate wooden kitchen with oven and two foot-mills, a thatched building for storing flour, a house with clay daub walls, and granaries. An African slave from Angola named Ambrosio and the mulatto overseer, Francisco Galindo, helped to run the ranch and were included in the inventory.

Also listed in the inventory were 22 oxen, 8 horses, and 45 head of swine. Tools, farm implements, and furnishings included a whetstone, auger and bits, spades or hoes, hatchets, sickles, hand adzes, saws, carpenter's planes, machetes, iron goads, iron chains, table and benches, an oil lamp, beds, one pewter dish, and two bricks of chocolate, the latter used to cure dysentery.

Following the rebellion, new haciendas were established in Timucua. Spanish citizens no longer were hindered by the necessity of having to obtain permission to use land from native chiefs. The St Augustine government saw the haciendas as a way to collect fees. Grants of land to Spaniards were made and taxes on those grants collected.

The descendants of Francisco Menéndez Márquez were especially prominent in the later haciendas in Timucua. One ranch was owned by Juan de Hita, married to Antonia, a daughter of Tómas Menéndez Márquez. That ranch was near mission San Francisco, perhaps at San Felasco Hammock, northwest of present-day Gainesville. Another ranch, Chicharro, was run by Francisco Romo de Uriza who was wedded to another of Tómas's daughters. Chicharro was on the opposite side of Paynes Prairie from La Chua and the residents could see one another across the flat, three-mile wide prairie.

The declining native population in Timucua must have created labor shortages for the ranch owners. One archaeological site in eastern Alachua County, the Zetrouer site, thought to be the location of a hacienda, contains a large amount of pottery thought to be associated with the Yamasee Indians who had moved into Guale on the Georgia coast from the interior of that state in the late seventeenth century. Perhaps Yamasee Indians were moved south into interior Timucua to work the ranch.

The Timucuan ranches were money makers for the Spanish colonists. They also contributed to feeding the residents of

St Augustine. As a consequence they were tempting targets for raiders who wanted to steal cattle and goods and sever a link in St Augustine's food supply. La Chua was raided in 1682 by French privateers who traveled up the Suwannee and Santa Fe rivers from the Gulf of Mexico. Two years later the raid was repeated. That time the raiders went inland from the central Gulf coast using the Withlacoochee River and then marching overland to the ranch.

Between 1703 and 1706, when militia from the Carolina colony were raiding the missions of Apalachee and Timucua (see chapter 8), La Chua again became a focus of hostilities. A blockhouse was built, but it was quickly abandoned when it was realized that it was ineffectual. La Chua was abandoned early in the eighteenth century, as were the missions which remained in Timucua province. By 1710 what had been the land of the western Timucuan groups was largely uninhabited.

Agents of Change

The Spanish and French explorations and attempts at settlement in the early and mid-sixteenth century certainly had a detrimental demographic impact on the Timucua Indians. Introduced diseases must have caused epidemics and many deaths. But, as yet, there is little archaeological evidence and no documentary reports of such epidemics prior to the settlement of St Augustine. This is due to two factors. First, archaeological studies focusing on demographic impact during the sixteenth century prior to the missions have only been carried out at one site believed to have been associated with the Ocale Indians. Second, the documentary record prior to St Augustine is discontinuous. During that period there were no European observers among the Timucua in interior Florida for more than a few weeks at a time; no one was there to record the presence of epidemics when they occurred.

As we shall see in chapter 8, the situation during the period of the Franciscan missions is quite different. There is archaeological and documentary evidence that epidemics regularly occurred in the seventeenth and eighteenth centuries and that the Timucuan population continued to decrease throughout that time.

Against this backdrop of declining Timucuan numbers, the missions were efficient agents of change. It was the intent of

Spain and the Church to change the Timucua, making them contributing members of the La Florida colony. As noted above, an expedient way to do this was to convert the Timucua into Catholic subjects of the Crown who were dependent on the Spanish empire. New aspects of culture were deliberately substituted for old ones.

Missionary friars instructed native villagers in the Catholic faith and introduced them to aspects of Hispanic culture, including new crops, the Spanish language, writing, metal tools, and other European-derived items, and new ways of thinking and behaving. Villagers were persuaded to change old patterns, especially things the friars deemed in conflict with Christian teachings, and accept new ones. We will examine this process in more detail in chapter 7.

One not-so-subtle way to gain the attention of potential native converts was to have their leaders visit St Augustine where they were given presents of European goods. In 1597 the chief of the town of Timucua and his entourage of 19 people received 30 lb of flour per day during their two-week visit to that town in addition to a hoe, axes, and complete outfits of clothes. The chief and his heir also received red hats, shirts, doublets, and shoes. Items given at other times to other native visitors included blankets, buttons, and more metal tools. The cost of these items was taken from the *situado*, the royal subsidy paid by the Spanish Crown to help in the support of the colony. The lure of European goods must have brought many Timucua to the missions and Catholicism.

Adults converted to Catholicism raised Christian children, enabling the missions to accomplish their goals. In 1620 Father Francisco Pareja at San Juan del Puerto wrote that the mission villagers did not remember the old ways and that the new generation made fun of people who occasionally still practiced them.

The first Franciscan missions among the eastern Timucua were established more than 70 years after Juan Ponce de Leon's 1513 voyage to Florida. The first western Timucuan mission was nearly 70 years after Hernando de Soto's army had marched through the territories of the Ocale, Potano, and northern Utinan groups. Native populations served by those missions had already suffered the impacts of living three generations with the presence of Spanish and French explorers and colonists. It must have been clear to the Timucua that the way of life that had served them so well for so long suddenly was not all that secure. Changes were being forced upon them. The missions found easy converts; old ways gave way to new.

The mission system controlled the Timucua by converting them to Catholicism, providing them with objects of Spanish material culture, and making them dependent on the Spaniards for access to those objects. The military government centered in St Augustine and the Spanish-owned haciendas in the interior of Florida could then use the Timucua in support of the colony. The missions indeed brought great changes to the Timucua, just as they were intended to do. In the next three chapters we will look at the lifeways of the Timucua and the extent of the changes brought by mission life and Spanish colonization.

5

Mission Settlements and Subsistence

Colonization brought changes to the Timucua. Indigenous patterns of life were altered as populations decreased due to diseases and as Spanish missions were established among the various native groups. The Timucua became a part of the Spain's American empire, Catholic subjects of the Crown.

The Missions

Most of the earliest Timucuan missions, including those in interior northern Florida established prior to the Timucuan rebellion, were located adjacent to existing native villages, apparently the larger or more important ones. As we saw in chapter 4, some of those Potano and northern Utina villages, for example, Aguacaleyquen (San Martín) and Cholupaha (Santa Fé), probably were the same ones the de Soto expedition had been at in 1539.

What would become other mission villages also had been subjected to de Soto's passage nearly 70 years earlier. Santa Ana just west of modern Gainesville and associated with the San Francisco *doctrina* was probably at the village of Utinamocharra. Indeed, in 1606 the chief of that village, who had been a boy when de Soto had been to the village, still remembered the cruelties inflicted by the Spanish army. Santa Cruz, most likely the Indian Pond site in western Columbia County mission, may have been the town of Uriutina and San Miguel de Asile probably was at Asile; both Uriutina and Asile were northern Utina towns where de Soto's army had camped.

Each mission *doctrina* had one or more missionary friars who lived in the mission village in the *convento*, their residence. Clustered around each mission village were additional native towns whose residents were served by that mission's friar and who went to the mission for services. For instance, in 1602 San Juan de Puerto on Fort George Island served nine satellite towns which were from about half a mile to 13 miles, one day's travel, from the mission.

This clustering of towns around a mission was observed by archaeologist Kenneth Johnson in Timucua province, who noted that the pattern resembles the precolumbian clustering found in both the Alachua and Suwannee Valley cultures. Johnson's archaeological surveys indicated that during the seventeenth century the clusters were more linear than circular, as they had been prior to the missions. He attributes this change to a desire by the Spanish to make the outlying towns more accessible by placing them along the road leading into and out of the main mission village. Even so, at least one friar complained that the distances he had to travel to reach ailing parishioners resulted in their dying before he could arrive and administer last rites.

Missions did not always remain in one place. They could be moved because all of the readily available firewood was used up or because nearby fields had lost their fertility. Likewise, as we saw in chapter 4, some of the Timucuan missions were moved after the rebellion of 1656.

Various documents provide hints at what the mission complexes looked like. Those descriptions have been enhanced by archaeological excavations in northeast and northern Florida, although we still have much to learn from archaeology about the missions.

Each mission consisted of a rectangular church and the *convento* (Figure 5.1). Some, if not all, also had a separate kitchen structure in which the friars' food was prepared. If Spanish soldiers were stationed at a mission they might be housed in a separate barracks. In a few instances soldiers staffed a stronghold constructed at or near the mission compound. Mission buildings fronted one or more plazas, on the opposite

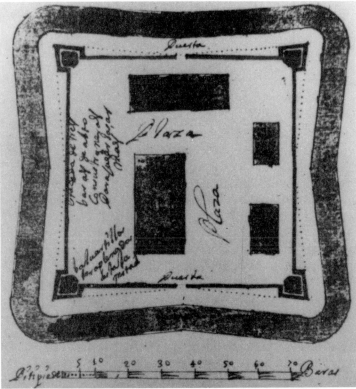

Figure 5.1 This 1691 map depicts mission Santa Catalina on Amelia Island, Florida. It shows four rectangular buildings: the church (lower left), the *convento* and kitchen (on the right), and a garrison house for Spanish soldiers (top); the four are positioned around plazas within a moat and wooden palisade with ramped, corner bastions. The moat and the palisade were never constructed
Source: courtesy P. K. Yonge Library of Florida History, University of Florida.

sides of which were the houses in which the Timucuan villagers lived. Some, possibly all, of the villages also had a large circular council house. Storage buildings and cribs, bell and lookout towers, and still other buildings also were found in the mission village.

The church itself was probably the largest of the mission buildings, averaging about 60 feet by 35 feet. Construction details varied. Some churches were constructed with vertical board walls; others had walls of wattle and daub – clay placed

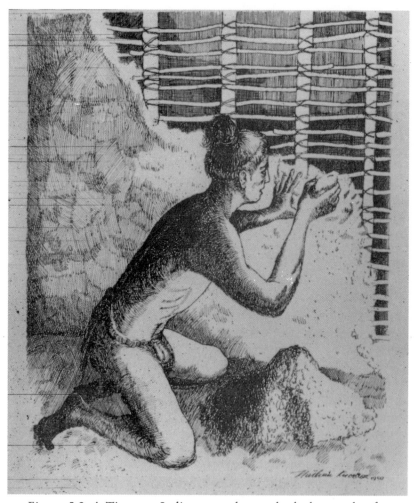

Figure 5.2 A Timucua Indian uses clay to daub the wattle of a mission church wall
Source: Boyd, Smith, and Griffin (1951: Plate 7); courtesy University Press of Florida.

over a latticework of posts and twigs (Figure 5.2). When dried, the daubed, clay walls could be plastered and even painted. Still other churches apparently were open pavilion-like buildings with no walls at all. It has been suggested that the first church built at a mission might be a small structure or a pavilion-like building. Later, more elaborate or larger churches were built.

Floors of church naves were packed earth or clay. Archaeological evidence from the small church or chapel at San Martín suggests the sanctuary end where the altar was situated and the santos and other religious items were displayed had a board floor.

As anyone who has observed posts or stakes pounded into the Florida or south Georgia soils can attest, buried wood rots quickly. Perhaps to counteract the natural soil acidity and the action of organisms that attack wood, villagers packed clay or shell along the bottoms of the church walls to protect posts and wall boards. Shells or clay also were used occasionally as filling in the holes used to anchor large wall- and roof-support posts. These support posts, usually cut from pine trees, were placed in holes more than three feet deep.

Similar construction techniques were used for the *conventos*, which normally were smaller and were subdivided into many small rooms. Some of the *conventos* had open porches attached to them.

Roofs of churches and *conventos* were supported by beams that rested on support posts. Palm thatch covered the roofs. The buildings were held together in part by wrought iron nails and spikes, hundreds of which have been found at some mission sites. Iron tools, including saws and hammers, were used in constructing the buildings, which combined Timucuan and Spanish construction practices.

Unfortunately, like the wooden houses of the Timucuan villages, the thatched mission buildings were highly inflammable, especially the roofs. The charred evidence of mission buildings found by archaeologists is mute testimony to accidental fires as well as fires deliberately set by raiders using flaming arrows or spears to ignite dry thatched roofs. It is ironic that the very act of burning the buildings helped to preserve the evidence of their existence, remains which can be interpreted by archaeologists.

The church at mission Santa María on Amelia Island excavated by Rebecca Saunders appears to have had a wooden construction at one end, perhaps an elaborated entry façade with balcony and/or bell tower. The doorway into the nave from the outside was an important place within each church. Marriages and other Catholic rites were performed there. Each church also had a font for holy water.

Table 5.1 Furnishings and ornaments for a typical late seventeenth-century *doctrina*

1 monstrance, either of silver or gilded (to hold the Host)
2 silver chalices
2 missals, including one used for Requiem Mass (books containing the Mass, prayers, devotions, etc.)
1 wooden missal stand and coverlet
9 or 10 sets of chasuble, stole, and maniple (vestments worn by priests at Mass) in various colours
7 or 8 antependiums (cloths hung down the front of the altar) in various colors
6 albs of white linen (outer garment worn by priests when saying Mass)
7 hand bells
8 brass candlesticks
1 or 2 choir-copes (robes)
5 or 6 altar cloths
7 amices (part of the priests' vestments)
7 or 8 palls (linen cloth for covering the chalice)
11 corporals of starched linen (cloth on which the bread and wine to be consecrated are placed)
5 burses (cloth pocket used to store the folded corporals)
11 or 12 chalice veils
2 surplices (a vestment)
3 or 4 rochets (a vestment)
5 cinctures (rope-like belt)
1 long decorated stole (a vestment)
1 coverlet for the altar
1 silver lunet for the Viaticum (to hold it upright in the monstrance)
  ceramic or glass cruets (for communion and for washing the priest's fingers during the Offertory section of the Mass)
1 or 2 silver chrism vials (for holy oils)
1 altar lamp of silver or brass
1 silver procession cross
1 thurible and incense boat and spoon of silver or brass
2 religious banners (which could be mounted for use in processions)
2 engravings each depicting some religious motif
5 or 6 statues (of Our Lady, Infant Jesus, and various saints)
13 pictures or paintings depicting religious motifs
4 *cornialtares* (possibly altar cards displayed during Mass)
1 cedar chest for storing vestments (a few missions had more than one)
1 silver crown or halo
1 procession lantern[a]
1 cloth communion paten
1 silver communion paten[a]
1 silk humeral cloth[a] (a vestment)
1 or more linen handcloths

1 ritual[a] (a book of prayers)
1 veil or curtain
1 host press[a]
1 mirror[a]

---

[a] Not present at all missions.
Source: Based on Hann (1986a)

At the opposite end of the nave was the sanctuary, where carvings of saints and other religious icons were displayed behind and to the sides of the altar. Off the sanctuary was a sacristy, a separate room where the extensive array of vestments and sacred vessels and other accoutrements used in services were stored (Table 5.1 presents a typical list of these). The magnificence of the carvings and the vestments and the pageantry of the rites conducted by the friars must have brought the beauty and splendor of Catholic ritual to the native villagers and their small wooden churches.

The large brass bells which hung at *doctrinas* served to signal time and call villagers to Mass. They were important symbols of the ecclesiastical authority of the Catholic Church and the missions and mission friars. Some even received names. Bells were literally the voice of the missions. As historian Amy Bushnell has noted, mission villagers lived "beneath the bell." When the Florida missions were destroyed early in the eighteenth century (see chapter 8), these symbols of Catholicism and Spanish might were pounded into pieces by the Carolinian Protestant raiders and their native allies.

Within the complex of mission structures constructed "beneath the bell," fences or walls were used to demarcate areas and buildings. Some were daubed in the same fashion as the walls of buildings. Similar walls sometimes surrounded the church, or the *convento*, or both. Walls also might have been placed around the mission cemetery if one were present. Investigations at mission Santa Fé in Timucua suggest that a wall or fence surrounded a cemetery there. Mission gardens tended on behalf of the friars by mission Indians also were walled.

Interring the Dead

Timucua Indians of the seventeenth century lived as Christians and, when they died, they were afforded Catholic burial rites in sanctified ground, either in the floor of the mission church or in the mission cemetery, the *campo santo*. People who died at satellite villages were taken to the mission church for burial.

Christian Timucua were nearly always interred extended on their backs in individual, shallow graves. Each individual's arms were folded on his or her chest, at times with hands clasped. In a few instances archaeologists have found interments made in small oval or round graves. In those cases the person was buried on his or her side in a flexed position with knees bent and arms bent and drawn up close to the torso. Such flexed burials were much more common in the precolumbian period when the ancestors of the Timucua interred people in sand mounds. Perhaps, in the absence of a mission friar, villagers may have opted to bury a deceased friend or relative in the traditional way.

Some mission villagers were interred wrapped in cloth shrouds secured with brass straight pins. A very few burials have been found in wooden coffins. In Apalachee at mission San Luís bioanthropologist Clark Larsen and archaeologist Bonnie Mc-Ewan found coffin interments in the church floor close to the altar, suggesting the people interred in that fashion were important individuals with high social status.

Some of the Timucua were buried holding or wearing items of Christian piety, such as small crosses, religious medallions, and reliquaries. Individuals also have been found clutching rosaries. Jewelry and beaded clothing and ornaments also occasionally accompanied the dead into their graves. Early in the seventeenth century the Timucua were admonished by friars not to place objects within the shrouds. Apparently some villagers were interring their deceased relatives with items the Catholic friars deemed non-Christian. On the Commemoration of All Souls day, November 2, Christian Timucua made offerings of pumpkins, beans, maize, or toasted (wheat?) flour in reverence to the dead.

Within the churches and the cemeteries the graves and the bodies they contained all were aligned in the same direction. Excavations at San Martín and Santa Catalina, the latter a late seventeenth-century mission on Amelia Island serving Guale Indians, suggest that the graves were in rows (Figure 5.3). Over time, as more villagers died and were interred, what had been ordered rows became more chaotic, perhaps as exact locations of previous burials were forgotten. In such cases new burials often intersected older ones, at times creating a jumble of bones and

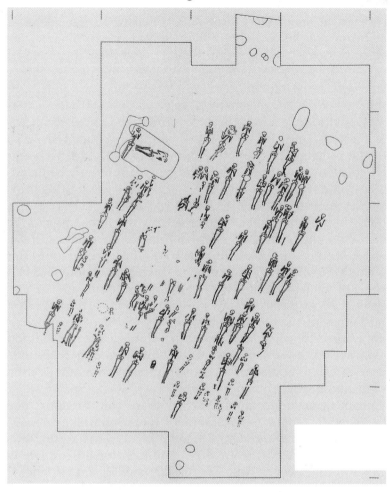

Figure 5.3 Christian burials in the floor of the Santa Catalina church on Amelia Island. The rectangular area encompassed by the burials is about 33 feet by 55 feet

graves. In churches, which had only a limited amount of floor for interment, burials were extremely packed with as many as ten people buried in one 10-foot by 10-foot space in graves 3 feet deep or less.

Some archaeologists have suggested that all mission burials were inside churches. Areas containing interments which originally were interpreted as cemeteries may actually have been open, pavilion-like churches. At San Martín, however, in Timucua province the small, open church first constructed at the mission had burials placed around (outside) it. No interments were made within the area covered by the roof. And at the Baptizing Spring mission site, also in Timucua province, interments were not made within the church.

The most remarkable thing about the mission burials is that much of the story about the health, diet, and causes of death of the mission Timucua can be reconstructed from analysis of their skeletal remains. Employing a number of analytical techniques, biological anthropologists are allowing the mission Timucua to, at least in part, tell their story. A lifetime of ill-health and hard work as well as epidemics took a devastating toll.

The Catholic interments afforded the mission Timucua were quite different from the mound burials of their ancestors who lived in the precolumbian and early colonial (pre-mission) times. As we saw in chapter 1, mound interments were practiced by the people of the Suwannee Valley, Alachua, St Johns, and Savannah cultures. Most often, burials in mounds were of cleaned bones. The bodies of the deceased had been allowed to decompose or they were stripped of flesh, then they were cleaned and stored in a charnel house or temple before being buried in a mound. In fewer cases the bodies were interred directly in mounds, usually in a flexed position.

European accounts note that, prior to the missions, native priests and leaders were afforded special burial ceremonies. When either died their houses and possessions were burned. Their bones were cleaned of flesh and kept for a period of time when offerings were made. There is archaeological evidence that the bones later were buried in a mound along with offerings and goods, such as shell drinking cups, that these important personages might need in the next life.

In a document written in 1630, a Franciscan friar described the traditional burial customs of the Timucua:

They are a most pious people toward their deceased . . . [A]s soon as the one who is ill expires, they all cry with great tenderness for the time of 30 days, the women with high and doleful tone, the men in silence . . . [W]hen the principal cacique [chief] died, they buried some children from the common . . . people along with his body. For this benefit, their mother and father are held and esteemed as leading people from then on . . . And all the rest offered a portion of their hair as a sign of sorrow, which they cut for this purpose, along with the most precious ornaments that they had. They always kept these graves separate from the rest and all on the highest hills, distanced from the settlements. In other provinces, all the blood relatives, both men and women, cut themselves with sharp flints on the upper arms and thighs until they shed a great deal of blood. And after they know that the flesh [of the deceased] is consumed, they remove the bones and, (after being) purified at the fire, they keep them in some small leather trunks . . . [T]hey maintain them in their tombs or little houses, separated from those in which they live. And they visit them there every day and they offer them a small amount of everything that they eat. (Hann, 1993a: 99)

Much of the detail in this account is very similar to that recorded by the French in 1564–5 and by other Spanish observers. One of the latter added the information that chiefs were buried directly in mounds while the bones of other people, once cleaned, were stored. Another person stated that a chief was buried after a three-day period of fasting. Then for six months to a year villagers mourned the chief by daily ceremonial wailing.

During the period of mourning relatives of the deceased did not eat food gathered from the fields of the departed. Instead the crops were given away. After interment relatives were ritually cleansed and did not eat fish for a period. Widows and widowers who had cut their hair as a sign of mourning did not remarry until their hair had once again grown (Figure 5.4).

When a chief or other important individual died in his or her house, the death was believed to have polluted the structure, which then had to be destroyed. To avoid having to burn down or otherwise destroy a house, a chief who was near death was moved to a new house constructed specifically to house that individual while he or she died.

The practice of burning the house in which a chief had died may have a long history among the ancestors of the Timucua. At the McKeithen site, the fifth century precolumbian Weeden Island village in Columbia County, Florida described in chapter 1, the village leader, perhaps a woman, was found interred in a shallow grave dug into the floor of a house which had been erected on a low mound. A small tomb of logs and sand had been built atop the grave and then the house was destroyed by being burned.

All of the archaeological evidence on hand indicates the construction and use of burial mounds by the Timucua halted by the late sixteenth or early seventeenth century, the same time as the

Figure 5.4 A de Bry engraving depicting grieving widows scattering their newly cut hair on the graves of their husbands; the shell drinking cups (erroneously shown as nautilus snails, not *Busycons*) and bows and arrows of the dead were also laid on the graves
Source: de Bry (1591).

first missions. Mission friars actively sought to halt those native ceremonies and beliefs which they felt were not in concert with Catholic doctrine. Mound burial would have been high on that list.

Native Villages

Accounts from the later half of the sixteenth century from both the eastern and western Timucuan regions indicate a typical village contained about 25 houses and a population of 200, about eight people per household. These figures are very similar to those derived from excavations at the Richardson site, the early Alachua culture village described in chapter 1. Very early in the mission period one friar noted that three villages he was serving had a total population of 1,200 people, but that figure seems out of place with the others we have.

Were precolumbian villages larger? Pertinent archaeological evidence from the precolumbian period is lacking. However, site surveys in the Potano and northern Utinan areas show that precolumbian sites were not significantly larger in extent. About 20 to 30 houses and 200 to 250 people seems to have been an optimal village size. When villages grew larger than this number, some of their residents may have moved to a nearby location and established a new village. Such a process of "budding off" villages would account for the clusters of sites observed among the Timucuan groups and described in chapter 1.

But these village figures did not remain constant during the mission period, a time when epidemics continued to reduce the Timucuan population. Demographic data from eastern Timucuan villages recorded in 1602, very early in the mission period, listed only 200 Timucua living in three villages in the St Augustine vicinity. And although the size of individual mission period villages fluctuated, perhaps in part because the populations of individual groups were consolidated around *doctrinas*, the trend throughout the seventeenth century was for smaller village size. As we shall see in chapter 8, epidemics and the hardships presented by colonization led to smaller and smaller Timucuan populations over time. The villages of the eighteenth century often had fewer than 50 people living in them.

Population reductions also led to fewer Timucuan villages. Settlements grew less densely distributed across the land. And following the 1656 rebellion it became common for small villages to be consolidated. As we shall see in chapter 8, it ultimately became necessary to consolidate different groups in the same towns. As a consequence, the ethnic makeup of early eighteenth-century Timucuan villages was quite different from the villages of the early seventeenth century.

Not all of the Timucua lived full time in villages. Special-use camps were present in some locales. Archaeologists have found small shell midden sites along the coast south of St Augustine, presumably camps occupied at times when fishing was optimum. A 1595 Spanish account may describe this pattern. It noted that there were only clusters of huts along the coast, while the villages were further inland.

Even in non-coastal areas hamlets consisting of several houses were present apart from villages. Such hamlets are mentioned in a 1602 Spanish account. And a French account from the 1560s indicates that during the winter some of the Timucua went to live in small thatched houses that were in the woods away from villages. Small archaeological sites probably corresponding to these small hamlets have been found in both the eastern and western Timucuan regions. The households living at such sites may have been engaged in seasonal hunting or other specialized subsistence activities, and the houses probably were not occupied full time.

With the onset of the missions and the desire of the Spanish to control the Timucua, populations were consolidated in mission villages. Only rarely is the presence of Timucua not living in established villages noted in the mission provinces in the seventeenth century.

At least some of the Timucuan villages may have been protected by a palisade. One of the 1591 engravings of Theodor de Bry, which was based on French accounts from the 1560s and on paintings or sketches done by the Frenchman Jacques Le Moyne, shows a Timucuan town, probably one located near Fort Caroline, surrounded by a wooden-post palisade. Palisades also are mentioned in other sixteenth-century European accounts of the eastern Timucua. But as yet no archaeological evidence for palisaded villages has been found and none of the extensive documentation from the later sixteenth and the seventeenth centuries mentions palisades. Most likely the security-conscious Spaniards would not have allowed the mission Timucua to fortify their villages. To do so presented a military threat.

Native Buildings

Within the mission villages there were several types of structures, the most numerous of which were the houses of individual households. Archaeological evidence from eastern and western Timucuan mission villages indicates that, although many new ideas and practices were introduced to the missions, the native people continued to build houses in the old ways. Even though iron tools are found in Timucuan houses, those houses contain almost no iron construction hardware, such as spikes and nails. The old tools and methods of building structures were retained, in contrast to the mission churches and *conventos* where such hardware is common. The Spaniards must have overseen the construction of the mission buildings; they left the construction of native houses to the Timucua.

Descriptions of Timucuan houses were provided by various European observers between 1564 and 1675 and all are reasonably consistent with one another. Features described in common include a circular shape, palm thatch and wooden pole construction, and very small doors. In appearance, one Franciscan observer noted the houses resembled a pyramid. Probably the rounded structures came to a point on top.

Within the houses there were reed benches for sleeping, under which small smudge fires were lit to ward off insects. Excavation of a Potano house at the Richardson site located such smudges, each of which was in a small depression 4 to 6 inches across and several inches deep. Cane mats or mats woven from other plants, such as palmetto, were placed on the benches. Each house also had a large, central fire. The latter was probably used to provide light and for cooking and warmth. Torches also were used for light.

At the Richardson site in Alachua County one house pattern and several partial ones were excavated. The circular to slightly oval houses were about 25 feet in diameter. Wall posts were about 8 inches in diameter and were set in the ground two to three feet apart. The walls were probably thatched with palm fronds; no evidence of wattle and daub construction was present. Individual houses were spaced about 70 feet apart.

Multiple fire and refuse pits were located inside the houses, the latter containing refuse from meals and other garbage. Other garbage was swept up against the interior of the walls under the sleeping benches.

Excavations at the Fountain of Youth Park site in St Augustine also uncovered portions of colonial period houses. Some of the houses were slightly oval, measuring 20 feet by 15 feet. The wall posts, about 6 inches in diameter, were set in pairs with each pair about 3 feet from the next. Within the village houses were more closely spaced than at the Richardson site. Each was about 10 feet from its neighbour. No daub was found and the walls and roof were probably palm thatched.

Investigations in one of the Fountain of Youth Park houses revealed a central hearth nearly 6 feet in diameter. Two small interior fire pits may have been used a smudges. The interior of the house was quite free of debris; perhaps it was used in warmer months when most activities took place outdoors. Beside the house was a cluster of small postmolds encircling one side of a large pit containing shells. This may have been part of a storage area or even a drying rack.

Additional excavations at the same site had earlier discovered two other structures, both slightly oval and only 7 feet long. Wall posts were only 3–4 inches in diameter and were placed one to two feet apart. Both had a central hearth kindled in a shallow pit 3.4 feet across. These may have been built for special purposes, perhaps as sweat lodges or seclusion huts or even as structures for smoking food.

In addition to the houses of individual families, each Timucuan village contained a large circular council house with wooden wall posts. Such council houses were the locus of village communal activities, including many ceremonial and political activities. Sacred teas were typically drunk in the house, and when divisions of harvested produce were made by a chief, that might also be done in the communal structure. The council house also served as the village chief's office, the place where he conducted the village's business. They also functioned as men's lodges where adult males lounged and made bows and arrows and tanned deerskins. Visitors to a village were usually housed in the council house during their stay. And when Spanish officials held meetings with native leaders, the individuals involved met in the council house. Council houses continued to be built and used throughout the seventeenth century.

Historical sources agree that council houses were circular, although estimates of size vary widely. One account describes a council house only large enough to hold as many as 300 people; another says 3,000. Another from 1695 describes a council house as circular, 81 feet in diameter. A second circular row of interior support posts was 50 feet in diameter.

Nearly all of the firsthand European accounts mention the benches around the interior walls; council houses with a second ring of support posts probably also had a second ring of benches concentric within the outer ring. In one house the benches are said to have been painted red, yellow, and blue. In at least some council houses the interior of the outside walls were daubed with clay. Murals were painted on the clay with natural pigments.

Within the houses torches were lit for light. In addition, a large fire was built in the center of the floor. The smoke from the fire

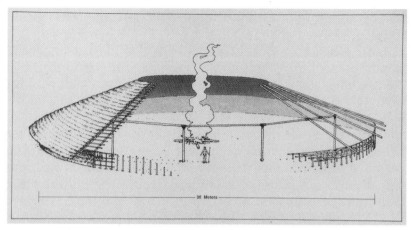

36 Meters

Figure 5.5 Artist's view of the council house at San Luís in
Apalachee. The second row of benches is not shown
Source: courtesy of the Florida Division of Historical Resources.

exited upward through an opening in the roof. Doorways were
short and wide, about a yard high and a yard and a half wide.
People entering the hut had to stoop. Europeans found the
doorways peculiar, not at all like the doorways with which they
were familiar.

Archaeologists working at the Apalachee Indian mission of San
Luís have located and excavated the council house associated
with that mission village and found it almost exactly like the
historical accounts. The circular San Luís building was round,
120 feet in diameter with a circle of low benches built around the
interior of the outside wall (Figure 5.5). Within that outer circle
of benches were eight large support posts arranged in a second
circle with a second circular row of low benches. Eight large
rafters radiating in from the outside wall posts rested on the
eight posts and supported the roof. Excavators concluded that
the council house, including the roof around the central opening,
was thatched.

Within the two concentric rings of support posts and benches
at the exact center of the structure was a hearth marking the
location of the council house fire. A large circular roof opening
is thought to have been present over the center of the structure;
that opening may have been as large as 46 feet across. The floor
area around the central fire was most likely a dance ground
measuring more than 65 feet across.

Excavation of portions of the council house, directed by Gary Shapiro, showed that in all there were 64 benches and 136 support posts. Historical accounts state that individual benches were separated from one another, perhaps with partitions which are described as "cabins." In the San Luís house small fires had been lit on the floor of the house in front of some of the individual benches or cabins.

Under the benches were numerous small corn cob-filled pits which probably function as smudges. The floor of the mission period Apalachee council house was littered with broken pottery, beads, and pieces of small brass bells. The pottery pieces had been swept up against the interior wall and into the central hearth, while the beads and bells probably were lost by dancers. Apparently people in the council house occasionally passed the time chipping arrow points; both points and the debitage from making them were found.

Timucuan council houses probably were very similar to the San Luís structure. In 1675 a Spanish bishop visiting Florida described one:

Each village has a large council house called the great *bujío* [a word brought to Florida from the Caribbean by the Spaniards], constructed of wood and covered with straw, round, and with a very large opening at the top . . . They are furnished all around the interior with niches called *barbacôas* [another Caribbean word adopted by the Spaniards], which serve as beds and seats for the . . . chiefs, and as lodging for soldiers and transients. Dances and festivals are held in them around a great fire in the center. (Wenhold, 1936: 13)

Another Spanish account, one from 1639, described the interior seating in a Timucuan council house. Each of the chiefs, sub-chiefs, and other respected individuals (see chapter 6) knew their own status and the location of their seat relative to the chief's:

In this community house . . . they have its seats placed around with great order and arrangement, with the one belonging to the principal chief being the best and highest . . . Those of the remaining leading men follow after this seat, without there being any confusion in it, while also having seats for the remaining common people, where they seat themselves without this order or arrangement. (Hann, 1993a: 94)

Other structures present in precolumbian Timucuan villages included drying racks, corn storage cribs, menstrual seclusion huts, and a granary or storehouse which held the chief's share of corn and other crops. And outside individual houses there must have been work areas where many day-to-day activities took place, especially in the warmer months.

Making a Living

During the late precolumbian period and into the sixteenth century the Timucua Indians had a mixed economy, one which combined hunting, gathering plants and animals, and fishing. They also farmed and gardened, although the relative import- ance of agricultural products varied among the different groups. Where extensive wetlands provided sufficient wild foods, such as among the Ocale and some the groups living along the Atlantic coast, farming was not as large a part of the economy as it was among the northern Utinan groups, the Potano, or some of the eastern Timucuan groups living in the St Johns River drainage in northeast Florida.

Relative to native societies living in the interior of the South- east, such as the groups ancestral to the Creek Indians or the Apalachee Indians in northwest Florida, the Timucua did not rely so intensively on cultivated crops. Corn, squashes, and other domesticated plants did not comprise as large a percentage of their diet. Crops were not planted in fields as large as those found among the northern groups, nor were plants cultivated as intensively.

The major factor behind these difference is that the region of the Timucua is not blessed with the rich, annually replenished soils that are found in the river valleys of the interior Southeast. The soils of northern Florida and southern Georgia were not as fertile as those found to the north. Nor were they replenished by annual floods that deposited new layers of silt atop old fields. It was the natural environment, not conscious decisions, that caused the Timucua to evolve their particular economic system.

Because the Timucua produced a smaller portion of their diet and were more reliant on wild foods, they differed from the interior native groups in several important ways. First, the Timu- cuan economy, one based largely on hunting, gathering, and fishing and less on farming, could not support the dense large populations found in the piedmont and interior river valley regions of Georgia, Alabama, Tennessee, and much of the Mississippi Valley.

Smaller populations meant the Timucua lived in smaller villages which were less densely distributed than the interior groups. And, in part because relatively larger percentages of the population were needed to help collect the food necessary to support the villagers, the Timucua did not develop the complex political apparatus so common to the north. Less social and political complexity and fewer societal institutions were needed to organize society and assure agricultural endeavors. And the customs and practices, myths and rituals surrounding extensive agriculture and its concomitant social and religious institutions were not present among the Timucua. Instead they developed lifeways well suited to their environment and the economic patterns they used to assure their well-being.

The Timucua did copy some aspects of the social, political, and ideological systems of the farming groups who lived to their north and northwest. But they applied those ideas to their own circumstances. They undoubtedly also borrowed ideas from their other neighbors, and they originated many other cultural practices as well. But the cultural systems of the Timucuan groups were not mere reflections of those found among their native neighbors. The Timucua developed a way of life that allowed them to live and prosper in the natural world in which they lived.

Europeans among the Timucua in the sixteenth century noted some of the plants which were grown in fields or gardens surrounding the villages: corn, beans and peas, pumpkins, citrons, and gourds. Those plants had probably been cultivated for hundreds of years prior to the early colonial period. Some European accounts indicate that agricultural plots were planted and tended by both men and women. Others suggest that women not only did most of the work related to planting and harvesting, but they collected most of the wild plants and smaller game that the Timucua used as well.

The French living in the region of the eastern Timucua in the 1560s described two planting seasons for corn, one in March and one in June. A mission period Spanish account gives April as the time for sowing. Probably different groups sowed at different times in the spring. Fields were cleared by cutting down the trees and then burning them, a practice which flushed animals out of hiding and made them easy prey. Chiefs and native priests performed ceremonies in conjunction with planting, harvesting, and using corn and other plants.

The fields were prepared and then planted with seed. Periodically while they were growing the crops were hoed to keep down weeds. The hoes made of wood were tipped with large fish bones or chert blades. It also was common to build a house in the corner of the each field so a lookout could be posted to keep an eye on animals that might eat the crops. Harvested ears of corn were husked and then shelled. Then the kernels were ground into meal in log mortars which were 15 to 18 inches in diameter and about two feet high. They were used with wooden pestles five or six feet long. Women did the hard work of shelling and grinding the corn into meal. Similar log mortars and wooden pestles were used by nearly all southeastern native farmers.

Corn meal was eaten in a variety of ways, sometimes mixed with other meals or foods. Most frequently it was served in a porridge or gruel mixed with water. Small cakes of corn meal dough about an inch in diameter were cooked in the ashes of fires. These baked corn cakes, the predecessor of our cornbread, and other corn meal recipes also were common among all southeastern native peoples.

In addition to cultivated plants a significant portion of the Timucuan diet was provided by wild plants, including acorns, hickory nuts, palm berries, may pop, wild grape, walnuts, hazelnuts, wild cherries, plums, persimmons, blueberries, huckleberries, elderberries, peppervine, groundcherry, amaranth, bristlegrass, pokeweed, broomweed, smartweed/knotweed, bulrush, nut sedge, buttonbush, water shield, spatterdock, and various roots. Hickory nut meal was mixed with parched corn meal to make a sort of "trail mix" that could be easily carried and eaten by people on the move.

Another wild food was a root called *ache*, which grew in wet areas. Rather than being a single species, *ache*, a Spanish term, may have been a generic term for several different edible roots. The roots were collected when other food were in short supply. As when plants were harvested, collection of at least some wild plants involved ceremonies and incantations.

Father Escobedo, a Franciscan friar, described how meal ground from acorns was made into cakes called *gacha* or *ogacha*:

They gather large amounts of the acorn which is small and bitter and peel the hull from the meat. They grind it well and during the time they bury it in the ground the earth is warm from the heat of the sun. Since low temperature spoils the dough, they do this about noon. After the dough is taken from the earth, they sprinkle it with water so intensely hot that it cooks the dough into the form of a loaf. By the above water and earth process the acorn loaf acquires a pleasant taste. The cacique [chief] of Florida eats this dish and it is usually is one of his most appreciated delicacies. It is reserved for gentlemen only, and, of course, "la gacha" is greatly relished by all. (Covington and Falcones, 1963: 150–1)

Another account indicated the dough or meal was buried for eight or more days, apparently to allow the bitter tannin in it to leach out. The dough was then put on a wooden stick and cooked over a fire. *Gacha* traditionally was presented to chiefs as a sign of welcome.

By the third quarter of the seventeenth century, during the mission period, the recipe for *gacha* had changed or the same word was used to describe more than one dish. A document from that time noted it contained corn, ashes, squash, and beans in a succotash-like stew. Ashes were mixed with maize to soften the hard kernels, making them more digestible.

In general the agricultural Timucua tried to store enough food to provide at least a portion of their diet through the winter. But this may have not always been possible if the harvest was bad. When that occurred families moved out of their villages and took up residence in palm-thatched houses built in forests where game, fish, shellfish, and acorns were more easily accessible and could sustain them.

In addition to the plants that were collected for food, a number of other wild plants and trees were used for tools, firewood, construction material, canoes, and for other purposes. As noted in chapter 1, at the Hontoon Island site south of Lake George in the St Johns River drainage 30 wood species and 82 species of seeds and other plant parts were identified. The Timucua and their neighbors made wide use of the natural resources of northern Florida and southern Georgia. They knew which plants and herbs were best for specific purposes, whether food or tools.

Herbs, including tobacco, were used in a variety of ways, including in curing ceremonies (see chapter 7). Rubbing the juice of certain herbs on one's body before battle was thought to ward

Figure 5.6 Timucuan hunters in deer disguises
Source: de Bry (1591).

off enemy arrows. Other herbs were used by women as contraceptives and abortifacients.

Herbs also were used in love charms. One herbal charm attracted a woman. By magically perfuming her Spanish moss skirt with a herb a woman could similarly attract a man or could cause her own spouse to remain true to her. Bathing with certain herbs could bring a wandering husband home.

Perhaps as important to the Timucua as plants were the wild game, fish, and other animals which lived in northern Florida and southern Georgia. Deer were a major source of meat. At times they were hunted by men in antlered deer disguises (Figure 5.6). They also were hunted in fire drives, as were rabbits. Deer were butchered at the kill site and the haunches and other choice parts, such as the lower jaws with tongues attached, were taken back to the village. Other usable parts, such as sinews, antlers, and hides also were removed and transported to villages. During the period of the missions when deer hides became a valued trading commodity, village chiefs were able to claim a share of the skins from hunters.

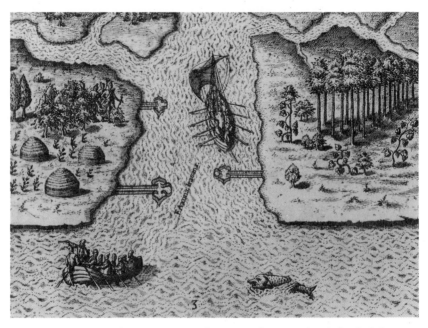

Figure 5.7 Ribault's 1562 expedition at the mouth of the St Marys River, which they called the River Seine. Three fish weirs are shown on the banks of the river
Source: de Bry (1591).

Another important meat source was fish, which were caught using fish traps, weirs, and nets as well as with spears or gigs. Some of the weirs were apparently elaborate wooden constructions that were used to trap quantities of fish (Figure 5.7). One, probably constructed of posts or reeds, was said to be 250 yards long. The weirs were placed both in saltwater and freshwater locations. Streams draining into the marshes or the coastal lagoon rose and fell with the tide. As the water dropped, fish were trapped in back of the weirs.

Apparently some weirs could be opened to allow the fish to swim in with the tide. Then the opening was closed and the fish were trapped. Large nets could be pulled through the water toward the weir, literally harvesting the trapped fish. On occasion fish were hunted with bows and arrows, sometimes from canoes, or they were caught in casting nets.

As in the precolumbian period a large variety of species was taken from saltwater and freshwater habitats. From one sixteenth-century Timucuan village in St Augustine the remains of catfish, drum, croaker, perch, gar, grouper, and trout – all marine species – were found. Many more species have been found at other coastal archaeological sites in the Timucuan region.

An equally long list of freshwater fish has been identified from sites in the St Johns River drainage and from sites in northern Florida. Freshwater catfish, gar, bass, and mullet were especially popular. Fish could be eaten fresh or dried (by smoking?) and saved for later use. Some fish were rendered down and the resulting fat used as a food supplement. A number of charms and rituals surrounded hunting and fishing (see chapter 7).

Coastal and inland wetlands also provided shellfish – especially oysters along the coast and snails and freshwater mussels along the St Johns River – as well aquatic turtles, shrimp, wading birds, migratory ducks and geese, and other animals, such as alligators. Wetlands, whether coastal or inland, were veritable larders of food.

Forested areas surrounding the rivers and lakes of the region and those adjacent to the coast were home to still other animals which were hunted, snared, or collected. In addition to deer some of these were gopher tortoises, turkeys, rabbits, and raccoons. Occasionally, other mammals were taken, including bears, foxes, bobcats, and panthers.

With the establishment of missions changes began to occur in the economies of the Timucua. Subsistence strategies were altered as plants and animals from Europe were introduced. And because the Spaniards living in St Augustine as well as the Franciscan friars and Spanish soldiers residing at the missions relied on Timucuan crops for part of their own subsistence, mission villagers probably began to place more emphasis on the cultivation of corn. Some mission corn was exported by the Spanish as well. What had been a subsistence crop became a source of revenue.

Plants brought from Spain and grown in mission gardens found their way into the diet of the mission villagers. Preserved remains of watermelons, peaches, figs, hazelnuts, oranges, and garbanzos were used to supplement traditional foods and all have been identified from mission sites. Archival materials mention an even larger number of plants brought by the Spanish to Florida: European greens, aromatic herbs, peas, sugar cane, garlic, melons, barley, pomegranates, cucumbers, European grapes, cabbages, lettuce, and sweet potatoes. All of these also could have been grown at the missions.

Wheat, identified from several mission sites, was cultivated at Spanish ranches in the Timucuan region and may have been grown in some mission fields as well. Unlike the native plants, wheat was planted in the fall, in October, and harvested in June. Wheat grains were ground into flour for bread, a valued Spanish commodity. Unleavened flour also was used to make the host for communion, a must in Catholic ritual. The wet flour was shaped into round wafers with a metal, tong-like press device which could leave an embossed religious motif on the surface of each wafer.

As noted above, at each mission crops were cultivated for the support of the mission friars and corn was grown for export directly to St Augustine or it was transported to the Gulf of Mexico coast and shipped out. At times the mission Indians could sell corn to the Spanish; in 1592 one native chief sold 263 arrobas of maize – about three tons – for fifty silver ducats, six axes, three hoes, nearly fifty yards of burlap cloth, and thread.

The ability to increase the production of corn was due to a larger number of fields being placed under cultivation and the use of metal tools – machetes, axes, and hoes – which increased efficiency. Iron hoes have been found at several mission villages.

Archaeologists have found thousands of charred corn cobs at mission sites in Timucua. On the other hand, only very small amounts of corn have ever been found at late precolumbian and early colonial sites in the same region and even then most have been charred kernels. The reason so many corn cobs are found as opposed to charred kernels may reflect the method of "packaging" the corn for transportation to St Augustine. Probably it was only the kernels or the ground meal that were transported in baskets, not the whole cob. The cobs with kernels removed were left at the missions where they provided a ready source of fuel. Many of small smudge pits at mission sites, pits thought to been used for insect control, are filled with charred cobs. Apparently they were a readily available smudge fuel.

By having only the kernels or meal sent to St Augustine, the Spaniards could increase the amount of corn each native bearer carried. And having the kernels already removed from the cobs and then ground into meal meant further processing did not need to be done after the corn left the missions.

New species of animals were brought to the missions along with new plants. Chickens, pigs, cattle, and, occasionally, horses, were kept at the missions, and used for food or transportation. In Apalachee province the export of livestock products – tallow, pork, cowhides, and beef – provided income for Spaniards and the Apalachee Indians alike.

Even though they added European plants and animals to their diets, the mission Timucua continued to hunt, trap, and fish and to collect wild plants. Many of the same animals found at precolumbian sites have been identified at the missions along with many of the same wild plants (maypop, acorn, hickory nuts, persimmons, and cabbage palm and palmetto berries).

Hunting was done with bows and arrows. The bowstrings were made of gut or leather, while the arrows were shaped from reeds or slender pieces of wood. They were tipped with fish or sharks' teeth and fish bones, as well as with small triangular points chipped out of chert, a local flint-like stone. Occasionally they were made from other stone. The Spaniards marveled at the archery abilities of the Timucua.

One aspect of the introduction of new foods was that new methods of food preparation were required. Traditionally most foods were boiled or stewed over an open fire in earthenware bowls. Cooking might also have been done in earth ovens. Meat was roasted and eaten or dried or smoked for later stewing or boiling. Broths were common. Fish were prepared in much the same ways as meat. They were first cleaned and hung to dry or they were smoked. Drying racks were made of wooden posts.

Acorns, like corn, were ground and made into a meal, and both acorn and corn flour were probably used in preparing gruels and in breads. Acorns and other nuts probably were ground in log mortars as was corn. Some seeds or other plant foods also were ground and processed. Other plant foods were probably dried or parched to preserve them for storage and later use. Gruels or porridges were cooked in ceramic bowls and served in smaller ceramic bowls or wooden ones. Shell and gourd dippers or cups were used also (Figure 5.8).

At all of the mission sites excavated thus far archaeologists have found native-made ceramics in the shape of Spanish plates, pitchers, bowls, and other dish ware. This colono-Indian ware

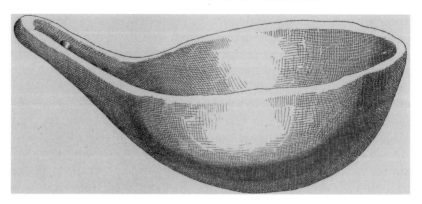

Figure 5.8 A ceramic dipper from the Mount Royal site. The gourd-shaped dipper is 5.5 inches long. It could be hung by a thong passed though a hole in the end of the handle
Source: Moore (1894b: Plate XVII).

was made for Spanish use, but at least some of the items found their ways into native households, perhaps those of high-ranking families. Like their diets, the ceramics of the Timucua became a combination of the old and the new.

During the period of the missions the technology used in hunting, tool making, and the like apparently changed less than did aspects of food technology. At the San Martín and the San Juan mission sites, both in western Timucua province, a variety of traditional stone, bone, and antler tools were found in the native villages, although a few iron tools and scraps of brass were present. Shell also was used for tools and implements. At one site in St Augustine Spanish glass was fashioned into a traditional native scraper.

Baskets and mats woven of cane and other fibers were widespread. One seventeenth-century account describes boxes made from leather, but these may have been copies of Spanish chests.

Dugout canoes, almost always made from cypress logs shaped by using fire and stone and shell tools, provided transportation for the Timucua. Thousands of cypress chips, most likely debris from canoe-making, were found at the Hontoon Island site preserved in wet deposits. Dugout canoes have been found throughout Florida, preserved in wet deposits. A canoe also has been recovered from the Georgia coast. All are shallow, narrow craft with platform-like protruding prows and sterns. Fishermen could have stood on the end platforms while looking for fish to spear or while poling the canoe in shallow water. At times two canoes were lashed to a connecting, mat-covered wooden platform to make a catamaran which could carry more people and cargo then two single canoes. Such catamarans may have been used as the "ferries" manned by mission Indians at the river crossings along the mission road and at the crossings connecting the coastal islands in Mocama.

Canoes were normally propelled with wooden paddles, portions of which have been found preserved in archaeological wet sites. Timucuan paddles were of various lengths. A Spaniard noted one type of paddle was nearly two yards in length with a blade about 6 inches wide and 18 inches long.

The range of tools and other implements used by the Timucua and their precolumbian ancestors to make a living was equal to that found in an modern American's kitchen and tool drawers. Over hundreds or even thousands of years the native people had invented, borrowed, and improved the items they used to hunt and fish, gather and grow plants, prepare and serve food, and carry out all the many other activities that occurred in the course of a day. Europeans items of metal were added to the Timucua's material culture, but such items never replaced the traditional tool assemblage. One reason may have been that the Timucua were never provided with Spanish tools in large quantities. Even the Franciscan friars had to beg the Spanish authorities for the loan of tools to build their missions.

Trade

The ancestors of the various Timucuan groups had been engaged in trade for many generations before the appearance of people from Europe. Trade brought exotic items that had prestige and value. Copper, a prized metal, was traded south into Florida from the Appalachian Mountains. Most likely, it was not raw copper which was traded, but objects made of copper. Certain stones – for instance, greenstone and argillite – used for tools and other objects also were brought south from the mountains. A French account from the 1560s indicates that access to trade routes was at least part of the reasons the Saturiwa and Utina alliances were at war. Chief Utina's geographical position allowed him to control the east–west route into western

Timucua that probably connected with the routes into the Appalachians. Control of that same route helped to give the western Timucua control of the chert outcroppings in interior north Florida, chert which was needed by the eastern Timucuan groups for tools.

Traditional trading among the Timucuan groups served to transfer resources from one area to people who did not have direct access to those items. For example, eastern Timucuan groups could trade with the Utina or Potano in western Timucua to obtain the chert they desired. In return they could offer marine resources: shell from whelk shells useful for tools and ornaments.

The French and Spaniards offered new opportunities for the Timucua to gain valued or needed items through trade. The eastern groups living near Fort Caroline traded food to the French for clothing and other items originating in Europe. Mission Timucua bartered foodstuffs or labor to the soldiers stationed at mission garrisons or they traded deer hides, a particularly valuable commodity which the Spaniards exported. In exchange they received other goods.

Adult males from the mission villages were conscripted as labor to work in St Augustine on various projects (see chapter 7). For these efforts they were paid a minimum daily wage. The wage was not paid in cash but in goods. The mission villagers could then trade a portion of these items – beads, scraps of brass, clothing, and the like – to Indians living in Georgia and Alabama and who, at least during most of the seventeenth century, did not have access to such goods. In return the Florida Indians received deer hides and other goods that could then be traded to the Spaniards for highly valued metal fishhooks, knives, axes, hatchets, and scissors.

Deer hides also were used by the Timucua to make moccasins that were highly valued by both native people and Spaniards alike. One Spanish friar reported that he had seen Pedro Menéndez de Avilés wearing just such a pair of moccasins, perhaps acquired from native traders. The Florida Indians, especially those living along the Atlantic coast, collected ambergris, used in Europe in perfumes, and traded that for European items as well as for tobacco.

At times the Spaniards did not live up to their end of the trades. In 1677 villagers at mission San Juan de Aspalaga in Apalachee complained to Spanish officials that seven or eight years earlier their chief, who had since died, had traded 100 arrobas (one arroba equals 25 lb) of beans and maize to a Spaniard for money plus a horse, but had never been paid. On another occasion mission villagers traded maize for blankets, but again the goods due them were never paid.

Had the native people been able to control the sale or trade of corn to the Spanish, native entrepreneurs might have profited handsomely. But the Spaniards could not afford that. Early in the period of the missions, by 1598, the governor of St Augustine had instituted a policy requiring native people to pay a tribute of corn to the Spaniards, presumably on an annual basis. In that year Governor Canzo reported that the tribute had been reduced to one arroba of corn per married man and six arrobas per single man. But this system of tribute did not last throughout the mission period, although the use of conscripted labor did.

Because trade with the Timucua and other native peoples was one way the colony could turn a profit, the government of La Florida sought to regulate it. A large fine was imposed on those Spaniards who traded with the Indians without official permission. Smuggling, however, was common, especially up the rivers that led into north and northwest Florida from the Gulf coast.

The Indians were not shy when it came to trading. They actively hawked their wares during festival days in early seventeenth-century St Augustine. On occasion they paddled canoes out to meet Spanish boats along the coast, trading turtles, turkeys, ducks, corn, fish, fruits, and ambergris for European goods.

The presence of the Spanish missions brought new objects and circumstances to the Timucua, and the Timucua were not hesitant to try to turn those new ways to their advantage. The Timucua, as much as possible, adjusted to the missions and the new world of which they were an important part.

6

The Organization of Societies

As we saw in chapter 5, the Spanish missions brought changes to traditional Timucuan settlement and subsistence systems. The European presence affected the political and social organization of the Timucuan groups as well. These changes were set against the backdrop of the disease-caused decline in population and Spanish manipulation of traditional Timucuan political and village organization, the latter intended to benefit the Spanish need for labor and to assist mission efforts.

The Sixteenth Century and Before

Narratives penned by members of the Hernando de Soto expedition and by colonists at the short-lived French Fort Caroline settlement twenty-five years later provide important information about Timucuan political organization in the sixteenth century prior to the establishment of Franciscan missions. But as we saw in chapter 3, even the 1539 de Soto *entrada* followed by eleven years the earlier invasion of Pánfilo de Nárvaez. And members of the Ayllón expedition and other Spaniards had been among the coastal Timucua in Mocama a full two generations before Laudonnière founded Fort Caroline. As a consequence some scholars would argue that even by 1539 and certainly by 1564 the presence of European soldiers and sailors already had caused change in traditional Timucuan political organization.

Why might this have been? Faced with Spanish and French military might under highly organized, centralized, and efficient chains of command – ultimately reaching back to monarchs in Europe – the Timucua were forced to attempt to similarly organize themselves. Separate villages or groups of villages may have joined alliances as a way to provide military protection. Such alliances appear to have been dominated – one might say commanded – by war chiefs who previously may not have had the great importance and power they assumed in the colonial period. Simply put, European military might led to an escalation in the military capabilities and political complexities of the Timucua, an escalation intended to counter the invading armies and bureaucracies from Spain and France.

Unfortunately, we cannot be sure of this because firsthand accounts of the time before the appearance of people from Europe do not exist. In order to try to shed some light on this dilemma let us again go back in time to the years when the Spaniards and French first sought to conquer and colonize the Timucua.

It is clear, as noted previously, that the Timucua were never organized as a single political unit. The various groups which spoke Timucua were organized around individual villages, each with its own chief and other village leaders. Over time, perhaps hundreds of years, existing villages had budded off new villages as the population of the parent villages increased to levels that made such a fission economically feasible. Because of this process, groups of contiguous villages shared common histories, populations which retained kin ties, and other characteristics which drew them together and gave them a sense of identity. Within such ethnic Timucuan groups the parent villages and their chiefs may have had greater importance and respect, status derived from the historical events of the past.

The Timucua apparently had several words for their village chiefs (Figure 6.1). One was *holata*, another was *utina*, and a third was *paracusi*. There may have been subtle differences between the use of these terms, or one usage may have been more common in one Timucuan region than another, but this was not apparent to European observers. It might also be that the war chiefs, described below, were the *paracusis*.

Although within any one group most chiefs were equal in status to one another, the reality of the situation was that one chief, that of the most important village, often held the greatest power and influence. Power grew out of the respect and prestige afforded that chief's village. It may be that these more important

Figure 6.1 Chief Athore and Laudonnière beside the stone marker erected by the French near the mouth of the St Johns River in 1562
Source: de Bry (1591).

chiefs received the title *utina* (or *paracusi*), which signified their traditional ties to a specific parental village and the territory it controlled.

The status of chiefs was ritualized in their own behavior and in the behavior of their villagers toward them. For instance, in 1562 when the Frenchman Jean Ribault landed at the mouth of the St Johns River he met a Timucuan chief who was seated on boughs of green laurel and palm fronds. The chief refused to stand to acknowledge Ribault; apparently chiefs did not stand to address those they thought were beneath them in status.

On the same journey Ribault met two other chiefs, one of whom also did not stand. The second refused even to come out of his thatched house to greet the French leader. In each case, however, gifts were given to Ribault, a symbol which meant the chiefs sought if not friendship, at least a situation of non-enmity. The gifts, probably valued items often given to native chiefs in similar situations, included a red-dyed egret plume and well-tanned and painted hides.

Figure 6.2 Seated on benches a Timucuan chief and his principal
men take cassina; the drink would have been taken from *Busycon*
shells, not the nautilus snails shown here
Source: de Bry (1591).

The status of chiefs was manifested in other ways. Within their
houses, structures larger than those of their villagers, chiefs were
afforded special seating platforms. They took similar special
seats in their village council houses where they conducted the
business of their villages (Figure 6.2). When greeted in the council house chiefs were given a special salute. The greeter ap-
proached the chief with both hands twice raised to the level of
the head (palms open and forward?) and intoned "Ha he ya ha
ha." Other people who were present then responded, "Ha ha."
A chief who had been away was welcomed home with ceremonial wailing, a sign of greeting.

Chiefs and some members of their families were heavily tattooed. On certain occasions they were carried in litters hoisted
on the shoulders of villagers whose own high status qualified
them for the task (Figure 6.3). The use of litters is documented
for both eastern and western Timucuan groups. Flute players
accompanied the litters, playing to announce the chiefs'
presence.

Figure 6.3 The wife-to-be of a chief is transported in a litter. A canopy of boughs built atop the litter was a symbol of her status
Source: de Bry (1591).

Special paraphernalia and ornaments were worn by chiefs, including shell beads and copper ornaments, the latter highly prized (Figure 6.4). Chiefs also were entitled to a share of certain resources and to a share of the labors of their villagers. Bearskins belonged to the chief, as did a share of deer hides. Perhaps these valued items would be redistributed to other individuals as a tangible symbol of their favor with the chief. Villagers cultivated crops which were placed in the chief's storehouse; this surplus apparently was kept as a hedge against lean times, when it was distributed to the villagers.

Another way in which the status of a chief was emphasized was in his or her interactions with other individuals. Chiefs could choose not to communicate directly with other people, but to pass along orders and information through an individual called an *inija*. This chiefly assistant was selected from the same kin group of the chief and may have been a close relative. Father Francisco Pareja observed that there were other chiefly officials as well, counselors who performed specific duties and

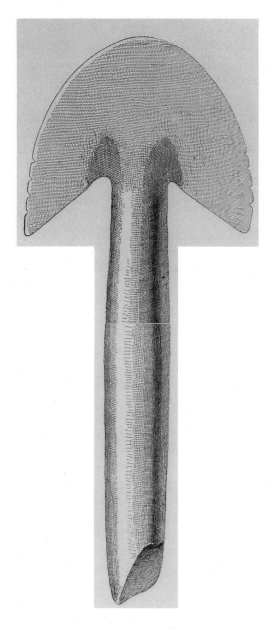

Figure 6.4 This greenstone celt from the Shields Mound in Duval
County probably was a symbol of status and was used by chiefly
officials. Shown broken here, the intact specimen is 14 ½ inches long
Source: Moore (1896a: 461).

tasks, but whose status was not as high as that of the *holatas* and *inijas*.

Writing in 1630 one friar reported that a chief had four such counselors. Along with the *inija*, these may have been the offices called *anacotima*, second *anacotima*, and *afetema*. These counselors – it may be more correct to call them chiefly officials – may have been included with respected village elders and other high-status individuals in the group referred to as "principal men" by the Spaniards.

The chiefly officials shared certain leadership duties with the main chief. However, the prominence of that chief was recognized by all, including the Spaniards, who referred to the individual as the "principal chief." All of these individuals were assigned specific places to sit in the council house, a reflection of their relative importance. Most likely a wise chief listened closely to his aides and the other principal men. The most successful chiefs were those who led with the support of those they governed.

Part of the respect afforded a chief came from his or her ability to pass along status to these officials. No doubt those officials reciprocated with shows of respect, tangible or otherwise. The balance of power in Timucuan societies was supported by and symbolized in verbal behavior, ceremonies, paraphernalia, the exchange of gifts and mutual respect.

Chiefs, *inijas*, and, perhaps the other chiefly officials in the hierarchy, came from specific clans or kin groups, with the chiefs coming from the White Deer clan. Their positions were inherited. But unlike Spanish or French patterns, the Timucua calculated kin-group membership and inheritance through the female line. In this matrilineal form of determining descent, a person belonged to the same kin group as his or her mother, not the father. Because marriage within the same kin group or clan was forbidden, this meant that each individual's inherited titles, such as that of the *inija*, were passed down from one's uncles (one's mother's brother), rather than one's own father.

When first observing this pattern of descent the French and Spaniards were at times thoroughly confused. Familiar with their own descent patterns in which the eldest male child inherited the father's titles and property, they did not always correctly identify native familial relationships. One Frenchman incorrectly recorded that a chief married his own sister to produce an heir.

That apparently was how the observer explained that the chief's heir was his sister's child, not a child from the union of the chief and his wife. In reality the chief's sister's child, his nephew, was a White Deer clan member, the same clan as the chief. Consequently it was the sister's child who inherited the title; the chief's own child belonged to the clan of his wife and was not a member of the White Deer clan and could not be chief.

Other Timucuan clan names were Panther, Bear, Fish, Earth, Buzzard, and Quail. An early seventeenth-century account noted that the system of clan ranking was slightly different in the Potano and Fresh Water districts from that of other Timucuan groups.

Numerous accounts of the Timucua note that chiefs could be women. Women may have inherited the position when there was no male in the proper kin group suitable to hold the office. There may have been no males in the line of succession, or no one of suitable age (or abilities?) to hold the office. However, there are a few hints in documents that some villages traditionally had chiefs who were women. Every indication is that chiefs who were women wielded the same powers as male chiefs. When a woman presided in the council house, other women sat in attendance, which they did not normally do when a male chief presided:

Women are not permitted to enter into this house, except when there is a dance (or) other such assembly or that the *cacica* [a woman chief] is the one in charge and the lord of the land. And then she sits alone on her seat and the rest of the women [sit] separated from the men. (Hann, 1993a: 94–5)

Unable to fully understand the native system of matrilineality and chiefly succession, French and Spanish observers sometimes thought that a specific woman chief was the widow of a male chief who had died. This was probably never the case, however.

As they had done elsewhere in the Americas, the French and Spanish sought to ingratiate themselves with native chiefs. If they could coerce or convince a native leader to behave in some fashion or agree to some outcome, that leader could almost assure the same outcome among his or her followers. Missionary friars often sought first to baptize chiefs so that individual villagers similarly would agree to conversion. Throughout the colonial period the Spaniards supported the native chiefs even while trying to use them for their own purposes.

Writing in 1630, after the mission system was well established, Father Francisco Alonso de Jesus summarized the Spanish view of Timucuan chiefs:

> They have their natural lords among them . . . These govern their republics as head with the assistance of counsellors, who are such by birth and inheritance. [The chief] determines and reaches decisions on everything that is appropriate for the village and the common good with their accord and counsels, except in the matters of favor. That the cacique [chief] alone is free and absolute master of these, and he acts accordingly; thus, he creates and places other particular lords, who obey and recognize the one who created and gave them the status and command that they hold. (Hann, 1993a: 95–6)

Chiefs held important powers, but that power was diluted in part by other chiefly officials and counselors. Chiefs gave their largesse; in return they received their power.

The terms *holata*, *utina*, *paracusi*, and *inija* were not always used by the Spanish, who more frequently employed other terminology to refer to Timucuan chiefly officials. *Cacique*, or its female equivalent *cacica*, was used instead of *holata*, *utina*, and *paracusi* and *mandador* was used in place of *inija*. *Cacique* was an Arawakan word for chief, one brought to Florida by the Spaniards from the Caribbean, home of Arawak-speaking Indians and where the Spaniards had first established colonial towns. *Mandador* was a Spanish term, meaning a person who gives orders.

Caciques and other chiefly officials were concerned both with the secular and sacred aspects of village life. In Timucuan society the supernatural was the natural; there was no separation of the two as in our modern societies. Religious beliefs and everyday life were one. Consequently, chiefs were both civil and religious leaders.

Caciques and their chiefly aides were not the only Timucuan leaders. There also were war chiefs, chiefs who planned and led warriors on raids against other groups. The prefix *irri-* – sometimes given as *uri-* or *iri-* – meant war. Thus *uriutina* or *irriparacusi* meant war chief.

It is likely that war chiefs led not only when an actual battle was to take place, but when the threat of such action presented itself. Because the invading French and Spanish colonists presented the threat – often the reality – of military action, war chiefs may have assumed more importance in the sixteenth century. The French and the Spanish probably did not recognize the existence of a dichotomy between war and civil chiefs. Indeed, many of the chiefs with whom the French had interactions in 1564–5 may have been war chiefs.

The war chiefs, like other chiefs, apparently also had aides and counselors, some of whom had specific titles. These people probably were included among a village's principal men. Names of these statuses may be the ones given by a Franciscan missionary friar as: *ibitano, toponole, bichara, amalachini,* and *itorimitono* (Figure 6.5). It is not certain if the positions of war chief and the associated offices were always hereditary ones or if the individuals were selected because of their military skills. Most evidence points toward the former.

In 1564 the Frenchman René de Laudonnière observed Saturiwa conducting a ceremony in preparation for an attack on his enemies, whom he called Thimogona:

Seated beside the river and surrounded by ten other paracousis, he commanded that he be brought some water quickly. When this was

Figure 6.5 Three chiefly officials associated with Chief Utina
accompany the chief and his warriors
Source: de Bry (1591).

done, he cast his eyes up at the sky and begin to speak of many things and deeds, showing no other emotion but a burning anger which sometimes made his head shake from side to side, and sometimes . . . caused him to turn his gaze toward the land of his enemies and threaten them with death. He often gazed toward the sun, requesting of it a glorious victory over his enemies. Having done this for half an hour, he poured some of the water from a vessel he was holding onto the heads of the paracousis and threw the rest, as if with fury and anger, into a fire which was prepared there expressly for this purpose. As he did so he shouted three times, "Hey Thimogona!" and was echoed by at least five hundred Indians who had assembled there who all cried out in one voice, "Hey Thimogona!" (Lawson, 1992: 68–9)

Warriors regularly scalped and sometimes dismembered their enemies. Scalping was still practiced at the time of the Timucuan rebellion in the mid-seventeenth century. Saturiwa's warriors waged battle with bows and arrows and large wooden clubs. The latter were said to be 28 inches long and often were studded with embedded chert flakes. They were lethal weapons.

The Timucuan political structure, at least the presence of a hierarchy of chiefly village officials and the dichotomy of civil/religious and war chiefs, resembles that of other native groups who lived north of the Timucua all across the southeastern United States in the late precolumbian period. Indeed, the terms *holata* and *inija* used to refer to chiefly officials were not unique to the Timucua. The same names, in various forms, appear among the Apalachee as well as many other southeastern native peoples, including people who spoke Creek languages, Choctaw, and Caddoan.

Does this mean that the late precolumbian and early colonial period Timucuan groups had the same political systems as those found among their contemporary neighbors to the west and the north? Probably not. Let us briefly examine the nature of the political organization of those neighbors.

Anthropologists have learned a great deal about the political systems of those groups, calling them chiefdoms. Simply stated, southeastern chiefdoms are societies in which towns, often groups of towns, were governed by a group of the elite, including chiefs who were at the head of a ranked social system. Within each chiefdom the governing elite were arranged in a hierarchy of offices, each of which was hereditary. Certain lineage, clans, or other kin groups were ranked above others, and the elite selected from those kin groups were similarly ranked.

Chiefs and other officials had certain duties and responsibilities as well as specific powers. A rich assortment of paraphernalia and symbols surrounded the elite. Craftpersons, priests, and other important individuals also lived in the towns whose total population could number in the thousands.

Each chiefdom was associated with a well-defined geographical region. In the Southeast such territories generally were centered on a section of river valley. Such locales included swamps rich in plants and animals as well as extensive deposits of fertile alluvial soils that were replenished in annual floods. Today these chiefdoms are referred to as Mississippian chiefdoms after the Mississippi River Valley where they were studied early on by archaeologists.

The Mississippian people practiced intensive agriculture, cultivating corn, beans, pumpkins, and other crops on the rich alluvial soils of the river valleys. Cultivated foods provided a large portion of the diet. Even so, fish and other foods that could be collected from the forests and wetlands near towns also were important to the diet.

Mississippian towns were large, often covering several hundred acres. Special buildings – temples and residences for the elite – were constructed on the tops of flat-topped, artificial, earthen pyramids arranged around plazas. Houses of less important individuals surrounded the plaza-mound precinct. Often villages or portions of villages were moated and palisaded for protection. Other families lived in small agricultural homesteads scattered between towns. Those people traveled to the towns for markets and to witness or participate in various festivals and religious ceremonies.

John Walthall, an archaeologist, has described one such Mississippian town, the site of Moundville in Alabama (1980: 214, 216):

Moundville was a major ceremonial center with a large resident population, perhaps as many as 3,000 individuals, including nobles, friars, artisans, and commoners. The site covers some 300 acres. Within this area are extensive habitation zones, 20 truncated earthen pyramids, and a large central plaza. The mounds range from 3 to 60 feet in height . . . A wooden stockade and ditch may have surrounded a large portion of the site.

Similar archaeological sites are found all across the interior of the Southeast, from the river valleys of the Carolinas and Georgia west to Arkansas and eastern Oklahoma.

The members of the Hernando de Soto expedition who traveled through the heart of those Mississippian chiefdoms were often in awe of what they saw. One participant described the Spaniard's meeting with the chief of Coça, a huge chiefdom which extended 200 miles along river valleys from eastern Tennessee to Alabama:

[We] travelled six days, passing by many towns subject to the Cacique of Coça . . . until [we] . . . arrived at Coça . . . The Cacique came out to receive him [de Soto] . . . borne in a litter on the shoulders of his principal men, seated on a cushion, and covered with a mantle of marten-skins . . . ; on his head he wore a diadem of plumes, and he was surrounded by many attendants playing upon flutes and singing. (Smith, 1866: 75–6)

Coça was a complex chiefdom, one in which a paramount chief ruled over other regional chiefs who themselves were leaders of large chiefdoms which included many towns and village chiefs. Other of the Mississippian chiefdoms were not as large or complex.

On the one hand, the documentary record of the Timucua contains examples of many chiefly elements that are very similar to those of the Mississippian chiefdoms. Hierarchies of chiefly officials existed and the chief's office was inherited. The governing elite, including the chiefs, were selected from specific kin groups which themselves were hierarchically ranked. Other shared traits include use of the terms *holata* and *inija* and the practice of transporting chiefs in litters accompanied by flute players.

But on the other hand, none of the archaeological correlates of the Mississippian chiefdoms are found among the Timucua. Timucuan villages were much smaller because village populations were much smaller. Villages may have had central plazas, but they lack the truncated pyramidal earthen mounds upon which temples and houses for the elite were erected. Such mounds are found throughout the Mississippian world. Indeed it must be pointed out that were we basing our analysis of Timucuan political structure only on archaeological evidence we would have no clue that chiefs even existed.

The Timucuan political system was only a reflection of the system present among the Mississippian chiefdoms. The Timucua may have borrowed some characteristics of those chiefdoms – certain words and behavior – but the entire spectrum of traits associated with Mississippian chiefdoms was never present among the Timucua.

Chiefdoms and Chieftaincy

How can these similarities and differences between the Timucua and the Mississippian chiefdoms be interpreted? Why did the various Timucuan groups not exhibit the full range of traits present in those other societies?

One answer is that the situation may be confused by modern anthropologists who seek to describe these colonial period societies as either chiefdoms or not chiefdoms. Instead what we may be observing is a continuum in political complexity, from large Mississippian chiefdoms with multiple levels of village, regional, and territorial chiefs to smaller-scale, Timucuan chiefdoms which assumed some of the guises of the larger chiefdoms to solve their particular needs.

Such a continuum was closely tied to economic patterns. The economic base of the Mississippian societies, especially the employment of intensive farming methods which allowed the production of a significant proportion of food, allowed large populations. Larger, denser populations and the need to organize the system of intensive agriculture, as well as the need to protect populations, towns, and stored food and wealth from raids, created the need for a complex political system like that manifested in the Mississippian chiefdoms.

The Timucuan groups, who relied much less on agricultural production and had much smaller and less dense populations, consequently did not need or have the full array of Mississippian cultural traits. But the Timucua did need leaders to help organize and manage their societies. Also, interactions between Timucuan groups and Mississippian chiefdoms, such as between the Uzachile and their neighbors the Apalachee Indians, must have encouraged the Timucua and their leaders to adopt some of the trappings of Mississippian chiefs. In other words, the Timucua exercised chieftaincy.

Warfare, perhaps raids by the Apalachee on the Yustaga/Uza-chile or even warfare among Timucuan groups, could have led to the exercise of chieftaincy by war chiefs who sought to form inter-village and inter-group alliances. When the Spanish invaded northern Florida and the French occupied their colony at Fort Caroline, the presence of those Europeans also provided a greater need to exercise chieftaincy, to exercise more complex political entities.

In the region of the Timucua it was the realities of political interaction, especially warfare and the threat of warfare, that caused some native groups to act in a more complex fashion. To adjust to a threat or an opportunity posed by interaction with a politically more complex society, the Timucua found it in their own interest to try to act just as complexly.

One way in which the Timucua could emulate the Mississippian chiefdoms was by forming alliances among chiefs and villages, thus creating a larger political entity. This would have been an efficient way to raise a military force for offensive or defensive purposes. It may also have been a way to provide insurance against disruptions in food collection or production by spreading liability over a larger area. If Utina's village suffered a poor corn harvest due to a lack of rainfall, an alliance with other villages could provide a source of corn and seed to get Utina's villagers by until the next harvest.

Alliances might grow to include many villages and village chiefs, who themselves were somewhat ranked, deriving various degrees of relative importance for historical reasons. Relative chiefly importance might also have derived from military or economic power. An economically successful village – successful in terms of both food production and controlling resources and access to resources – probably was the most important one in an alliance and its chief could dominate the alliance's main leader. With the settlement of Fort Caroline, the ground rules may have changed somewhat, however. Access to the exotic goods brought by the French may have given prominence to local chiefs who could acquire those goods.

As we saw in chapter 2, a number of Timucuan alliances existed in the sixteenth century. The French at Fort Caroline interacted with several alliances in northeast Florida and southeast Georgia. The Utina and Saturiwa alliances were two such entities. Chief Saturiwa may have derived his importance in part because of his location near the mouth of the St Johns River, which would have allowed him to control traffic up river. He also may have benefitted from interactions with the French in 1562.

Chief Utina's importance might also have been in part due to his controlling lands off the St Johns River where fertile soils could have given his village a productive advantage over the villages and chiefs on the river proper. Utina also was able to control the trails into the Timucuan groups in northern Florida (and south-central Georgia?), a source of stone needed for tools.

The de Soto expedition accounts describe the alliance which existed among the Aguacaleyquen, Napituca, and other chiefs in Columbia, Suwannee, and Madison counties, an alliance that seems to have been dominated by Chief Uzachile of the Yustaga. That alliance may have been formed in response to the presence of the Apalachee Indians, a Mississippian chiefdom located immediately to the west of the Yustaga/Uzachile. The nature of that alliance might also have been influenced by the passage of the Nárvaez *entrada* eleven years earlier.

Both Spanish and French observers wrote that the chiefs in these various Timucuan alliances were brothers. Probably this was an example of fictitious kinship. Rather than actually being brothers, the term reflected a means for the chiefs to demonstrate ties to one another, to suggest equality within the alliance. If the chiefs were from the same clan, as probably was the case, the word given by the Spaniards and French as brother might better be translated as clansman.

The exact make-up of the Timucuan alliances may have changed through time. One example may be the alliance often called the Potano Indians. When the de Soto expedition marched through what is today Alachua County in north-central Florida in the summer of 1539 there was no Potano alliance. Instead, the picture that emerges from the narratives of that expedition is of a number of separate villages, one of which was named Potano. But by the time of Fort Caroline, a Potano alliance existed. Perhaps the people of that region sought to exercise chieftaincy – to form an alliance – for protection against the invading Spaniards and French, not to mention Chief Utina's warriors. The presence of soldiers and colonists from Europe could only have created a greater need for alliances, especially military alliances in which war chiefs assumed importance.

Did Timucuan alliances exist prior to the coming of the people from Europe? We may never know, since such alliances apparently have left little or no archaeological trace. There is still much to be done before we fully understand the nature of Timucuan political structure in the precolumbian period. What is certain is that the exercise of chieftaincy, including alliance building, was an adaptive tool used when Timucuan villages and groups needed more complex political unions. With the appearance of the Europeans, the need for such structures could only have increased. As we shall see in the next section the establishment of the mission system and the rapid decrease in population that took place negated the need for the alliances. Timucuan chiefly roles would change once more.

Effects of Seventeenth-Century Colonization

The military government of Spanish Florida sought to organize and control the Timucua by relegating them to missions. As noted above, both St Augustine military officials and mission friars sought to convince native leaders to convert to Christianity and to have their followers to do likewise. The Spaniards recognized the role and power of chiefs in the political structure of the Timucua.

Throughout the period of the missions the Franciscans and Spanish officials continued to work through the indigenous political system with its hereditary chiefly officials. The Spaniards understood that native leaders could be used to obtain the labor and cooperation of their people. It was also by befriending chiefs that the Spaniards could exercise control over the lands of La Florida. Economically, it was better to rely on native peoples to hold the land than to establish Spanish settlements to do the same. Using the mission villages and their native leaders allowed the Spaniards to control a huge region from a single settlement, St Augustine.

Chiefs were encouraged to visit St Augustine to receive gifts, in essence bribes to convince the chiefs to ask for missionary friars to serve their villages.

Governors of Spanish Florida regularly sent official delegations from St Augustine to visit the Timucuan missions, providing an opportunity to distribute gifts. The governor's representatives also adjudicated disputes relating to native inheritance and chiefly succession. With a high death rate and the consolidation of populations at specific Timucuan missions, determining exactly who had the traditional right to serve as a village chief may at times been a topic of debate.

In general the St Augustine officials supported the traditional native system, except when it was in their best interests to interfere or change it by selecting or appointing an individual whose chiefly credentials might be less bona fide than another's, but one who would benefit the Spaniards more.

Spanish support of village chiefs cleverly linked Catholic practices with traditional native respect for chiefs. When chiefs were baptized they received a Christian name, one taken from the day of the saint on which the baptism took place. For instance, if a chief from the village of Potano were baptized on the day of Saint John, San Juan, his name would become Juan de Potano. Yearly within the village of Potano the missionary friars would lead the people in celebration of the feast day of San Juan, a way of enhancing the chief's status and his ties to the friars and to Catholicism.

Another subtle way of controlling the chiefs and chiefly officials was to indoctrinate the male children who were their heirs. These heirs were given special attention by the friars, often receiving religious education beyond that afforded other youngsters. Historian Amy Bushnell has described this practice (1994: 106):

The education of native males at the hands of friars was strongly religious. Incipient caciques and principales, following a different career track than commoners, were groomed from an early age to serve at the altar and trained in the offices of sacristan, chorister, and catechist. The future lords of the land learned to speak Spanish . . . making them useful interpreters.

These chiefly officials-to-be often were boarded in the mission convents with the friars. As Bushnell notes, when they reached adulthood convent-trained native leaders were devoted to the friars, whom they addressed – with respect – as "My Father."

Loyal Christian chiefs were often handsomely rewarded by the Spaniards. One chief, Don Juan of mission San Pedro on Cumberland Island in Mocama, who had been educated by Baltazar López, served the Spanish so well he was awarded 200 ducats.

This was no small sum. At the time he received this gift it was estimated that the upkeep of each mission friar cost about 140 ducats a year.

But even while the Spanish colonial church and governmental officials supported village chiefs, their presence brought changes to Timucuan political structure. With the incorporation of Timucuan villages into the mission system there no longer was any need for the type of inter-village or inter-group alliances which were present in the sixteenth century. The emphasis in the seventeenth-century was on the village *caciques*, not on dominant chiefs who led alliances of several chiefs. In 1616 Father Pareja noted that native people were using the chiefly term *utinama* to refer to the Christian God "who is in heaven above" (Gerónimo de Oré, 1936: 107).

The threat of warfare was removed when the Spanish military occupied St Augustine and stationed soldiers at key garrisons in the mission provinces. This greatly diminished the role of war chiefs. The names *uriutina* and *irriparacusi* are not found in seventeenth-century documents dating after the initial founding of the missions. War chiefs and the hierarchy of chiefly officials surrounding them probably disappeared. Warfare became the purview of the Spanish military. It was Spanish soldiers who organized mission villagers into a militia, not the traditional war chiefs. The native beliefs and practices surrounding warriors and warfare no longer were given importance.

Although the Spaniards intentionally worked through village chiefs, the powers of those chiefs were diminished as chiefs were coopted into the colonial system. Indeed, the term *holata*, like the names used for war chiefs, was not used by the Spanish after the establishment of the Timucuan missions. *Cacique* was used instead. It was also in the Spaniards' best interest to treat village *caciques* as equal to one another. Even so, the Spaniards did recognize that certain chiefs were more important than others.

The use of *cacique* to refer to chiefs rather than use of the native term *holata* may reflect the diminution of chiefly powers as some of the traditional roles and rights of village chiefs were usurped by the Spaniards. For instance, at one time chiefs received tribute in the form of labor and gifts from their villagers. But those rights were transferred to the Spaniards to satisfy the needs of colonial St Augustine. Even though village chiefs helped to organize the labor drafts, no one could have missed that it was the Spaniards who benefitted from the production of corn at the missions and its transportation to St Augustine. In general, however, the Spaniards supported the *caciques*, keeping them placated by supporting them in their villages, buying them off when necessary.

When Spanish haciendas were established in Timucuan territory ranch owners no doubt were most supportive of those chiefs who granted permission for the ranches to exist on native lands. As populations declined and groups like the Potano all but disappeared, some chiefly entrepreneurs sought to take advantage of the situation, extending the geographical limits of their aegis. One of the best examples is Lúcas Menéndez, a chief of the northern Utina whom we learned about in chapter 4. It was he who granted permission for the La Chua ranch on the north side of Paynes Prairie in what had been Potano territory. As the Potano and their chiefs disappeared under the onslaught of disease, Lúcas Menéndez claimed control of lands well to the south of the northern Utina's traditional lands.

Even while supporting village chiefs the missions sought to change certain chiefly behavior. Chiefly ceremonial duties which the Franciscan friars deemed sinful, superstitious, or not in accordance with Christian doctrine were actively discouraged.

The *Confessionario*, the extraordinary book compiled by Father Francisco Pareja and printed in 1613, provides a glimpse of what some of those duties and rights were. The book was written to provide Franciscan missionary friars with lists of questions and other information to be used in administering the confession to Timucua Indians. The questions are written in both Spanish and Timucua.

The text by Pareja contains the following questions written for chiefs and chiefly officials:

Questions for Caciques:
Have you taken more tribute and other things from your vassals than is due you?
Have you taken the daily wages of those that work for you?
Have you made someone work on a fiesta day without the permission of the friar?
Have you arranged for someone to be married in the traditional ceremony without first notifying the friar?
Have you kept a black slave or servant as your mistress?

Have you said that no one should open the storehouse until a "sorcerer" (a native priest) prays?

Questions for Mandadors and Lesser Chiefs:
Because you are angry, not because someone did not work, have you ordered that person be punished by having their arm broken?

Other confessional questions addressed to chiefs have to do with the performance of ceremonies, especially prayers or charms offered in conjunction with hunting, fishing, planting, harvesting, and gathering wild foods. It is clear that chiefs were responsible for seeing that traditional ceremonies surrounding those subsistence-related activities were adhered to. It was precisely those ceremonies which the Franciscan friars actively campaigned against, associating them with non-Christian behavior. We will return to these rituals in the next chapter.

Father Pareja and the other missionary friars were successful in their efforts to change the Timucua and reshape their culture to serve Spanish interests. The *caciques* of the later missions were a different type of chief from the *holatas* of the sixteenth century. But even in the eighteenth century the Timucua themselves still recognized the traditional right of specific individuals from certain clans to be chief of certain villages, even when those villages were moved to new locations around St Augustine. The voices of the past were never completely obliterated.

7

Beliefs and Behavior

Before the arrival of the Spanish missionaries in La Florida Timucuan beliefs, ceremonies, and practices, things which a modern observer might call Timucuan religion, were an integral part of everyday life. Ideology was integrated with social and political systems and economic pursuits, providing the Timucua with the foundation to explain and use the world around them. These traditional ways had served them and their ancestors for many generations.

But with missionary endeavors came new beliefs and behavior. Ideology and practices associated with, for instance, the planting and harvesting of corn were suppressed. The efficacy of traditional curing beliefs and practices was denied. Once respected shamans were discredited. Much of Timucuan ideology was obliterated and Christian beliefs were adopted, at times replacing native ones. Often no new behaviors were taught which might help support and explain the new world being shaped by the presence of the colonists from Europe.

These cultural changes took place in only a generation or two. In that short period population levels continued to drop. Venerable patterns of culture which had worked for the Timucua for hundreds of years gave way to new gods, new standards of success, and even speaking, reading, and writing in a new language. The missions, backed by the strength symbolized in St Augustine's stone castillo, offered the Timucua the only alternative in what for them must have been grossly unsettling times. It is no wonder they were at times even eager to give up the old and adopt the precepts of what seemed a superior way of life.

Participation in the mission system, an arm of the Spanish empire, was the only realistic avenue open to the Timucua.

But conversion to Christianity was not always easy and it did have its almost comical moments. One friar, writing about the piety of the Indian converts, noted that it was with great devotion that they knelt in church. But in the beginning – until muscles adapted to this new position – men who knelt often toppled over. Kneeling was only one small part of the new world that was unfolding around the Timucua.

It is ironic that the Franciscan friars' desire to eradicate aboriginal beliefs and practices which the Church viewed as being pagan and non-Christian has provided students of the Timucua with one of our main sources of information on those aspects of Timucuan life. The *Confessionario* written by Father Pareja opens to us a very small look at the richness of traditional Timucuan ideology. Although archaeologists can excavate Timucuan houses, find the bones of animals the Timucua used for food, and study the ceramics created by Timucuan hands, modern scholars cannot reconstruct those facets of culture that Pareja included in his *Confessionario*, written in the early part of the seventeenth century. It is fortunate that a few copies of the *Confessionario* have survived to the present day.

Father Francisco Pareja originally came to Florida in September 1595, one of a group of twelve friars who would bolster the small contingent of three Franciscans – two friars and one lay brother – already there. Pareja, a native of the Spanish province of Guadalajara, was assigned to the mission San Juan del Puerto, a *doctrina* he apparently founded and served for more than three decades.

From that Timucuan mission Father Pareja traveled to nine nearby satellite villages on a regular basis to administer to their people. In his early years in Florida he traveled among other Timucuan groups in southeast Georgia and northern Florida. His knowledge of differences in the Timucuan dialects suggests he traveled even more widely than that, or that he used a number of Timucua Indians from various groups as linguistic informants.

Between 1595 and 1612 when the *Confessionario* was printed Father Pareja had been present while the first generation of Timucua were brought to Christianity. Consequently, his observations on Timucuan life are extremely valuable.

Another source of information on aspects of Timucuan culture was written in 1630 by another Franciscan friar, Father Francisco Alonso de Jesus, who served as *custodio*, or head, of the Franciscan Florida province. Father Alonso de Jesus, who prepared his account for the Spanish king, noted that he had been in Florida for about twenty years at the time. The document was translated by John Hann in 1992. It seems clear that by the time Alonso de Jesus wrote about the Florida Indians, many changes already had taken place and much of Timucuan culture which Father Pareja had observed earlier was gone.

In the sections which follow, Father Pareja's *Confessionario* and Father Alonso de Jesus's narrative, as well as other documentary sources, are used to recount aspects of Timucuan life, especially ideology, both prior to and after the missions.

Traditions in an Old World

As was noted in the previous chapter, Timucuan chiefs had specific rights and duties and were responsible for performing or ordering certain ceremonies and rites. For instance, when a new chief took office following the death of his or her predecessor a new fire was lit in the council house and kept burning for six days. The house was ritually cleansed with the smoke from burning "laurel," probably red bay.

Caciques would not allow villagers to eat the first harvested corn or other newly collected plants until the shaman, whom Pareja called a *hechizero*, or "sorcerer," first was allowed to taste the crop. The shaman was ordered by the chief to perform that ritual. He also could be ordered to use magic to find lost objects. In the relationship between a chief and a shaman, the former had the upper hand. However, it is clear that the chief always made sure that the shaman received his just compensation.

It was believed that if a chief did not drink cassina, a tea brewed from the yaupon holly (*Ilex vomitoria*) from a shell cup after eating bear meat, the chief would become ill. The yaupon holly, a plant native to the coasts of Florida and Georgia, one closely related to the plant maté which is brewed in South America, was often referred to as *la yerba* – the herb – in Spanish accounts. Modern scholars call it black drink, because the tea brewed from the dried leaves of the plant is a dark color.

The beverage, which contains caffeine, was drunk by many southeastern native people, including the Timucua, both as a ceremonial emetic and on other occasions. Usually it was drunk from a large conch shell cup. It may have been the herb taken by shamans during certain rituals, including casting spells or other magic.

The drink was usually served in the council house (see Figure 6.2), although sometimes it may have been prepared by women elsewhere and then taken to the council house. There the chief, other chiefly officials, and the rest of the principal men each drank from the shell cup in turn. One account says that after drinking the tea the men sweated profusely. On some occasions ritual drinking was combined with fasting.

People who drank black drink sometimes vomited, apparently intentionally. Sweating, fasting, and vomiting all were ways in which the cassina drinkers sought to ritually purify themselves. The taking of the tea was intended to remove bodily impurities and restore the drinker to a state of equilibrium within the world, allowing them to successfully complete or participate in another task. The latter might be performing a ritual, taking part in a ceremony, or simply returning to normal activities after having done something that was viewed as polluting, for instance participating in warfare or burial rites.

To brew the tea leaves of the yaupon holly were toasted over a fire, then broken up and placed in a special ceramic vessel containing water. The vessel was placed over a fire to heat. After brewing, the liquid was filtered and served. Special containers also were used in the serving and drinking of the tea. Several accounts indicate that the tea was taken from a shell cup, one probably made from a *Busycon* shell, though other containers were used as well. When a chief died, the shell cup that had been used by that individual in life was interred with the body in the burial mound.

The black drink ceremony has a long history in the southeastern United States. Evidence for the performance of the ceremony in conjunction with mound construction and use in Florida has been found by archaeologists at several sites, some dating back more than a thousand years before the colonial period. Some of those sites probably were occupied by the ancestors of the Timucua.

As noted in the previous chapter, chiefly duties included participating in, overseeing, or ordering the carrying out of a number of rituals surrounding hunting, fishing, food production, and the harvesting or collection of food. The performance of one such ritual or charm, one involving tobacco, was carried out before hunting. When deer hunters were going to use antlered, deerskin disguises to hunt, a charm was said over the disguise. Another charm was done before hunting turtles, and still another was performed by the chief before a fire drive was used to hunt deer. The latter involved putting six arrows and six oak splinters together in a woven cloth bundle(?) and then singing or chanting all night.

Deer hunting involved other magic as well. Once on site where the hunt was to take place, all the hunters' arrows were prayed over by the shaman. For this presumably successful service, the shaman received the first animal killed. Any arrow that only wounded, not killed, a deer was also the object of a special charm so it would be successful the next time it was used.

Charms and beliefs also surrounded the butchering and eating of animals. It was believed the person who killed a deer should not eat the meat or he would not be successful in hunting animals. Nor should the liver and lungs of a deer be cooked in cold water lest more deer not be killed. The bones of butchered and consumed animals, probably those of the legs and haunches, were not thrown away, but were hung by the ankles or put in the upper part of a house near the thatched roof. If this were not done, other animals would not be trapped.

Spilling the broth in which venison or quail were cooked similarly was thought to prevent other animals from being caught. One dietary taboo was against the eating of small quail – perhaps ones not yet full grown – during the winter.

Fishing also elicited a number of magical charms and incantations. Prior to a fishing expedition – probably one in which group nets were employed – the participants said prayers to the lake. Prayers also were said when a new fish trap was put in the water. Both these rituals were intended to ensure good fishing. Other things intended to invoke a similar result were the practice of releasing the first fish caught in a new weir (so it could bring others) and cooking the first fish that could be eaten in cold water, not hot.

The first catch of fish was smoked (and preserved?) on a wooden frame, and half of the fish were given to the shaman who had conducted the appropriate fishing rituals. There was a taboo against men who recently had sexual intercourse from entering a fish trap. To do so would cause eels and fish not to enter.

Just as hunting and fishing were surrounded with a rich variety of beliefs and ritual intended to bring success, so were planting and harvesting and collecting wild plants. People going to gather (hickory?) nuts and palm berries were cleansed in a ceremony involving praying and use (burning?) of laurel.

First harvests of both agricultural products and wild plant fruits received special attention, just as did the first deer and fish that were taken. Acorns and fruits were dried, and not immediately eaten. Other fruits that were to be eaten received prayers. Rituals also accompanied digging a field in preparation for planting. When the planting took place a bowl of *gacha* – the gruel described in chapter 5 – was eaten by six elderly men in a ceremony ordered by the chief. Then when the crop was harvested the first corn was not eaten (perhaps only by the people who had harvested it) and the maize was prayed over by the shaman. If lightning happened to strike a field of corn it was considered a bad sign and the corn was not harvested.

When corn previously stored in a crib was to be taken out and ground into meal, prayers and incantations were offered at several stage in the process. One ritual was performed before walking up to the storehouse, another when the storehouse was first opened, and another when meal was first ground.

Many of these prayers and rituals may have been quite simple and short and probably were second nature to the Timucua. To the Franciscan friars, however, they represented the invoking of non-Christian elements and were to be eradicated. Pareja even counseled people who might visit a village of non-Christians ("infidels") not to go near where ceremonies or prayers to the devil were being performed and try to learn them.

The Timucua believed in omens conveyed by animal behavior and by natural phenomena, as well as information conveyed in dreams. Information could also be obtained from diviners who, while in a state of possession, saw into the future.

Sayings, beliefs, and portents were associated with a wide range of behavior, just as they are in our own society today. For instance, lightning meant that warfare was going to occur. The popping sound of burning wood also was interpreted as a sign of impending warfare. Whistling could prevent a canoe from overturning because of chopping water, such as when the canoe was near a sandbar or other obstacle; whistling could similarly calm a storm.

A hunter believed that if he heard the bleating of a fawn, he should immediately put a specific herb in his nose to prevent nosebleed. Then he was to return home and cleanse himself with the water used to brew cassina. If he did not, he would die.

Owls were seen both as good and bad omens. If one heard an owl it was an evil omen; frightening the owl only made it worse. But the song of another owl – perhaps a different species – brought pity on the listener. Encountering a snake was also bad omen.

If a woodpecker was heard, the listener was to keep still or a nosebleed could result. Another omen was the song of a blue jay or other bird. If someone trembled while hearing the song, it meant either than someone was coming or that an important event was going to take place.

Facial tics held other portents. If a person's eyebrow twitched it meant food would be available, or someone was saying something bad about the person, or a bad event was about to take place. An eye twitch was an omen that something bad was going to take place which would cause crying. Belching was another sign that there would be food, although the same thing could be interpreted as meaning the belcher wished to die.

Dreams were thought to reflect reality. Father Pareja cautioned the Timucua against believing the bad that appeared in one's dreams:

Son, as one thinks during the day, thus he dreams at night; if he thinks good things then he will dream good things, and if bad, these will also be represented in his dreams; if the dream is about good things he should try to put them into practice, and if bad, don't pay any attention to them because the Devil is the stoker and cause of bad dreams and no matter what form they take, never give any credit to those dreams. (Milanich and Sturtevant, 1972: 24)

Pareja was especially concerned with the actions of Timucuan religious practitioners and curers. His *Confessionario* uses three different Spanish words to differentiate these individuals: *hechizero*, or sorcerer, mentioned above; *herbolario*, or herbalist, probably someone who cured using plants; and *medico*, or doctor, another type of curer. However, in the Timucuan text that accompanies the Spanish only two terms are used: the *isucu*, derived from the Timucuan word for herb (*isu*), was both the herbalist and the *medico*, a person referred to here as a curer; the *yaba* was the "sorcerer," the individual referred to here as a shaman or native priest who performed many of the rituals associated with garnering food. The latter could also use magic to cure people. Pareja's *Confessionario* makes it very clear that in his opinion, both the curers and the shamans performed certain rituals, chants, and charms that invoked the devil. He wished them instead to cure using the "name of Jesus and the sign of the cross."

Curers had a wide range of skills and could bewitch people. They could also use herbs to bring about good and bad outcomes, as well as to cure people. For instance, they could use herbs to slow down or speed up runners in foot races, thus influencing the outcome. Curers prayed over the sick and built new fires to aid cures. One cure involved an offering of corn left at the person's door.

Tobacco was one of several plants used in herbal cures which involved inhalation of smoke. Text accompanying a de Bry engraving – which is based on French-derived information – described the process:

They used to cure illness in the following way. They made long benches, . . . on which they laid their sick, either on their stomachs or backs according to the type of illness . . . Those who lay on their stomachs inhaled smoke through the nose and mouth from the burning of several seeds over hot embers. As the smoke spread through the whole body it would induce vomiting, and so destroy the cause of the illness, or at least reduce it. They also had a herb which the Indians of Florida call "Vbannoc", . . . and the Spanish "Tobacco." The leaves of this plant were carefully dried and put into the broadest part of a tube to be burnt, then they put the narrow end of the tube in their mouth and inhaled the smoke which came out again through the mouth and nostrils. This process helped to discharge the morbid fluids. (Lawson, 1992: 14)

Curers also aided midwives in childbirth deliveries. Herbal applications and other rituals were employed, and it was thought that the curer had the ability to use those herbs to speed up or retard delivery. Some curers were accused of retarding delivery to derive a higher fee. Women who were about to give birth marked the door of their house with a laurel branch and apparently delivered the child away from the house.

A person who was restored to health was required to pay the curer or else it was thought the sickness would return. Payments could consist of food, including acorn cakes. Some curers were accused of not working hard enough to remove a person's sickness, a ploy to derive additional payments.

Shamans, those whom Pareja called sorcerers, also performed a variety of rituals in addition to those surrounding subsistence activities. Shamans were thought to have great powers, including the ability to foretell the future and to find lost or missing objects, including identifying the person who had stolen something. Apparently a herb was used which allowed the shaman to enter into a state of possession so he could predict the outcome of war. The ceremony may have been the same one witnessed by the French when Chief Saturiwa's *jarva*, said to be a diviner, entered into a state of possession in order to foretell the outcome of the impending battle with Chief Potano (Figure 7.1). *Jarva* and *yaba* may be the French and Spanish versions of the same Timucuan word.

Figure 7.1 Chief Utina's *jarva* seeks to foretell the outcome of the pending battle at Chief Potano's village
Source: de Bry (1591).

The *yaba* could cause it to rain, thunder, and storm. Likewise, by blowing toward the heavens he could cause he clouds to go away and the rain to halt. Using herbs a shaman could bewitch someone. The same or a different spell could be given by the *yaba* to another person who wished use it to bewitch someone else. The effects of the black magic generated by these spells could be reversed if the bewitched person took the proper antidote.

One bewitching spell, intended to lead to the death of the person upon whom it was cast, involved the skin of a poisonous snake or of a black snake, black Spanish moss, other herbs, and water. While casting the charm and until it worked, the conjurer abstained from eating fish, shaving, and sleeping with his spouse. After a successful outcome – i.e. the death of the person – the conjurer then bathed, ritually cleansing himself. If the spell did not work, it could cause the death of the conjurer. In lieu of actually performing this death magic the *yaba* might go to the person who was to be its victim and threaten to carry out the spell unless he was paid off. Shamans also could perform other magic that caused harm, though not death, to people. Specifically, he could rupture someone and cause injuries to a person's legs or feet. He could also employ herbs to cause injury.

Acting as native friars, shamans performed marriage ceremonies, for which they were paid. A shaman also could use herbs or charms to draw a woman out of her house and cause her to love him. Another ceremony performed by the shaman was intended to cure a sick person by drawing out the sickness. The charm involved placing the following items before the person to be cured: white feathers, a new chamois, the "ears" of an owl (probably the feather tufts), and arrows which were stuck into the ground. As a part of this curing ritual the shaman sucked the illness out of his patient's body, removing the object that had caused the problem (Figure 7.2). He then exhibited the object which had been magically sucked out. This necessitated sleight of hand on the part of the shaman. Father Pareja described how it was done and explained to his fellow friars how to expose the shaman's deception, thus discrediting him:

Another counsel by which one can deceive those who cure in this way, that what he shows in the palm of his hand after having placed one [there], as if a leech sucking with his mouth (that usually is a little piece of coal, at other times a small lump of dirt and other unclean things, things alive or as if alive) that it cannot be, since no hole is left in the

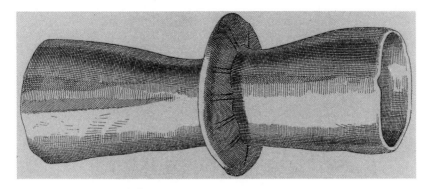

Figure 7.2 A clay biconical pipe, 5 inches long, from the Mount Royal site. Some archaeologists believe such pipes were used by curers to "suck" the illness out of individuals who were ill
Source: Moore (1894b: Plate XVIII).

body through which that can exit, and naturally there was deception and some substance where that was, or else the Devil must have managed it subtly, and this can be believed since from as hard a part as the forehead and arms and head and spine or back of the neck it is not possible, it is a secret not comprehended until now; when asked about such things they say with a look of surprise I do not know how this is done. (Milanich and Sturtevant, 1972: 32)

The traditional culture of the Timucua incorporated music and dance in community ceremonies. At least some of these activities included men and women and took place in the council house. Father Alonso de Jesus, looking back to the pre-mission period, offers one of the few descriptions of Timucuan dances, but even it contains few specifics:

Dances . . . are held only in the council houses and community houses, where they assemble at the time they are called, with the men always being separated from the women. The dances, the majority of them, are decent. They have their songs that they sing and they have certain little tambourines that they beat and sing along with in complete unison, to which the women, placed in a crescent and standing up, respond, dancing with the same rhythm. During their heathen days, these dances were very lengthy and drawn out; that they lasted for entire days and nights. (Hann, 1993a: 97)

What are translated as tambourines (*atavales*) may actually refer to small drums.

Figure 7.3 Excavated from a site on Murphy Island in the St Johns
River north of Lake George, this copper sheet, 7 inches long, may
have been used to cover and hold together a three-reed panpipe
Source: Moore (1896b: 507).

Another musical instrument played by the Timucua was the
flute. Both flutes which played only one or two notes and pan-
pipes were used (Figure 7.3). The latter were played by blowing
across the open end to make a tone, much like one makes a
sound by blowing across the open top of a soda bottle. Gourd
rattles were used, and large rocks beaten with clubs, to produce
rhythms to accompany dances and ceremonies.

The French who observed Timucuan people for more than a
year while they lived at Fort Caroline were quite taken with the
athletic abilities of the people. Villagers regularly competed in
games of archery, foot and distance races, and leaping contests.
In all these contests betting could be fierce. Still another game,
one which must also have involved betting, was similar to dice.
Winners of these almost ritualized sporting contests were ac-
claimed and drew respect for their performances.

Another sport – a ball game – was played by the Timucuan
groups living in interior northern Florida. The game, which has
been described as "a substitute for war," was also prominent
among the Apalachee Indians. Unlike the well-known southeastern Indian ball game played with sticks – a predecessor of
modern lacrosse – Timucuan ball game players scored by pro-
pelling the ball with their feet. Father Escobedo described the
game:

They arrange themselves twenty on a side and play the game in a brisk
athletic manner. The ball carrier handles it smartly and he plays such
an effective game with his sure shots that we can state that he scores
on each shot. They erect goal posts made from pine trees about seven
feet tall and on top of this goal they place a figure. Suddenly the forty

players dash to the field, commence playing, and the game has begun with a rush. It is a rough game which many times proves to be costly to some unfortunate player who gets seriously injured. These seasonal games last for one month.

Even if the one carrying the ball returns to the game on the following day, he will try to move in a different direction. His adversary, however, will be just as fast, attempting to intercept him with his hands and feet and throw him to the ground. While the other thirty-eight struggle among themselves, these two carry on the fight between themselves. Each one attacks his opponent and tries to cast him to the ground. if some persons assist the one who is carrying the ball because he is their friend, they are disqualified and never again will be allowed to play. The two teams fight as if they were in a real battle and each one tries to get a good grip on his adversary. The arms of the Indians in the game are as valuable as the net was to the gladiators.

In Castile [Spain] the hands are used in playing ball, these Indians play ball with their feet. They propel the ball with their feet directly at the goal. I have seen fifteen; then fifty direct shots, until the player gave up because he was exhausted. That number was the maximum allowed by the rules of the game. The Indian who is lucky and has good control over the ball plays eagerly but rather blindly like an inspired man. If he is playing against a strong opponent, he tries to overcome him and sometimes is full of tricks for the opponent.

Those assisting the one who propels the ball carry on such a quarrel that they do not respect brother, or even father or son. The opponent tries to break up the locking of arms. If one loses his grip, another will some to the rescue and clasp the arm. So it is a continuous war until time is called. The one holding the ball with his foot will kick the ball straight at the goal. If he makes the mark, his friends go wild because the reward is worth the struggle and it is considered an act of great skill to hit the mark. (Covington and Falcones, 1963: 148–9)

Father Alonso de Jesus, in a short description of the same ball game, added several other details about what was certainly a dangerous game, not the least of which is that it was occasionally played by women. He also noted that the game was played in a village plaza where the ground was well packed. Apparently one point was scored for hitting the goalpost and two were received for placing the ball in the target on the top. At times the sides might be 50 or even 100 people on a side. As with other games, betting was intense.

Historian John Hann has provided more details about the game, relying on a thorough description written by a Franciscan friar who witnessed it being played in Apalachee. The playing ball was slightly larger than a musket ball, perhaps the size of a modern golf ball or the ball used today in handball. Made from deerskin stuffed with dried mud, at times with human hair mixed in, the ball was very hard. The target on top of the goalpost, for which two points were awarded if the ball was kicked into it, was an eagle's nest. Eleven points won the game.

The playing season was during the summer growing season. Aspects of the game were dedicated to the supernatural beings associated with the sun, thunder, and rain, all elements important to a successful harvest. Like so much of everyday life, even the ball game was intimately entwined with the agricultural system of the native people.

Another type of game also was played with a ball, although in this case the ball was thrown at a target on a post, rather than propelled with the feet. It was this sport rather than the ball game described above that the French at Fort Caroline observed. One account says a square target made of woven reeds was placed atop a post eight or nine yards high. Another says the post

Figure 7.4 Timucua Indians engaged in various sporting contests; also depicted is a ball pole with its target on top at which balls were thrown
Source: de Bry (1591).

was 16 or 18 yards high (Figure 7.4). Participants threw small balls at the target, the winner being the person who hit it first.

The life of the precolumbian Timucua was a rich one. Knowledge about their environment and beliefs concerning their place within it helped to explain the world that had served the Timucua so well for so many years. The ritualized behavior of chiefs, shamans, curers, and ball players and the familiarity of a rich ceremonial life brought predictability and helped to assure harmony with the Timucua's social and natural environments.

A common theme in a number of these Timucuan ceremonies, those performed by herbalists and shamans as well as by other individuals in other contexts, was the lighting of a new or separate fire. The kindling of such a fire was an important act intended to focus power during rituals and to counter impurity and dissonance, such as resulted from illness.

Fire was the earthly representative of the sun, a supreme being in the religions of the southeastern Indians. The emphasis on the ritual lighting and use of fires by the Timucua mirrors similar beliefs and practices found across the Southeast. Other traditional Timucuan beliefs and ritual practices, such as the ceremonial use of black drink, also resembled those of their southeastern neighbors.

Many of those cultural traits must have a long history, dating back into the precolumbian period for hundreds, some perhaps thousands, of years. Living in proximity to one another for many generations and, perhaps, sharing common origins in the distant past must have led to many examples of similar behavior among the southeast Indians. But because of their natural environments, lesser reliance on intensive agriculture, and for other reasons, the Timucua developed a way of life that was distinct from that of their western and northern neighbors. As we shall see in the next section, that traditional life was greatly changed with the establishment of the missions and the new ideology brought by the Franciscan friars.

Living "Under the Bell"

With the Spanish missions came new ideas, new practices, new foods, and new technology. Traditional beliefs gave way to the Ten Commandments, the Seven Deadly Sins, and the Fourteen

Works of Mercy, as well as other articles of Catholic doctrine. Carved figurines and other art depicting beings and symbols from traditional Timucuan ideology were replaced by Catholic *santos*, portrayals of the Last Supper, and woodcuts of various devils.

The process of altering the culture of the mission Timucua was both subtle and direct. "Spiritual ideas were conveyed by . . . architecture, painting, statuary, [and] the symbolism of the liturgy" (Geiger, 1937: 29–30). Selected aspects of Hispanic culture, such things as food, clothing, material items, and standards of acceptable behavior, were introduced to the Timucua, gradually replacing or supplementing the old ways.

Heirs to chiefly offices were boarded in the mission convents and grew up in Christian piety, educated to the ways of Europeans. And aspects of traditional culture were suppressed through religious indoctrination, such as the questions asked in the confession, and the banning of native rituals and practices deemed in conflict with Christian ones. As Father Pareja admonished those who adhered to the traditional beliefs and practices – which he placed in a section of the *Confessionario* labeled "Ceremonies, Omens, and Superstitions That Are Still Used By Some" – "all these abuses and tremors of the body and signs of birds and animals, none of it is to be believed" (Milanich and Sturtevant, 1972: 23, 25).

More direct, or at least more dramatic, examples of direct culture change also occurred, such as that undertaken by Father Martín Prieto when began his missionary work in northern Florida. Initially he burned 12 wooden "idols" in the plaza of the main town (later the site of mission San Martín). Then he traveled to four other towns where he destroyed six more carved images in each.

In their place Christian symbols – crosses and *santos* – were introduced. One Franciscan friar wrote about the piety shown by the Timucua to the newly introduced Christian cross:

They respect the Holy Cross with such great love that they never step on its shadow, if they see it on the ground. Nor is it missing from their homes. And the first thing the heathens request of us when we arrive at their villages is that we raise it and hoist it on high. (Hann, 1993a: 101)

Crosses also have been found stamped on native pottery, and at a number of mission sites small crosses, religious medallions, rosary beads, and reliquaries have been found. What had been a rich tradition of Timucuan iconography was rapidly replaced by an equally rich Catholic iconography.

Not all traditional culture was to be suppressed. The friars allowed curers and villagers to continue to use some herbal remedies. But the rituals and ceremonies that accompanied their use in the past and which were thought in the light of church doctrine to be evil were stripped away.

The drinking of cassina – associated with ritual purification – continued throughout the mission period, when it was drunk by Indians as well as soldiers and friars. But even that ceremony could be used to teach Catholic doctrine. Father Pareja, in one of his religious tracts, advised his fellow Franciscans to offer this insight to their charges:

When you drink cassina and look into the cup, you see many reflections of your face in the bubbles, even though there is only one of you. So it is with God, although he is only one, he is everywhere. (Translated from Pareja, 1627: 18r)

The appropriateness of one native custom, the ball game played with the feet, was debated by the Franciscan friars at various times in the seventeenth century. Friars at both Timucuan and Apalachee missions sought to ban the game because of its association with non-Christian ceremonies and beliefs. They were not alone. Some of the Christian Indians who knew and understood the ball game much better than the Spaniards also admitted it should be banned. But still other friars argued to keep the game, calling it harmless. Ultimately the sport was allowed to continue.

The education of mission Indians included religious doctrine and, in many instances, instruction in learning to read and write Spanish. As early as 1595 individuals at the San Pedro mission on Cumberland Island could speak Spanish. Mission villagers, including children, also were taught to read and write in the Timucua language.

This was done in part using books Father Pareja and perhaps other friars wrote for that purpose. None of these books, described as primers and booklets of devotions, exists today. But Father Alonso de Jesus, writing in 1630, noted their use. He opined that literacy was a very efficient way to secure the devotion and conversion of the native people. Some of the Timucua even wrote letters to one another.

The importance of literacy continued to be recognized by the Spanish throughout the colonial period. One of Pedro Menéndez's initial plans had been to take sons of native leaders to a school in Cuba to educate them. And, as we have seen, Indian children were boarded in the convents to receive special education. Even as late as 1677–8, Spanish officials visiting the missions of Apalachee and Timucua continued to order the establishment of schools for the instruction of the native children. By the time of the refugee villages around St Augustine in the second quarter of the eighteenth century it is probable that Spanish was heard in the missions as frequently as Timucua.

The religious doctrine taught to the Timucua was extensive and comprehensive, even though Christian Timucua could only receive four of the seven sacraments (baptism, confession and penance, communion, and marriage). Confirmation was rarely conveyed to mission villagers, and extreme unction and ordination never.

Amy Bushnell's account of the religious doctrine taught at the Franciscan missions indicates that as *catecumenos*, the religious students learned the responses to the questions of the catechism as well as the *Pater Noster*, *Ave Maria*, and *Salve Regina*, prayers offered in Latin. Other doctrine learned for recitation included the Sign of the Cross and the *Credo*. There also were the Ten Commandments, the Seven Deadly Sins, the Fourteen Works of Mercy, and other items.

As *cristianos*, Christians, the villagers received a Christian, Spanish name, sometimes one which combined a native name with a Spanish one. A few of the chiefly officials were awarded the honorific title Don.

The mission Timucua became true Christians. They were ardent converts to Catholicism; their traditional belief system was replaced in large part by a new one. Village Indians knew how to sing Mass and they participated in morning and evening prayers. At mission San Juan del Puerto some even were given organ lessons.

Villagers aided the friars at Mass and they celebrated the appropriate festivals and feast days of obligation, including the days of the saints of their towns and their chiefs. On these days a Mass was said and the villagers were freed from labor. These days included Sundays; the feasts of Nativity (Christmas), Resurrection (Easter), and Pentecost; All Saints' Day; and the days of

Epiphany, the Lord's Circumcision, the Lord's Ascension, Corpus Christi, the Purification of Our Lady, the Annunciation of Our Lady, the Assumption of Our Lady, the Nativity of Our Lady, and the Apostles St Peter and St Paul (Bushnell, 1994: 90–1).

In addition, a number of fast days, all Fridays during Lent, the Saturday before Easter, and Christmas Eve were commemorated. On those special occasions villagers also were released from work obligations.

Mission villagers joined religious confraternities or associations like those present in other Catholic communities. Baptisms, marriage ceremonies, and burial rites were conducted in the church according to Catholic doctrine. Some of the Catholic rites were translated into Timucua by Father Gregorio de Movilla, who drew on approved doctrine written by friars in Mexico who had translated Spanish ritual into the Nahuatl language. Baptism ceremonies could well have included words said in Spanish, Latin, and Timucua.

The path to achieving religious instruction could be harsh at times, as well as profitable. Friars could whip those who skipped services or did not participate in schooling. Only chiefly officials and married women were spared. On the other hand, in order to attract adults to seek religious instruction, gifts might be handed out by the friars. But once the missions were established and a generation of children grew to adulthood living "under the bell," that was no longer necessary.

Under the guidance of the Franciscans the Timucua became as devout as other Catholics in Spain's transatlantic empire. Father Pareja, whose views were recorded about 1614, thought that in performing some religious duties, the Timucua were better Christians than were the Spaniards:

Among them are Indian men who have sufficient knowledge to give instructions while there are Indian women who catechize other Indian women, preparing them for the reception of Christianity. They assist at Masses of obligation on Sundays and feast-days in which they take part and sing; in some districts that have their confraternities and the procession of Holy Thursday, and from the mission stations they come to the principal mission to hear the *Salve* [the *Salve Regina*] which is sung on Saturdays . . . They take holy water and recite their prayers in the morning and evening. They come together in the community house to teach one another singing and reading . . . Do they confess as

Christians? I answer yes . . . Many persons are found, men and women, who confess and who receive (Holy Communion) with tears, and who show up advantageously with many Spaniards. And I shall make bold and say and sustain my contention by what I have learned by experience that with regard to the mysteries of the faith, many of them answer better than the Spaniards. (Gerónimo de Oré, 1936: 152–3)

Serving New Masters

Mission villages served as centers for the religious education of the Timucua. They also were a system for organizing mission villagers – generally adult males – to supply labor in support of the colony. That support was not only for the needs of the Spaniards living in St Augustine and at the missions. The mission Indians were drawn into a much larger network, one stretching far beyond the shores of La Florida. Although on the very northern fringe of Spain's American empire, the colony and its people were a part of that empire, one subject to many of the same international factors influencing Spanish colonial policy elsewhere.

For instance, a drop in the *situado* paid by the Crown for support of Florida which was caused by economic problems in Spain could increase St Augustine's need for mission-grown corn. Or the rising value of deer hides on the international market could influence the immediate aims of friars and soldiers stationed at the missions. In each case, the responses to extra-Florida events directly impacted the need for mission labor.

And, as we have seen, much of the day-to-day lives of the Spaniards in Florida, whether mission friar, garrison soldier, or St Augustine resident, depended on native labor. Timucua and other Indians supplied food, worked as domestics, and aided in construction projects. The need for the Timucua to serve the colony transformed their lives as surely as their religious instruction. Indeed, living and laboring "under the bell" went hand in glove.

Mission friars knew the size of the adult male population associated with their respective missions. When authorities in St Augustine indicated conscripted labor was needed the friar could respond accordingly, probably conferring with the village chief who then assigned which villagers were to provide the hands and backs needed.

Adult males performed a number of tasks for the Spaniards. They were required to serve as burden bearers to transport corn and, at times, other foodstuffs or supplies from Apalachee and Timucua to the Gulf coast where they could be shipped. Or they were required to carry loads overland along the east–west trails, including the *camino real*, to St Augustine. One route to St Augustine from western Timucua was by canoe along the Wacissa River into the Gulf of Mexico, down the coast to the mouth of the Suwannee River, and then up the Suwannee and the Santa Fe rivers to a landing near mission Santa Fé. There the water route intersected with the overland *camino real*. The landing may have been near modern Oleno State Park.

At Santa Fé the goods were loaded on the backs of native people for the trek to St Augustine. On these endeavors the Timucua, led by their own leaders and by Spanish soldiers, were to be lodged and fed at missions along the way. Cost of their keep was to be paid from the royal funds paid yearly to support the colony. In reality, however, the funds were not always forthcoming and at times the laborers sometimes carried their own food and supplies.

Indians from the mission provinces were conscripted to go to St Augustine to provide labor for projects there, or they were required to remain in the town after transporting supplies to it. These conscriptions often took people away from their villages for four months and sometimes longer. Because laborers might move from one project to another, some individuals were away from their home villages for several months at a time.

In St Augustine the native labor gangs tended fields for the benefit of the soldiers stationed at the garrison there. At various times during the growing season shifts of laborers prepared and planted the fields, hoed the fields, and harvested the crops. If two corn plantings were to be made in a growing season, that much more labor was required. Timucua and other natives also worked on construction projects, such as building forts, timbering (often at some distance from town because of deforestation), and cutting stone (*coquina*) in the mine on Anastasia Island. As many as 300 native people were involved in the construction of the stone castillo in the 1670s. Most likely, nearly all manual labor in St Augustine was provided by Christian Indians.

It was intended that the conscripted laborers be paid for their work. Their salary, which was not paid in cash but in goods, was

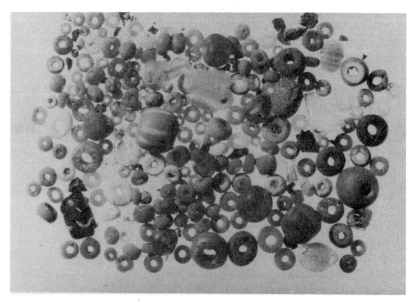

Figure 7.5 An assortment of glass beads of many colors and types
from mission sites. Trinkets such as these were paid to native
laborers by the Spaniards
Source: courtesy Florida Division of Historical Resources.

distributed to the village chiefs who passed it on to the laborers
once they had returned to their home village. Because the money
for the goods came from the royal subsidy, which often did not
arrive punctually or even at all, payment to the Timucua was
also not punctual and sometimes not at all. The standard payment was one *real* worth of goods per day. In 1678 the governor
of Florida bought the following to pay the native laborers constructing the castillo of San Marcos: two sizes of hawk bells,
knives, blue glass beads, multicolored glass beads, pieces of sheet
brass, razors, cloth, and scissors (Figure 7.5). The desire to
obtain these items by working for more than four months may
account in part for the long absences from home of some mission
villagers.

The items received by the workers could be traded to non-
mission Indians who did not have direct access to European-
manufactured trinkets and metal. In exchange the Timucua and
other mission peoples received deer hides and perhaps other
goods that could then be traded back to the Spaniards for more

goods. This system benefitted both the Spaniards and the Timucua.

Indians living in the villages adjacent to and near St Augustine were a ready source of labor. Because of their proximity to town, they were called to unload the cargoes of ships which made port in that town. Native people from those same towns worked as house servants for Spanish families in St Augustine. Food preparation and many other domestic tasks were probably done by the Timucua and other native peoples.

In the mission provinces some male villagers were organized into a native militia, reinforcements for the Spanish troops in St Augustine. The native troops were drilled and some were armed with arquebuses and shotguns. In the late 1620s and again in the 1650s the governor of the colony called up the native militia when it was thought St Augustine might be attacked by the English.

In the interior of La Florida the Timucua and other mission Indians also were required to labor in support of the colony. They maintained the road to St Augustine by clearing brush, repairing creek crossings, and even building bridges. Where the *camino real* crossed the larger rivers too deep to ford, mission natives maintained ferry services. People from the village at Salamototo complained about having to provide ferry service across the St Johns River, a task that often kept them away from home for several days in bad weather. Ferries also were maintained elsewhere in Timucua, and in Guale ferries allowed passage between the barrier islands.

Christian Indians also worked at the missions where they lived, providing food for the friars and working as servants for both the friars and soldiers who might be stationed at mission garrisons. The supplies not produced locally all had to be transported to the missions, a task which fell to the same villagers.

Mission villagers, including men, women, and children, provided services for the friars. They cooked, tended the convent gardens, looked after animals, did household chores, and provided maize, fish, deer, and other food for the friars' tables. Special fields and gardens were planted, hoed, and harvested and the maize husked, shelled, and ground, all for the benefit of the missionaries. As a result, friars living at the missions probably had access to a much more varied diet with higher amounts of meat than did the residents of St Augustine. Soldiers stationed at mission villages did not maintain the hold on the villagers that the friars did, and they were forced to pay or trade for the services they received. This led to abuses and a nearly constant source of conflict among the soldiers, the villagers, and the Franciscans.

Amy Bushnell (1994: 112) has described the range of activities villagers performed for the mission friars:

[Village men] were the friars' boatmen, burdeners, guides, bodyguards, and couriers. They hunted and fished, returning with food for the convent kitchen as for their families. They were the ones who went to the woods for charcoal or the timbers for buildings and fences. Women, for reasons of security, child care, and propriety, did most of the work in or near the town. With the help of the larger children, they collected the firewood, shelled and ground the maize, and gathered and processed the cassina, nuts, and oysters. They cleaned the church and its grounds. They planted and hoed the sabanas [fields] and gardens, guarding them against birds and other garden raiders. No doubt they raised pigs and chickens as part of their gardening routine, keeping the hogs in pens during the growing season and feeding them on plants culled or weeded from the gardens.

Under the guidance of the village chiefs and friars, maize was stockpiled and livestock raised in order to generate income, some of which was used for the support of the missions. When times were hard in St Augustine, the military government was known to turn to the missions and offer to buy this food. Because friars, who had taken vows of poverty, were not to run a cash operation, they instead received credit for the goods which could then be applied toward for supplies. Maize especially was a money-maker for the missions, as explained in a letter co-written by Franciscan friars:

In each doctrina they dig one sabana [field] for maize – in half a day they dig it, all of them [mission villagers] together. The harvest goes to sustain the ministers, helps cover the costs of maintenance and repair for the churches, and remedies the lack of ornaments and things necessary for divine worship or (buys) better ones. (Translated in Bushnell, 1994: 111)

The Timucuan missions, run by friars and the chiefly officials whom the friars had raised from childhood, were formidable economic enterprises.

But the mission way of life did not last. As we shall see in chapter 8, epidemics, new lifeways, and competition among European colonial powers would destroy the missions, turning the Timucua who survived into refugees whose numbers continued to decline until they were no more.

8

The End

European exploration, colonization, and the establishment of the missions all took place within the context of disease-caused epidemics that cut like a scythe through the Timucua. The cultural changes that occurred as the Timucuan groups adapted to the missions and the presence of first French and then Spanish colonists and soldiers were in part attempts to adjust to the fact of numerically fewer people.

Eventually, by the second quarter of the eighteenth century, the native population of Florida and southern Georgia was so reduced that the few native settlements that existed consisted of only small numbers of people, often less than a hundred, sometimes smaller. These villages were home to the remnants of the Timucuan groups that once had nearly filled the landscape. Although individuals in these villages still retained their language and ethnic identify, the villagers were refugees who were forced to live in towns which harbored non-Timucuan people with other languages and affiliations. There were no more Potano or Saturiwa or Arapaha villages and there probably were no distinctive Timucuan material assemblages.

By early in the third quarter of the eighteenth century there literally were only handfuls of Timucuan refugees still surviving. Later, in 1763–4, those few Timucua who had been living under the auspices of the Spaniards in St Augustine would be taken to Cuba.

The Beginning of the End

Juan Ponce de Leon's landfall on the Atlantic coast in 1513 sealed the fate of the Timucua. Located in what was to be the initial geographical focus of attempts by people from Europe to colonize the eastern United States, the Timucua and the other native groups in Florida and those along the Atlantic coast of modern Georgia and South Carolina would suffer the brunt of the initial invasion. The Timucua and their neighbors paid the ultimate price.

Disease epidemics and the hardships caused by colonization caused a demographic disaster. Fewer babies were born, fewer Timucua reached child-bearing age, and fewer Timucua lived to old age. The death rate exceeded the birth rate, and populations declined, then plummeted.

Scholars continue to debate the details and timing of this population disaster. Did the early Spanish and French excursions to La Florida bring European diseases to the Americas that led to pandemics, epidemics which swept through the native populations of the Caribbean and Central America, spreading down into South America and northward into North America? Did epidemics raging out of the Caribbean precede the actual presence of people from Europe in regions of the Americas? Did the Timucua suffer epidemics even before Juan Ponce de Leon landed among them in 1513? Or were epidemics brought to the Timucua by the early expeditions, those of Juan Ponce, Pánfilo de Narváez, Hernando de Soto, Jean Ribault, and René de Laudonnière?

These are difficult questions to answer because of a lack of both archival and archaeological information. If there were not yet people from Europe in a region, we do not have written, firsthand descriptions of what occurred. And even when there were such people who could provide information on the presence or absence of epidemics, those observers were not necessarily in one place for more than a few days or weeks. Juan Ponce and the members of other early Spanish voyages to the coasts of the Timucuan region were never in one place a sufficient length of time to observe much of anything. None of the respective accounts of the expeditions of the early explorers note the presence of epidemics among the Timucua.

Cabeza de Vaca, the chronicler of the Pánfilo de Narváez expedition, did write about members of that expedition suffering from sickness. But he does not tell us if the native people encountered by the expedition suffered from the same illness. And nothing is mentioned in the accounts of the Hernando de Soto expedition or the narratives penned by the French during their attempt to place a colony in northeast Florida.

Even though direct documentary evidence is lacking, most modern scholars would argue that epidemics impacted the Timucua prior to the time St Augustine was founded and the missions were established. Old World diseases must have been introduced into Florida and southeastern Georgia prior to the epidemics chronicled by the Franciscan friars and other Spaniards in the late sixteenth and seventeenth centuries.

It seems likely that such epidemics were restricted to specific groups and were not pandemics. For instance, records from the seventeenth century indicate that epidemics in the mission province of Timucua did not always spread to Apalachee. But the disease vectors along which epidemics might travel may have been different in the mission period when there were fewer villages and a smaller population. The bottom line is that until much more evidence is on hand we cannot say for certain what the nature and impact of early colonial period epidemics among the various Timucuan groups might have been.

There is at least some archaeological evidence that diseases did have a very negative impact on at least one Timucuan group in the sixteenth century. Tatham Mound is a site in easternmost Citrus County near the Withlacoochee River, the river named the River and Swamp of Ocale in the narratives of the de Soto expedition. Most likely the people who built the mound and who lived in the nearby area were the Ocale Indians.

The mound was excavated by archaeologist Jeffrey Mitchem in the 1980s. His research and analysis and those of bioanthropologist Dale Hutchinson indicated that more than 300 individuals, possibly Ocale Indians, had been interred in the mound. The bodies of more than 70 people first were laid down on clean sand deposited on the surface of an older, low mound. Then bundles of bones representing 240 additional individuals were placed on, around, and between those bodies. The bones previously had probably been stored in a charnel house. Ceramic vessels and shell cups were positioned around the bones and bodies. Then everything – vessels, bones, and bodies – was covered with a layer of sand.

Analysis showed that 12 individual bones from the bundled burials displayed probable sword cuts. Three were arm bones, six were leg bones, and one was a shoulder blade. The wounds had probably all been inflicted by Spanish soldiers, quite likely members of the de Soto expedition who had marched through the area in 1539. Further evidence of contact between the people buried in the mound and the Spaniards was present. Early sixteenth-century glass beads, metal beads, iron hardware, and a small piece of armor all were found in the mound, next to or even worn by the people interred there.

That more than 70 people had died at about the same time and were interred in the same burial ceremony is evidence that they died suddenly of disease, probably diseases brought by the de Soto expedition.

Exactly which disease or diseases may have been responsible for the epidemic cannot be determined at this time. Most fatal illnesses cause death too quickly to leave any evidence on our skeletons. But there is no lack of candidates. Spanish documents tell of the devastating effects of smallpox, measles, and other infections that ravaged native populations in the Americas in the colonial period (Figure 8.1). Smallpox was an especially widespread killer. Other inflections were chickenpox, scarlet fever,

Figure 8.1 Curing the sick using tobacco and by sucking the illness
out of the forehead
Source: de Bry (1591).

typhus, malaria, bubonic plague, pneumonic plague, influenza, typhoid, dysentery, diphtheria, and yellow fever.

Although individuals might survive any of these diseases and thus develop a lifelong immunity to that disease, there was always the possibility that another infection, perhaps one normally not as virulent (pneumonia, for example), might bring death to people who had suffered years of ill-health. This apparently did occur among Timucuan mission populations.

In addition to providing evidence for disease-caused deaths, Tatham Mound also serves to point out that the initial military invasion of La Florida resulted in battle casualties among the native people. Exactly how many of the people in the mound may have died from wounds is unknown. But what is certain is that the double-edged sword of disease and military might cut a swathe through those people. It is logical to think that same broad sword cut through other Timucuan groups in the sixteenth century as well.

Epidemics during the Mission Period

The establishment of the Franciscan missions among the Timucua was, among other things, a bureaucratic exercise that created a huge paper trail. Letters and reports written by mission friars to one another and their superiors, letters to the Spanish Crown and military governmental officials, official visits by representatives of the Governor of La Florida and by Franciscan bishops, transcripts of court proceedings and other hearings – all these activities provide information on the state of the missions and the Timucua who lived at them.

These mission-related archival materials are treasure troves of information about the Timucua. But the picture that emerges from the documents is not always a pleasant one. The story of the missions is also the story of the destruction of the Timucua. The seventeenth-century Spaniards were firsthand observers of the epidemics that killed literally thousands of Timucua. Historians, especially John Hann and John Worth, have delved into the documents and, as is not possible with the pre-1565 period, we can now put together an authoritative picture of the demographic disaster which took place during the mission period. It is ironic that it was the presence of the missions which generated so much of this paper trail of disease, yet it was those same missions that brought together people from outlying villages at a central location, unknowingly abetting the spread of diseases among the Timucua and other mission Indians.

Almost as soon as the first Franciscan missions were established among the eastern Timucua and the Guales, documents record the presence of epidemics. In 1595 a severe epidemic struck the coastal missions. Then between 1612 and late 1616 there were a number of what were described as "great plagues and contagious diseases" which affected half of the missionized Indians, as well as Spanish soldiers (Hann, 1988: 175). A first-hand observer, Father Francisco Pareja, wrote "a very great harvest of souls has been made" as a result of the epidemics (Hann, 1995: 346).

The 1612–16 epidemics struck the Timucua hard, especially the Potano. Some of the mission villages could not fill the labor quotas assigned by the military government in St Augustine. Adult male populations at the missions, and presumably the rest of their villagers as well, had been reduced severely in number. Potano, as well as parts of the lower St Johns drainage, already may have been severely depopulated. Comments by one friar suggest that the mission villages sending laborers to St Augustine suffered most in those epidemics. Perhaps the men brought back diseases to the missions or the laborers contracted illnesses and died in St Augustine.

Another epidemic struck St Augustine in 1649–50. One Franciscan friar wrote that several of his colleagues died at that time, suggesting the epidemic reached the missions. There was more death to come. In 1655 a particularly severe smallpox epidemic ravaged the provinces of Timucua and Guale as well as St Augustine itself. Other epidemics also hit about that time. In 1657 the Spanish governor wrote that the Indians of Guale and Timucua were few in number "because they have been wiped out with the sickness of the plague [*peste*] and smallpox which have overtaken them in the past years" (Hann, 1986d: 111). Nombre de Dios near St Augustine was devastated by the epidemic, which also halved the population of San Martín in western Timucua.

The mid-seventeenth-century decision by Governor Rebelledo to reorganize the Timucuan missions following the rebellion of 1656 was in part due to the demographic devastation that had taken place in Timucua. The eastern Timucuan missions had only small populations left and those in western Timucua had been ravaged by disease and could not provide enough labor to fill Spanish needs, especially for farming. Instead, as we saw in chapter 4, Governor Rebelledo reorganized western Timucua so those native people still living at those missions could be used to maintain the transportation link between St Augustine and Apalachee. Apalachee became the colony's bread basket and main labor source.

Toward that end the mission and town of San Luís was established in the heart of Apalachee immediately after the rebellion. Throughout the remainder of the seventeenth century San Luís was the largest Spanish settlement in La Florida outside of St Augustine. Living in that town were elite Apalachee Indians and their families as well as Spanish soldiers and families of colonists.

And still the deaths continued. In 1659 the new governor, Francisco de Corcoles y Martínez wrote that 10,000 Indians had died in a measles epidemic. The scope of the devastation of the Timucua must have been tremendous.

Demographic data provided by Spanish visitations and surveys of the missions reflect the devastation. A 1689 census providing a village-by-village count of mission Indians in La Florida lists a total of 646 Timucuan families. If an average family was five people the total Timucuan population at that time was only 3,230 people. That number is less than 2 percent of the 200,000 total Timucua estimated for 1492. Ten generations after Juan Ponce de Leon's first voyage to Florida, one Timucua Indian remained for every fifty who had lived then.

Faced with what they must have viewed as an inconvenient situation, the Spaniards sought ways to cope with a lack of laborers in Timucua. The reorganization of the inland Timucuan missions after the 1656 rebellion was one solution. Another was to shift people among missions, from areas and missions with larger populations to ones with fewer people. For instance, a 1645 account states that Timucua-speaking Oconi Indians were to be moved from their home to mission San Diego de Elaca. The latter was located where the *camino real* reached the St Johns River; presumably the plan was to use the Oconi to staff a ferry across the river. It is not certain if this move took place, however.

Another example occurred in 1657. Arapaha Indians were to be moved to the south and relocated at mission Santa Fé. That move was not successful, however, and two years later Yustaga

Indians were slated to be moved to that same mission to repopulate it. Later, by 1670, documents indicate that Arapahas again were moved into Yustaga. Still another shift had occurred in the 1650s when native villagers from the Timucuan missions of San Francisco de Chuaquin and Santa Cruz de Cachipile, both located in southern Georgia and both subject to the same chief, Chief Lazaro of San Ildefonso de Chamile, were moved to the former site of the San Martín mission near the Ichetucknee River. Significantly, all of the Timucua-speakers who were to be moved southward were from southern Georgia. In the mid-seventeenth century Timucuan population levels in southern Georgia must have been larger than those in northern Florida.

How many such moves may have occurred and how successful they were is not certain. The Timucua themselves may have resisted being moved from traditional locales to villages formerly associated with other groups.

At about the time these movements were taking place native people who previously had been living north and west of Apalachee province were moving into that area, where they began living at missions. Nuestra Señora de Candelaria de Tama and San Carlos de los Chacatos were two such "foreign" missions, occupied, respectively, by native people from Tama and by Chatot Indians, the latter from the Apalachicola River region. The population of Apalachee had declined during the first three quarters of the seventeenth century. But after about 1675 the total population appears to have stabilized at about 10,000. That stabilization may have resulted in part from the relocation of non-Apalachee to the region. Its larger population was one reason Apalachee rather than Timucua was the main arena for Spanish colonial efforts in the later seventeenth century.

From the point of view of the military government the efforts to maintain the mission system, including Rebolledo's reorganization of the Timucuan missions and the emphasis placed on Apalachee province, were successes. The total number of missions in La Florida in 1675 was the same as the number that had existed in 1655, about forty. Consolidation of populations and establishing new missions with people brought from elsewhere resulted in what appears on paper to have been a thriving colonial effort.

But, as we have seen, behind that figure of 40 missions is the specter of the demographic catastrophe affecting the Timucua.

What had been 23 missions serving Timucua Indians in 1655 prior to the rebellion was reduced to 17 in 1675 and 13 in 1689. At some of those 13 missions, ones in Mocama and in what had traditionally been eastern Timucuan territory, at least some of the 3,230 mission villagers were not Timucua-speakers, but people who had moved south from the Guale missions.

By the 1680s southern Georgia and northern Florida east of Apalachee province had been devastated of its native population. The Timucua, once so important to Spain's colonial efforts in La Florida, could no longer fill the needs of the Spanish, beyond simply helping to maintain the vital overland link between Apalachee and St Augustine. To the Spaniards the potential of what once had been the region of many Timucuan groups was unrealized.

By the century's end the *camino real* trail, once featuring mission stations a day's travel apart from Apalachee to St Augustine, offered none of the amenities it had offered two generations before:

Epidemics, rebellions, and fugitivism had turned many of the places along the camino real into ghost towns that offered a traveller nothing but feral cattle, neglected fruit trees, and "old fields" covered with second growth. Bandits made it unsafe to travel alone. (Bushnell, 1994: 115–16)

It may be no coincidence that at about this same time the military government and the Franciscans began to look further south to other native groups. After 1675 unsuccessful efforts were made to establish missions in central Florida among the Mayaca, Jororo, and Ais Indians. The Mayaca and Jororo were encouraged to become farmers. Most likely the plan was to move them north to agricultural lands in the province of Timucua, helping to repopulate the region and increase the food available to St Augustine. In the 1690s friars were sent to the Calusa on the southwest Florida coast. But none of these late seventeenth-century missions' efforts succeeded.

The Destruction of the Missions, 1680–1707

We will never know whether the remaining Timucuan population might have become consolidated at several missions and achieved numerical stability, as appears to have been the case in

Apalachee. During the last quarter of the seventeenth century and the first half of the eighteenth the Timucua, the Apalachee, and the other native peoples of Florida, as well as those of coastal Georgia, became pawns in an ongoing international conflict involving the colonial powers which were vying for the Americas. Between 1670 and the end of the first decade of the 1700s, that conflict would be played out across La Florida, leading to the destruction of the Spanish mission system and, ultimately, to the annihilation of the native peoples who had once lived in those provinces.

Raids against the Spanish missions in Guale actually began in 1661 when Chichimeco Indians, who had been living in Virginia and probably had received arms from English traders, attacked. Over the next two decades raids by these same well-armed Indians, also known as the Rechahecrians, drove native groups living in the interior of Georgia and in South Carolina to the coastal Georgia missions where they sought protection from the Spaniards. The refugees, who became known as Yamasee Indians, greatly increased the coastal population and, for a time, provided an additional source of native labor for St Augustine.

In 1670 English colonists founded Charles Towne (modern Charleston). That same year the Treaty of Madrid had been signed by England and Spain, giving each country the right to lands in America that they controlled at the time. Spain, with its missions and outposts in Guale, Timucua, and Apalachee, held the Georgia coast and Florida. The English colonies included the Carolinas, Virginia, and others to the north.

But England disputed Spain's claim to the Georgia coast, and that region, down to St Augustine, remained an area of contention. It was the intention of the English to force Spain out of Georgia and Florida and to expand its colonial holdings down the eastern seaboard. The ensuing disagreement blossomed into military confrontations, what one historian has called "an undeclared war." The Chichimeco Indians, whom the new Carolinian colonists called Westos and who had settled on the middle Savannah River, initially were used as a weapon by those same colonists against the Spanish missions in Guale. In 1680 a raiding party of Chichimecos/Westos, abetted by the Carolinians, attacked a mission on St Simons Island, then moved north to attack Santa Catalina on modern St Catherines Island, then the northernmost Spanish mission in Guale. More attacks on the Georgia coastal missions followed, some by French and Spanish pirates.

In the conflict with England the Spanish military in St Augustine was outnumbered by the Carolinian forces. Worse, the native allies of the Carolinians were both numerous and reasonably well supplied with firearms, while the Guale, Yamasee, and Timucuan villagers were not. The raiders from the north could attack the Florida missions at will; those Spanish garrisons posted in the mission provinces were never staffed with more than handfuls of soldiers, and they could offer almost no resistance.

Trying to defend the Georgia coastal missions was futile. In 1683 the Spanish governor ordered all of the missions from Cumberland Island north to be abandoned. By the end of 1684 that had been accomplished and the Guale and Timucuan mission villagers had been relocated at other missions closer to St Augustine where it was hoped they could be protected by the soldiers stationed at garrisons on Amelia Island and the larger force at the castillo. With the retreat from the Georgia coast

Figure 8.2 A large hole dug in the corner of the nave of the Santa Catalina church on Amelia Island served as an ossuary for the mass burial of 59 people, 80 percent of whom were female. The remains may represent people who, after death, were first stored in a charnel house and then moved into the church when it was built

Amelia Island became the site of the northernmost coastal missions (Figure 8.2). The northern frontier of the colony on the Atlantic coast once had been at the Chesapeake Bay; by 1700 it was only 50 miles north of St Augustine.

Not all of the villagers from the coastal missions were relocated to old and new missions between Amelia Island and St Augustine (Figure 8.3). Many of the Yamasee Indians had simply fled, abandoning the area when they realized the Spanish could no longer protect them. Some sought refuge among the Carolinians, whom they may have perceived as the eventual winners in the conflict and who harbored other Yamasees.

The Yamasees living under the auspices of the Carolinian colony had quickly learned that raids and slaving paid well.

Figure 8.3 A restored Yamasee Indian pottery vessel from a site on Amelia Island. The distinctive stamping on this and similar vessels is quite different from that present on Timucuan vessels

Villagers living at the poorly defended inland Florida missions
could be captured and taken back to Charleston where dealing
in slaves had been made legal in 1671. The profits which could
be made from slaving had been one of the reasons the Westos
had raided the mission settlements.

In 1685 Carolinian-abetted Yamasee Indians bent on captur-
ing villagers to be sold as slaves raided the mission of Santa
Catalina de Afuica located in southern Suwannee County.
Twenty-two Timucua were taken. Some of the slaves were taken
to Charleston and sold to slave dealers for 30 shotguns and
cutlasses; others were shipped to the English colonies in the West
Indies; and still others were sold to an Irish slave ship at Stuart's
Town near Charleston.

The next year soldiers from St Augustine retaliated for these
blatant infringements on Spanish territory by marching north to
attack Stuart's Town. Although that town was not reached,
nearby Port Royal was attacked.

A decade earlier, foreseeing that such conflicts were sure to
come, the Spaniards in St Augustine had set to work on a stone
fort to replace the older wooden one. The fort was constructed
of blocks of coquina stone mined from nearby Anastasia Island.
That fort – the Castillo de San Marcos – still stands. Today, a
national monument, the fort still dominates St Augustine's
waterfront. But the fort did little to protect the missions. The
raids continued, helping to further decimate already disease-
impacted mission villages.

In 1691 San Juan de Guacara on the Suwannee River was
raided. Then Pedro y San Pablo de Potohiriba and Santa
Fé in western Timucua were attacked in 1702. The Apalachicola Indians who raided Santa Fé were armed by the Carolinians. Although the small contingent of Spanish soldiers
stationed at Santa Fé successfully defended the mission, an ill-
advised counterattack resulted in the deaths of Timucuan villagers.

From the bureaucracy that was the military government of La
Florida, a letter was sent to the Spanish sovereign by Governor
Joseph de Zuñiga y Zerda, who sought to explain what had gone
right and what had gone wrong:

they [the Apalachicola] entered in the dawn watch and burned and
devastated the village of Santa Fé . . . , making an attack on the convent with many firearms and arrows and burning the church, although

not the images which with some risk were saved. Finally, the fight having lasted for more than three hours, our force repulsed them, after the hasty strengthening of an indefensible stockade which served as a fence to the gate of the convent. The enemy retired with some injury, and although our side had some killed and wounded, it would not have been large if the adjutant deputy, Juan Ruíz de Cañiçares, had not left, with small prudence and but few men, in pursuit of the enemy, whose number had increased. After pursuing them for six leagues [nearly 20 miles], they overtook them the same day after dusk, engaging them briskly, and one soldier that got away (reports) that one and another up to ten of our Indians died in the skirmish, because the enemy received them in a half moon (a crescent) and, closing it, caught many of them in the center, only a few Indians escaping . . . [T]he opinion exists that an Englishman led the band which entered Santa Fé. (Boyd, Smith, and Griffin, 1951: 46)

In November of that same year, Carolinian soldiers and their native allies, including Yamasee Indians, sailed from Port Royal to attack Spanish interests, including St Augustine itself. This would be the largest military force assembled to date in the conflict. The army, led by the governor of South Carolina, James Moore, landed on the northern end of Amelia Island and quickly scattered the small garrison of Spanish soldiers stationed there in what is now Fernandina Beach. The wooden tower defended by the Spaniards could offer little more than token resistance.

The Carolinian militia and native warriors then marched down the island to Santa Catalina, one of the missions moved from Guale in the 1684. That mission was located on the inland side of the island fronting the salt marsh and lagoon. The out-manned handful of Spanish soldiers stationed at the mission and the Franciscan friars fled just ahead of the attackers. Friars hastily grabbed what they could from the church before fleeing to the south end of the island and a ferry that provided transportation to next island south. When the attackers arrived at Santa Catalina they shot flaming arrows that ignited the mission buildings, destroying them (Figure 8.4). The charred remains of the mission, located on Harrison Creek, have been discovered and excavated by archaeologists. Included in the mission artifacts recovered during the investigations was the brass seal used by the friars to emboss the wax placed on their correspondence (Figure 8.5). It was found near the wall of the mission convent, perhaps where it had been lost by the fleeing friars.

Figure 8.4 The thatched roofs of mission buildings and the houses
of villagers were inflammable. Using fire arrows raiders could ignite
an entire town, burning it to the ground
Source: de Bry (1591).

After capturing Amelia Island the Carolinian army continued south, routing the Spanish soldiers at San Juan del Puerto
on Fort George Island. Soon Moore's men completed their
march through the remaining missions and outposts that lay
between San Juan and St Augustine. Mocama had been devastated.

The Carolinians laid siege to St Augustine, burning most of the
wooden buildings in the town. They could not breach the thick
walls of the stone fort, however. Although the siege continued
into December the coquina castillo was never taken and the
residents of St Augustine were saved. The native people living in
the refugee towns did not fare as well. Five hundred were taken
back to Charleston. Spain's hold on La Florida was loosened
that much more.

One way to put further pressure on St Augustine was to cut off
the food and other goods supplied by the north Florida missions.
In 1703 a force of Carolinian soldiers and Indians marched into
Apalachee and destroyed at least one mission. The next year two

Figure 8.5 The face of the brass seal from Santa Catalina on Amelia Island (printed backwards so it is legible). It reads (abbreviated): Saint Catherine, Martyr of Alexandria. Legend has it that at the end of the third century Catherine was tortured on a spiked wheel, but miraculously survived, only to be beheaded by the Roman emperor in AD 305

additional raids effectively destroyed the entire province. Mission buildings were burned and the native people either fled or were captured and taken back to South Carolina. Three hundred men and 1,000 women and children were forcibly relocated outside Charleston where they were to provide a human barrier to anticipated Spanish raids. Another 325 men and 4,000 women and children who had been captured were sold into slavery. Apalachee also was devastated.

Charred remains of the burned Apalachee missions have been found by archaeologists at a number of sites in Leon and Jefferson counties. One of the largest of the Spanish settlements in Apalachee, the mission and town of San Luís with its Spanish quarter and a moated and palisaded fort, is presently being excavated by archaeologists from the Florida Bureau of Archaeological Research. Time has been kind to the remains of the San Luís church and *convento* and other buildings. Investigations directed by Bonnie McEwan literally are providing wheelbarrow-loads of new information on the missions of Spanish Florida.

The Carolinian raids on the missions of Timucua and Apalachee were successful in bringing about a cessation of ranching and farming operations in those provinces. From 1705 to 1707 several additional raids completed the destruction of most of the remaining missions and the enslavement or scattering of the villagers. According to the governor of La Florida, 10,000–12,000 Indians were taken as slaves in the Carolinian raids during the first decade of the 1700s. By 1710, observers noted that north Florida was essentially empty of population.

A few Timucua had fled west to escape the raids. But most of the refugees from the missions were moved to the vicinity of St Augustine, where they were living in small villages. Some of the villages retained names taken from their old mission towns, while others received new ones. Survivors from the Santa Fé mission relocated at a village which optimistically was named Esperanza, Spanish for "hope." But there was to be little hope for the Timucua.

A People No More

The destruction of the missions and garrisons in northern Florida left the peninsula open to more raids from the north. Yamasees, various Lower Creeks, Westos, Savannahs, and other native groups raided the length of Florida, enslaving and looting. The native settlements south of the former mission provinces were tempting targets for the raiders. In 1709 it was said that the Florida Indians, other than those living around St Augustine, had been pushed southward to the tip of the peninsula.

The raids had even reached down into the Florida Keys causing havoc among the native people of that region who, like their neighbors to the north, were largely defenseless. In 1711 the Bishop of Cuba wrote:

In the past month . . . a ship entered this port [in Cuba], which had come from the keys . . . The heathen Indians of the chiefs, Carlos, Coleto, and others live in those keys. And some of the above-mentioned Indians who came in the aforesaid ship told me about very serious persecutions and hostilities, which they are experiencing and which they have experienced on other keys, which the Indians whom they call Yamasees have destroyed. That the Yamasees have killed some of the aforementioned Keys Indians; have made others flee; and that they have captured the greater part of the latter, whom, it is said, they carry off and sell, placing them into slavery at the port of [Charleston]. (Hann, 1991: 46)

These eighteenth-century raids by Yamasees and other Indians, like those of the late seventeenth century, were in large part a result of British colonial endeavors. After the establishment of the Virginia and Carolina colonies, British entrepreneurs had sought trading partners among the native peoples in the southeastern United States. Such trade, especially trade in deerskins which were exported to Europe, was very profitable.

One result of the trade was that firearms continued to be obtained by native people. Rifles, power, and shot gave these individuals a huge advantage in raids against people armed with bows and arrows and clubs. The attacks against Spanish interests in Florida were encouraged and, in some instances, aided by the government of South Carolina. In those attacks the raiders destroyed villages and enslaved the people, taking them to sell to the Carolinian entrepreneurs who then resold the slaves at a profit.

Ironically, the Yamasees, who played such a visible role in the slave trade, would themselves suffer the same fate as the Florida natives they had raided. In 1715 the Yamasees living in South Carolina rebelled against their Carolinian allies. To escape military retribution many of the Yamasees moved south to Florida where they were well received by their former allies, the Spaniards. Some of the Yamasees settled in towns around St Augustine among the refugee Florida Indians, while others moved into Apalachee and other locales in northern Florida abandoned during the mission raids.

But once settled in Florida the Yamasees only became prey for other raiders. Once slavers themselves, Yamasees were captured by the new Indian allies of the Carolinians and sold into slavery.

Franciscan friars traveled to the refugee villages around St Augustine to administer to the Yamasees and the other refugees, including the Timucua who had survived the raids of earlier decades. Historian John Hann has found census data that chronicle the histories of these eighteenth-century villages and their occupants. One census made in 1717 by a Spanish army officer lists ten refugee villages, three of which included Timucua Indians: San Buenaventura de Palica, Our Lady of Sorrows, and Nombre de Dios. Another three villages were home to Yamasee Indians who had only recently moved to Florida, while two others were home to Guale Indians. Apalachee and Mayaca Indians lived in the remaining two. Of the 942 total people living in the towns, only about 250 were Timucua.

Census figures collected from the refugee towns in 1726 reveal that the number of Timucua had declined to 157, a drop of 40 percent, probably the result of disease and, perhaps, slave raids. One of the three Timucuan towns which apparently had been particularly hard hit by disease also housed 20 refugee Pohoy Indians from Tampa Bay who were living with the 25 surviving Timucua. Although the number of the Timucua still surviving had declined precipitously, the total number of refugee villages actually increased to 12 and the total refugee population stood at 1,011. The larger number of villages and people (compared to 1717) reflected the movement of more refugees to St Augustine seeking Spanish protection.

The presence of the refugee towns continued to attract native slave-raiders. Yuchi and Tallapoosa Indians raided the villages, even those literally in the shadow of St Augustine. One Yamasee town apparently had been wiped out by raiders in 1725. In 1727 an epidemic had hit some of the towns. A report from the next year indicates only about 70 Timucua still remained, most living at Nombre de Dios.

In 1728, 200 Carolinian soldiers and Indians raided Nombre de Dios on the northern outskirts of St Augustine. That small village contained a stone church or *convento* which probably had been built earlier in the eighteenth century. Afraid that future raiders might fortify and occupy the stone buildings the Spaniards ordered them destroyed. However, the mission continued to exist.

By 1738 eight refugee villages with a total population of 340 people still remained. Only two of the villages had Timucuan residents. Some of the villagers worked in St Augustine as domestic servants. Proximity to St Augustine caused alcohol abuse problems among some of the native villagers.

Missionary efforts within the refugee towns would continue to mid-century. Five or six villages still existed in 1752, but only one, Palica, had Timucua Indians living in it. The 29 Timucuan residents included 12 men, 7 women, and 10 children. Juan Xímenez, the village chief, was 75 or 76 years of age.

At least some if not all of the Timucua living at Palica may still have spoken Timucua. The copy of Father Francisco Pareja's 1613 *Confessionario* which is in the library of the New York Historical Society has stuck between its pages a sheet of paper on which is written (Milanich and Sturtevant, 1972: 18): "*En* [blank] *dias del mes de* [blank] *de 1755. Confessó* [blank]. *Sabé la Doctrina.*" ("On the [blank] day of the month of [blank] in 1755 [blank] confessed. He knows the doctrine.") Apparently the *Confessionario*, with its bilingual Spanish–Timucua format, still was being used in 1755 by the Franciscan friar who administered to Palica.

As late as 1759 only two refugee towns still were served by Franciscans: Tolomato and Nombre de Dios, the latter also known as Nuestra Señora de la Leche. Apparently all the surviving native people were consolidated in one or the other of these towns whose populations totaled 95 people living in 19 households. Twelve Timucua were included in a census of the villages' residents.

One of the Nombre de Dios villagers was Juan Alonso Cabale. In addition to the dozen Timucua, the census identified Yamasee, Guale, Costas (Ais), Chickasaw, Chiluque, and Casipuya Indians living in one or the other of the two towns. Because the number of adults from one ethnic or linguistic group was so small, inter-ethnic marriages must have been the norm. It is for that reason that Juan Alonso Cabale had married a Yamasee woman; probably there was no suitable Timucuan mate.

In 1763 Spain and England signed a treaty, one provision of which gave St Augustine to the English in exchange for Havana, which had been captured by England during the Seven Years War. Joining that conflict between France and England had cost Spain the La Florida colony.

After the treaty was negotiated and signed the Spaniards withdrew from St Augustine to Cuba, taking with them the 89 Indians who lived in that town and in Tolomato and Nuestra Señora de la Leche. In Cuba the Indians were sent to the town of Guanabacoa. There Juan Alonso Cabale and the few other Timucua from Florida would live out what remained of their lives. Two and a half centuries after Juan Ponce de Leon's voyage opened La Florida to colonization the Timucua were no more.

Bibliography

Adam, L. and Vinson, J. (eds) 1866: *Arte de la Lengua Timuquana, Compuesto por El P. Francisco Pareja*. Bibliotheque Linguistique Américaine, Paris.

Allen, H. 1896: Crania from the mounds of the St John's River, Florida: a study made in connection with crania from other parts of North America. *Journal of the Academy of Natural Sciences of Philadelphia*, 10, 365–448.

Arnade, C. 1959: *The Siege of St Augustine in 1702*. University of Florida Press, Gainesville.

—— 1965: Cattle raising in Spanish Florida: 1513–1763. *St Augustine Historical Society Publication*, 21, 1–11.

Baker, H. A. 1993: Spanish ranching and the Alachua Sink site: a preliminary report. *Florida Anthropologist*, 46, 82–100.

Barrientos, B. 1965: *Pedro Menéndez de Avilés, Founder of Florida*, trans. A. Kerrigan. University of Florida Press, Gainesville.

Bartram, W. 1928: *Travels of William Bartram*, ed. M. Van Doren. Dover Publications, New York.

Bolton, H. E. and Ross, M. 1925: *The Debatable Land*. University of California Press, Berkeley.

Boniface, B. 1971: A historical geography of Spanish Florida, circa 1700. Unpublished MA thesis, University of Georgia.

Boyd, M. F. 1938: Map of the road from Pensacola to St Augustine, 1778. *Florida Historical Quarterly*, 17, 1–23.

—— 1948: Enumeration of Florida Spanish missions in 1675. *Florida Historical Quarterly*, 24, 181–8.

Boyd, M. F., Smith, H. G. and Griffin, J. W: 1951. *Here They Once Stood, the Tragic End of the Apalachee Missions*. University of Florida Press, Gainesville.

Bushnell, A. T. 1978a: That demonic game: the campaign to stop Indian pelota playing in Spanish Florida, 1675–1684. *The Americas*, 35, 1–19.

—— 1978b: The Menéndez-Marquez cattle barony at La Chua and the determinants of economic expansion in 17th century Florida. *Florida Historical Quarterly*, 56, 407–31.

—— 1981: *The King's Coffer: Proprietors of the Royal Treasury, 1565–1702*. University Presses of Florida, Gainesville.

—— 1989: Ruling "the Republic of Indians" in seventeenth-century Florida. In P. H. Wood, G. A. Waselkov and M. T. Hatley (eds) *Powhatan's Mantle, Indians in the Colonial Southeast*, pp. 134–50. University of Nebraska Press, Lincoln.

—— 1994: *Situado and Sabana, Spain's Support System for the Presidio and Mission Provinces of Florida*. American Museum of Natural History, Anthropological Papers 74. University of Georgia Press, Athens.

Cabeza de Vaca, A. Núñez 1922: *The Journey of Alvar Núñez Cabeza de Vaca and his Companions from Florida to the Pacific, 1528–1536*, ed. A. F. Bandelier, trans. F. Bandelier. Allerton Book Co., New York.

Covington, J. W. 1959: Trade relations between Southwestern Florida and Cuba – 1600–1840. *Florida Historical Quarterly*, 38, 114–28.

—— 1967: Some observations concerning the Florida–Carolina Indian slave trade. *Florida Anthropologist*, 20, 10–18.

—— 1968: Stuart's Town, the Yamasee Indians and Spanish Florida. *Florida Anthropologist*, 21, 8–13.

—— 1970: The Yamasee Indians in Florida: 1715–1763. *Florida Anthropologist*, 23, 119–28.

Covington, J. W. and Falcones, A. F. 1963: *Pirates, Indians, and Spaniards: Father Escobedo's "La Florida."* Great Outdoors Publishing Co., St Petersburg, Florida.

Davis, T. F. 1935: Juan Ponce de Leon's voyages to Florida. *Florida Historical Quarterly*, 14, 5–70.

Deagan, K. A. 1972: Fig Springs: the mid-seventeenth century in north-central Florida. *Historical Archaeology*, 6, 23–46.

—— 1977: The search for sixteenth century St Augustine. *Conference on Historic Sites Archaeology Papers*, 12, 266–85.

—— 1978: Cultures in transition: fusion and assimilation among the eastern Timucua. In J. T. Milanich and S. Proctor (eds) *Tacachale, Essays on the Indians of Florida and Southeastern Georgia during the Historic Period*, pp. 88–119. University Presses of Florida, Gainesville.

—— 1979: Timucua 1580: research and exhibit plan for a 1580 Timucua village near St Augustine, Florida. Report submitted to the

St Augustine Restoration Foundation, Inc. MS on file, St Augustine Historical Society Research Library, St Augustine, Florida.

—— 1983: *Spanish St Augustine: The Archaeology of a Colonial Creole Community.* Academic Press, New York.

—— 1987: *Artifacts of the Spanish Colonies of Florida and the Caribbean, 1500–1800.* Vol. I: *Ceramics, Glassware, and Beads.* Smithsonian Institution Press, Washington, DC.

—— 1993: St Augustine and the mission frontier. In McEwan (1993b), pp. 87–110.

De Bry, T. 1591: *Brevis narratio eorum quae in Florida Americae Provincia . . .* Frankfurt.

Dickinson, M. F. 1989: Delineating a site through limited research: the mission of San Juan del Puerto (8Du53), Fort George Island, Florida. *Florida Anthropologist,* 42, 396–409.

Dobyns, H. F. 1983: *Their Number Become Thinned, Native Population Dynamics in Eastern North America.* University of Tennessee Press, Knoxville.

—— 1993: Disease transfer at contact. *Annual Review of Anthropology,* 22, 273–91.

Ehrmann, W. W. 1940: The Timucuan Indians of 16th century Florida. *Florida Historical Quarterly,* 18, 168–91.

Elvas (Gentleman of Elvas) 1922: True relation . . . . In E. G. Bourne (ed.) *Narratives of the Career of Hernando de Soto in the Conquest of Florida, . . .* Vol. 1, pp. 1–222. Allerton Book Co., New York.

Gannon, M. V. 1965: *The Cross in the Sand: The Early Catholic Church in Florida, 1513–1870.* University of Florida Press, Gainesville.

Gatschet, A. S. 1877–80: The Timucuan language. *Proceedings of the American Philosophical Society,* 16, 625–42; 17, 490–504; 18, 465–502.

Geiger, M. J. 1937: *The Franciscan Conquest of Florida, 1573–1618.* Catholic University of America Press, Washington, DC.

—— 1940: *Biographical Dictionary of the Franciscans in Spanish Florida and Cuba (1528–1841).* Franciscan Studies 21. St Anthony's Guild Press, Paterson, New Jersey.

Gerónimo de Oré, L. 1936: *The Martyrs of Florida (1513–1616),* trans. M. J. Geiger. Franciscan Studies 18. Joseph F. Wagner, New York.

Goggin, J. M. 1952: *Space and Time Perspectives in Northern St Johns Archeology, Florida.* Yale University Publications in Anthropology 47. New Haven.

—— 1953: An introductory outline of Timucuan archaeology. *Southeastern Archaeological Conference Newsletter* 3(3), 4–17.

Granberry. J. 1956: Timucua I: prosodics and phonemics of the Mocama dialect. *International Journal of American Linguistics,* 22, 97–105.

—— 1993: *A Grammar and Dictionary of the Timucua Language.* University of Alabama Press, Tuscaloosa.

Hann, J. H. 1986a: Church furnishings, sacred vessels and vestments held by the missions of Florida: translation of two inventories. *Florida Archaeology*, 2, 147–64. Florida Bureau of Archaeological Research, Tallahassee.

—— 1986b: Demographic patterns and changes in mid-seventeenth century Timucua and Apalachee. *Florida Historical Quarterly*, 64, 371–92.

—— 1986c: Translation of Alonso de Leturiondo's Memorial to the King of Spain. *Florida Archaeology*, 2, 165–225. Florida Bureau of Archaeological Research, Tallahassee.

—— 1986d: Translation of Governor Rebolledo's 1657 visitation of three florida provinces and related documents. *Florida Archaeology*, 2, 81–145. Florida Bureau of Archaeological Research, Tallahassee.

—— 1987: Twilight of the Mocamo and Guale Aborigines as portrayed in the 1695 Spanish visitation. *Florida Historical Quarterly*, 66, 1–24.

—— 1988: *Apalachee: The Land between the Rivers.* University of Florida Press, Gainesville.

—— 1989: St Augustine's fallout from the Yamassee war. *Florida Historical Quarterly*, 68, 180–200.

—— 1990a: De Soto, Dobyns, and demography in western Timucua. *Florida Anthropologist*, 43, 3–12.

—— 1990b: Summary guide to Spanish Florida missions and visitas with churches in the sixteenth and seventeenth centuries. *The Americas*, 46, 417–513.

—— 1991: *Missions to the Calusa.* University of Florida Press, Gainesville.

—— 1992a: Heathen Acuera, murder, and a Potano *cimarrona*: the St Johns River and the Alachua prairie in the 1670s. *Florida Historical Quarterly*, 70, 451–74.

—— 1992b: Political leadership among the natives of Spanish Florida. *Florida Historical Quarterly*, 71, 188–208.

—— 1993a: 1630 Memorial of Fray Francisco Alonso de Jesus on Spanish Florida's missions and Natives. *The Americas*, 50, 85–105.

—— 1993b: Visitations and revolts in Florida, 1656–1695. *Florida Archaeology*, 7, 1–296. Florida Bureau of Archaeological Research, Tallahassee.

—— 1995: *A History of the Timucua Indians and Missions.* University Press of Florida, Gainesville. In press.

Hardin, K. W. 1986: The Santa María mission project. *Florida Anthropologist*, 39, 75–83.

Hernández de Biedma, L. 1922: Relation of the conquest of Florida. In E. G. Bourne (ed.) *Narratives of the Career of Hernando de Soto in the Conquest of Florida,* . . . Vol. 2, pp. 1–40. Allerton Book Co., New York.

Hoffman, P. E. 1980: A new voyage of North American discovery: the voyage of Pedro de Salazar to the Island of Giants. *Florida Historical Quarterly,* 58, 415–26.

—— 1990: *A New Andalucia and a Way to the Orient: The American Southeast during the Sixteenth Century.* Louisiana State University Press, Baton Rouge.

—— 1994a: Lucas Vázquez de Ayllón's discovery and colony. In Hudson and Chaves Tesser (1994), pp. 36–49.

—— 1994b: Narváez and Cabeza de Vaca in Florida. In Hudson and Chaves Tesser (1994), pp. 50–73.

Hoshower, L. M. 1992: Bioanthropological analysis of a seventeenth century native American–Spanish mission population: biocultural impacts on the northern Utina. PhD dissertation, University of Florida.

Hoshower, L. M. and Milanich, J. T. 1993: Excavations in the Fig Springs mission burial area. In McEwan (1993b), pp. 217–43.

Hudson, C. 1976: *The Southeastern Indians.* University of Tennessee Press, Knoxville.

—— (ed.) 1979: *The Black Drink – A Native American Tea.* University of Georgia Press, Athens.

—— 1990: *The Juan Pardo Expeditions: Spanish Explorers and the Indians of the Carolinas and Tennessee, 1566–1568.* Smithsonian Institution Press, Washington, DC.

—— 1994: The Hernando de Soto expedition, 1539–1543. In Hudson and Chaves Tesser (1994), pp. 74–103.

Hudson, C. and Chaves Tesser, C. 1994: *The Forgotten Centuries: Indians and Europeans in the American South, 1521–1704.* University of Georgia Press, Athens.

Hudson, C., Smith, M. T., DePratter, C. B. and Kelley, E. 1989: The Tristán de Luna expedition, 1559–1561. *Southeastern Archaeology,* 8, 31–45.

Hulton, P. 1977: *The Work of Jacques Le Moyne de Morgues, a Huguenot Artist in France, Florida and England.* 2 vols. British Museum Publications Ltd, London.

Hutchinson, D. L. 1991: Post-contact native American health and adaptation: assessing the impact of introduced disease in sixteenth-century Gulf coast Florida. PhD dissertation, University of Illinois, Urbana.

Johnson, K. W. 1990: The discovery of a seventeenth century Spanish mission in Ichetucknee State Park, 1986. *Florida Journal of Anthropology,* 15, 39–46.

—— 1991: The Utina and the Potano peoples of northern Florida: changing settlement systems in the Spanish colonial period. PhD dissertation, University of Florida.

—— 1993: Mission Santa Fé de Toloca. In McEwan (1993b), pp. 141–64.

Johnson, K. W. and Nelson, B. C. 1990: The Utina: seriations and chronology. *Florida Anthropologist*, 43, 48–62.

Kapitzke, R. 1993: The "Calamities of Florida": Father Solana, Governor Palacio y Valenzuela, and the desertions of 1758. *Florida Historical Quarterly*, 72, 1–18.

Keegan, W. K. 1992: *The People Who Discovered Columbus*. University Press of Florida, Gainesville.

Knight, V. J., Jr. 1990: Social organization and the evolution of hierarchy in southeastern chiefdoms. *Journal of Anthropological Research*, 49, 1–23.

La Grasserie, Raoul de. 1888: Textes analysèes et vocabulaire de la langue timucua. *International Congress of Americanists, Proceedings*, 7, 403–37.

Lankford, G. E. III 1984: Saying hello to the Timucua. *Mid-America Folklore*, 12, 7–23.

Larsen, C. S. 1993: On the frontier of contact: mission bioarchaeology in La Florida. In McEwan (1993b), pp. 322–56.

Lawson, Sarah (trans.) 1992: The notable history of Florida . . . . In S. Lawson and W. J. Faupel, *A Foothold in Florida, The Eye-Witness Account of Four Voyages made by the French to that Region . . .*, pp. 1–148. Antique Atlas Publications, East Grinstead, England.

Lorant, S. 1946: *The New World, the First Pictures of America*. Duell, Sloan & Pearce, New York.

Loucks, L. J. 1978: Political and economic interactions between the Spaniards and Indians: archeological and ethnohistorical perspectives of the mission system in florida. PhD dissertation, University of Florida.

—— 1993: Spanish–Indian interaction on the Florida missions: the archaeology of Baptizing Spring. In McEwan (1993b), pp. 193–216.

Lyon, E. 1976: *The Enterprise of Florida*. University Presses of Florida, Gainesville.

—— 1977: St Augustine 1580: the living community. *El Escribano*, 14, 20–33.

—— 1988: Pedro Menéndez's strategic plan for the Florida peninsula. *Florida Historical Quarterly*, 67, 1–14.

Marrinan, R. A. 1985: The archaeology of the Spanish missions of Florida: 1566–1704. In K. W. Johnson, J. M. Leader, and R. C. Wilson (eds) *Indians, Colonists, and Slaves, Essays in Memory of Charles H. Fairbanks*, pp. 241–52. Florida Journal of Anthropology Special Publication 4, Gainesville.

Marrinan, R. A., Scarry, J. F. and Majors, R. L. 1990: Prelude to de Soto: the expedition of Pánfilo de Narváez. In Thomas (1990), pp. 71–82.

McEwan, B. G. 1991: San Luis de Talimali: the archaeology of Spanish–Indian relations at a Florida mission. *Historical Archaeology*, 25, 36–60.

—— 1993a: Hispanic life on the seventeenth-century Florida frontier. In McEwan (1993b), pp. 295–321.

—— (ed.) 1993b: *Spanish Missions of La Florida*. University Press of Florida, Gainesville.

McEwan, B. G. and Poe, C. B. 1994: Excavations at Fort San Luis. *Florida Anthropologist*, 47, 90–106.

McMurray, J. A. 1973: The definition of the ceramic complex at San Juan del Puerto. Unpublished MA thesis, University of Florida.

Milanich, J. T. 1971a: *The Alachua Tradition of North-central Florida*. Contributions of the Florida State Museum, Anthropology and History 17. Gainesville.

—— 1971b: Surface information from the presumed site of the San Pedro de Mocamo mission. *Conference on Historic Site Archaeology Papers*, 5, 114–21.

—— 1972: Excavations at the Richardson Site, Alachua County, Florida: an early 17th century Potano Indian village (with notes on Potano culture change). *Florida Bureau of Historic Sites and Properties Bulletin*, 2, 35–61.

—— 1978: The western Timucua: patterns of acculturation and change. In J. T. Milanich and S. Proctor (eds) *Tacachale, Essays on the Indians of Florida and Southeastern Georgia during the Historic Period*, pp. 59–88. University Presses of Florida, Gainesville.

—— (ed.) 1991: *The Hernando de Soto Expedition*. Garland Publishing, New York.

—— 1994: *Archaeology of Precolumbian Florida*. University Press of Florida, Gainesville.

—— 1995: *Florida Indians and the Invasion from Europe*. University Press of Florida, Gainesville.

Milanich, J. T. and Hudson, C. 1993: *Hernando de Soto and the Florida Indians*. University Press of Florida, Gainesville.

Milanich, J. T. and Sturtevant, W. C. 1972: *Francisco Pareja's 1613 Confessionario: A Documentary Source for Timucuan Ethnography*. Florida Department of State, Tallahassee.

Miller, J. J. 1991: The fairest, fruitfullest and pleasantest of all the world: an environmental history of the northeast part of Florida. PhD dissertation. University of Pennsylvania.

Mitchem, J. M. 1989: Redefining Safety Harbor: late prehistoric/protohistoric archaeology in west peninsular Florida. PhD dissertation, University of Florida.

Moore, C. B. 1894a: Certain sand mounds of the St Johns River, Florida. *Journal of the Academy of Natural Sciences of Philadelphia*, 10, 3–103.

—— 1894b: Certain sand mounds of the St Johns River, Florida. *Journal of the Academy of Natural Sciences of Philadelphia*, 10, 128–246.

—— 1896a: Certain river mounds of Duval County, Florida. *Journal of the Academy of Natural Sciences of Philadelphia*, 10, 449–502.

—— 1896b: Two sand mounds on Murphy Island, Florida. *Journal of the Academy of Natural Sciences of Philadelphia*, 10, 503–16.

Pareja, F. 1627: *Cathecismo, y Examen para los que Comulgen, en Lengua Castellana, y Timuquana* . . . . Imprenta de Juan Ruyz, Mexico City.

Pearson, C. 1977: Evidence of early Spanish contact on the Georgia coast. *Historical Archaeology*, 11, 74–83.

Pearson, F. L. 1968: Spanish–Indian relations in Florida: a study of two *visitas* 1657–1678. PhD dissertation, University of Alabama.

Priestley, H. I. (ed.) 1928: *The Luna Papers, Documents Relating to the Expedition of Don Tristín de Luna y Arellano for the Conquest of La Florida in 1559–1561*. 2 vols. Florida State Historical Society, Publication 8. Deland.

Purdy, B. A. 1987: Hontoon Island, Florida (8Vo202) Artifacts. *Florida Anthropologist*, 40, 27–39.

Ranjel, R. 1922: A narrative of de Soto's expedition . . . . In E. G. Bourne (ed.) *Narratives of the Career of Hernando de Soto in the Conquest of Florida*, . . . Vol. 2, pp. 41–158. Allerton Book Co., New York.

Reitz, E. J. 1990: Zooarchaeological evidence for subsistence at *La Florida* missions. In Thomas (1992), pp. 543–54.

—— 1993: Evidence for animal use at the missions of Spanish Florida. In McEwan (1993b), pp. 376–98.

Ribau[l]t, J. 1964: *The Whole & True Discoverye of Terra Florida*. University of Florida Press, Gainesville.

Ruhl, D. S. 1990: Spanish mission paleoethnobotany and culture change: a Survey of the archaeobotanical data and some speculations on the Aboriginal and Spanish agrarian interactions in *La Florida*. In Thomas (1990), pp. 555–80.

—— 1993: Old customs and traditions in new terrain: sixteenth- and seventeenth-century archaeobotanical data from *La Florida*. In C. M. Scarry (ed.) *Foraging and Farming in the Eastern Woodlands*, pp. 255–83. University Press of Florida, Gainesville.

Saunders, R. 1990: Ideal and innovation: Spanish mission architecture in the Southeast. In Thomas (1990), pp. 527–42.

—— 1993: Architecture of missions Santa María and Santa Catalina de Amelia. In McEwan (1993b), pp. 35–61.

Seaberg, L. M. 1955: The Zetrouer Site: Indian and Spanish in central Florida. Unpublished MA thesis, University of Florida.

Shapiro, G. and McEwan, B. G. 1992: Archaeology at San Luis, Part One: The Apalachee council house. *Florida Archaeology*, 6, 1–173. Florida Bureau of Archaeological Research, Tallahassee.

Smith, B. (trans.) 1866: *Narratives of the Career of Hernando de Soto in the Conquest of Florida as Told by a Knight of Elvas and in a Relation by Luys Hernández de Biedma, Factor of the Expedition.* The Bradford Club, New York.

Smith, H. G. 1948a: Two historical archaeological periods in Florida. *American Antiquity*, 13, 313–19.

Snow, F. 1990: Pine Barrens Lamar. In M. Williams and G. Shapiro (eds) *Lamar Archaeology, Mississippian Chiefdoms in the Deep South*, pp. 82–93. University of Alabama Press, Tuscaloosa.

Solís de Merás, G. 1964: *Pedro Menéndez de Avilés. Adelantado, Governor and Captain-General of Florida*, trans. J. T. Connor. University of Florida Press, Gainesville.

Spellman, C. W. 1948: The agriculture of the early north Florida Indians. *Florida Anthropologist*, 1, 37–48.

Sturtevant, W. C. 1977: The ethnological evaluation of the La Moyne–De Bry illustrations. In Hulton (1977), Vol. 1, pp. 69–74.

Swanton, J. R. 1922: *Early History of the Creek Indians and Their Neighbors.* Bulletin 73, Bureau of American Ethnology, Smithsonian Institution, Washington, DC.

—— 1929: The Tawasa language. *American Anthropologist*, 31, 435–453.

—— 1946: *The Indians of the Southeastern United States.* Bulletin 137, Bureau of American Ethnology, Smithsonian Institution, Washington, DC.

—— (ed.) 1985: *Final Report of the United States De Soto Expedition Commission.* Smithsonian Institution Press, Washington, DC.

Symes, M. I. and Stephens, M. E. 1965: A-272: The Fox Pond Site. *Florida Anthropologist*, 18, 65–72.

Thomas, D. H. (ed.) 1990: *Columbian Consequences.* Vol. 2: *Archaeological and Historical Perspectives on the Spanish Borderlands East.* Smithsonian Institution Press, Washington, DC.

True, David O. 1944: The Freducci map of 1514–1515, what it discloses of early Florida history. *Tequesta*, 4, 50–5.

Varner, J. G. and Varner, J. J. (eds and trans.) 1951: *The Florida of the Inca.* University of Texas Press, Austin.

Vinson, J. 1884: Sur la langue timucua. *International Congress of Americanists, Proceedings*, 5, 362–5.

Wallace, R. L. 1975: An archaeological, ethnohistorical, and biochemical investigation of the Guale Indians of the Georgia coastal strand. PhD dissertation, University of Florida.

Walthall, J. A. 1980: *Prehistoric Indians of the Southeast: Archaeology of Alabama and the Middle South*. University of Alabama Press, Tuscaloosa.

Weber, D. J. 1992: *The Spanish Frontier in North America*. Yale University Press, New Haven.

Weddle, R. S. 1985: *Spanish Sea, the Gulf of Mexico in North American Discovery, 1500–1685*. Texas A&M University Press, College Station.

Weisman, B. R. 1992: *Excavations of the Franciscan Frontier, Archaeology of the Fig Springs Mission*. University Press of Florida, Gainesville.

—— 1993: Archaeology of Fig Springs mission, Ichetucknee Springs State Park. In McEwan (1993b), pp. 165–92.

Wenhold, L. L. (ed. and trans.) 1936: A seventeenth-century letter of Gabriel Díaz Vara Calderón, Bishop of Cuba. *Smithsonian Miscellaneous Collections*, 95(16), Washington, DC.

Widmer, R. E. 1994: The structure of southeastern chiefdoms. In Hudson and Chaves Tesser (1994), pp. 125–55.

Worth, J. E. 1992a: Revised Aborginal ceramic typology for the Timucua mission province. In Weisman (1992), pp. 188–205.

—— 1992b: The Timucuan missions of Spanish Florida and the rebellion of 1656. PhD dissertation, University of Florida.

—— 1995: *The Struggle for the Georgia Coast, an Eighteenth-Century Spanish Retrospective on Guale and Mocama*. American Museum of Natural History, Anthropological Papers 75. New York.

Index